ONE WEEK LOAN

This book is due for return on or before the last date shown below.

Education at SAGE

SAGE is a leading international publisher of journals, books, and electronic media for academic, educational, and professional markets.

Our education publishing includes:

- accessible and comprehensive texts for aspiring education professionals and practitioners looking to further their careers through continuing professional development

- inspirational advice and guidance for the classroom

- authoritative state of the art reference from the leading authors in the field

Find out more at: **www.sagepub.co.uk/education**

REFLECTIVE PRACTICE for TEACHERS

Maura Sellars

SAGE

Los Angeles | London | New Delhi
Singapore | Washington DC

Los Angeles | London | New Delhi
Singapore | Washington DC

SAGE Publications Ltd
1 Oliver's Yard
55 City Road
London EC1Y 1SP

SAGE Publications Inc.
2455 Teller Road
Thousand Oaks, California 91320

SAGE Publications India Pvt Ltd
B 1/I 1 Mohan Cooperative Industrial Area
Mathura Road
New Delhi 110 044

SAGE Publications Asia-Pacific Pte Ltd
3 Church Street
#10-04 Samsung Hub
Singapore 049483

Editor: James Clark
Editorial assistant: Rachael Plant
Production editor: Nicola Marshall
Copyeditor: Elaine Leek
Proofreader: Katie Forsythe
Indexer: Martin Hargreaves
Marketing manager: Catherine Slinn
Cover design: Naomi Robinson
Typeset by: C&M Digitals (P) Ltd, Chennai, India
Printed in India at Replika Press Pvt Ltd

First edition published 2014

Library of Congress Control Number: 2013937560

British Library Cataloguing in Publication data

A catalogue record for this book is available from the British Library

ISBN 978-1-4462-5650-3
ISBN 978-1-4462-6740-0 (p)

Contents

List of Figures

About the Author & Acknowledgement

After twenty-eight years of classroom practice in the UK and Australia, Maura Sellars now lectures at the University of Newcastle, NSW. She has worked in the area of professional experience for the last ten years and includes intrapersonal intelligence, pedagogy, inclusive practices and numeracy among her major areas of interest.

I would like to thank everyone who has offered support and advice during the production of this book, especially my publishing editor, James Clark.

Preface

The understanding that teachers need to be reflective practitioners is not new. In order to demonstrate many of the professional attributes that characterise successful educators in the twenty-first century, a substantial capacity for authentic reflection must be developed. The requirement for students preparing to teach to engage with this reflective process, however, raises a number of questions. These may include concerns about the notion of reflection itself, the identification of issues, events and interactions that may merit this specific type of focused thinking, and the impact of individual values, attitudes and belief systems. This book offers some answers to these questions and presents opportunities for you to develop a deep understanding of some of the key issues that the teaching profession is currently facing in this current climate of globalisation, change and technological advancement. It presents a model of reflection that requires individual responses while challenging the notion of complete objectivity in favour of self knowledge and understanding, acknowledgement of the origins of personal beliefs and values, and commitment to utilising a strengths-based approach to reflecting on several aspects of teachers' work. In order to engage with this personal model of reflection, you need to be well-informed about your chosen profession. Teaching is a many-faceted interactive activity and requires a commitment to ongoing professional learning and reflection in a number of areas, including the following, which are discussed in this text:

- understanding the importance of ethics and teacher professionalism as currently proposed and the resultant challenges these present
- acknowledging teachers' work as including mentoring, facilitating and caring in addition to the many established roles identified

- engaging with multidisciplinary approaches to the learning process, including those from areas not always customarily associated with learning, such as the findings of neuroscientists and positive psychologists
- considering personal beliefs regarding the nature of intelligence and the consideration of the potential of other, less traditional perspectives of intelligence, such as multiple intelligences and emotional intelligence
- developing an awareness of the impact of globalisation and skills in customising strategies to accommodate diversity and promote inclusion
- integrating technology in ways that are meaningful and supportive of the discipline and pedagogies with which they are implemented
- deliberating about the unique challenges and rewards of teaching at specific stages of your career, especially as a beginning teacher.

In order to facilitate reflective process relating to these aspects of teachers' work in an authentic manner, a number of theories and approaches to teaching and learning have been selected for discussion. The book offers samples of what has been written in each area. The intention is to be thought-provoking, challenging and informative, and to provide the necessary catalyst for further reading, examination and reflection. The book is structured with a number of recurring features designed to help you access the content in a way that is both personally significant and professionally relevant. These include reflective questions, suggestions of how the content may impact on education generally and on your personal practice. Additionally, the scenarios allow you to engage with the application of reflective practice in real school settings.

It is hoped that this book will support your capacity for thinking and reflection in relation to your unique ideas and understanding of teachers' work.

Chapter 1: Reflective Practice

In preparation for reading this chapter, it is important to consider what you already know and what attitudes and belief systems you bring to the activity. To help you do this, the following questions are provided to focus your reflections.

- Q1. What is reflection?
- Q2. Who needs to reflect?
- Q3. Is it important for me?
- Q4. How does it help me?
- Q5. Do I think reflection is important for teachers? Why?

Introduction

Teaching is very demanding work. It requires a lot of energy, stamina and fortitude. Among all the physical activity however, it is important to remain focused on what may be identified as the more 'intellectual' aspects of the teaching profession. This is significant for several reasons. Arguably the most important of these is your obligation as a beginning teacher or an aspiring teacher to make increasingly well-informed decisions in the context of your everyday practice. This is because teaching is a profession in which demanding situations arise on a daily basis. Frequently there are no right or wrong answers, no procedures to follow, no time or opportunity to consult with supervising staff or colleagues. In some cases you may have the possibility of discussing with and receiving advice about incidents or concerns from appropriate others. Often, however, as a certified teacher (or even as a student teacher), you may simply be advised or expected to use your professional judgement. This may be a reasonable expectation, as it allows you to develop your skills in relation to decision making and problem solving in your specific educational context. However, it does assume that you are well-informed or have some experience of the reflective process. It assumes that you have a framework within which to consider your options and determine any possible action. Robins et al. (2003) describe reflective practice as a tool that allows teachers, student teachers and teaching assistants to understand themselves, their personal philosophies and the dynamics of their classroom more deeply. While acknowledging the critics who argue that there is little evidence that reflection actually changes behaviour, they propose that the process of engaging in reflection not only provides a personal resource that can be accessed in other similar contexts, but is also a tool that empowers individuals who use it. This is because engagement with the process of focused thinking supports self knowledge and understanding (White, 2004; Wieringa, 2011).

The capacity to engage with your professional work in this manner is not always easy. One reason is that classrooms are busy, fast-moving work environments within which pupils of diverse characteristics are engaging in an extremely important undertaking: that of learning new knowledge, skills and strategies. Another is that any framework or other tool to support your professional development is only as beneficial as the user is proficient. In order to develop the skills and competencies of an expert teacher, you need to engage in reflection. Reflective practice, over time, allows you to become skilful in making informed judgements and professional decisions, and is empowering (Robins et al., 2003). Authentic engagement in reflection supports your efforts to become contemplative, to improve your professional competencies and to identify your personal strengths and relative limitations as a teacher. It is because of its potential to impact positively on individual practice that reflection is arguably the most important of the many professional attributes that characterise successful teachers at every stage of their careers (White, 2004).

What is Reflection?

Reflection is very broadly able to be defined as the deliberate, purposeful, metacognitive thinking and/or action in which educators engage in order to improve their professional practice. Different theories, models and levels of reflection have most commonly focused on differentiating the major elements of this construct:

- the conditions, situations or circumstances that prompt engagement in the reflective process
- the process itself, different types of reflection, different concepts or opinions on how this is undertaken
- the content of the reflection, what exactly needs to be analysed, examined, discussed, challenged in the reflective process and with what perspectives or ideologies
- the product of the reflection, improved understanding of professional practice, action taken as a result of the reflective thinking.

The brief overview of understandings of reflection in educational practice that follows illustrates some of these differences as proposed by various writers in this field.

What Does the Literature Say about Reflection?

It is not possible to discuss all the writings about reflection, but a variety of ideas are presented here to provide some background for your own reading and research and to establish some common understanding of different ways of engaging with the reflective process.

No introduction to reflection in education, however brief, would be possible without discussing the early work of Dewey. His 1933 work *How We Think* is considered to be seminal in this area and was based on the ideas of a number of earlier philosophers and educators. Dewey's own definition of reflection as a cognitive *process* – 'the active, persistent and careful consideration of any belief or supposed form of knowledge in the light of the grounds that support it and the further conclusions to which it tends' (1933: 9) – indicates some of the basic characteristics that underpin almost all models and theories of reflection. However, he stresses the active, conscious, deliberate *thinking* in this particular type of problem solving. He also emphasises the rational, logical analysis of the problem, in which ideas are ordered and then linked together in a meaningful way. It was then intended that this 'chain' of thoughts was rigorously examined for any assumptions, underlying beliefs or knowledge that had been utilised in the formulating of a solution and any evidence that supported these ideas (Calderhead, 1989). This process relies heavily on the use of scientific theory to guide teaching practice and so the current and emerging scientific theories of that time are the predominant criteria in the evaluative processes of reflection. As a deliberate, reasoned, almost scientific activity, Dewey (1933) distinguished reflective thinking from everyday, routine thinking and especially from impulsive thinking. Included in his notion of routine thinking was the thinking (and any subsequent actions) that resulted from an individual's automatic adherence to rules originating from authority or from tradition. He proposed instead that action taken as a result of reflective thinking was 'intelligent action' (Calderhead, 1989: 44), because the aspects of the issue had been considered rationally and the practitioner had undergone periods of doubt and uncertainty while working towards finding a solution. Dewey (1933) proposed that opportunities for reflective thinking were prompted mainly by *practical events* that created feelings of disquiet or confusion or by a sense of wonder and awe. These were to be resolved by the persistent, reasoned thinking that he identified as reflection, and this thinking was to be guided by the goal in mind. Dewey's understanding of the role of reflection is that it is undertaken to develop the knowledge and expertise of teaching.

Despite its importance and the heavy reliance of other theorists on his work, Dewey's notion on reflection has been challenged in several ways over the decades by other writers in this area. One of the most important critiques revolves around the notion that Dewey conceptualised reflection as the process of *thinking* about action and had not significantly linked it to action taken as the result of reflective thinking, despite introducing the term reflective action, which would complete what was identified as the 'reflective cycle' (Gore and Zeichner, 1991; Noffke and Brennan, 1988), which most theorists understand to be the *purpose* of engaging in reflection. Indeed, some writers (e.g. Calderhead, 1989) are openly dismissive of reflection that does not result in action. The very popular theory on reflection developed by Schon (1983, 1987, 1991) introduces some new ideas on the reflective process itself, most especially on the implication in Dewey's (1933) theory that reflection is necessarily a process embarked on after the event, is a long, ponderous undertaking and also on the content of reflection itself.

Schon (1983, 1987, 1991) suggests two levels of reflection: (i) reflection-in-action and (ii) reflection-on-action, partly based on Dewey's (1933) work. While Schon's (1983) theory differs in the criteria that constitute the content of reflection, in that he does not consider teaching to be the implementation of scientific theory in the sense that Dewey (1933) theorised, he, and others who are inspired by Dewey's work to support reflective teaching (e.g. Cruickshank, 1985), do not offer any suggestions regarding what precisely in their practice teachers do need to be reflective about. Reflection-on-action does have some of the same characteristics, specifically that the reflective process is undertaken after the event, problem or situation that initiated the process. However, Schon (1983) offers an interesting departure from the perception that problems for reflection are necessarily reflected upon after the event. He suggests that reflection-in-action is a concept that celebrates the art of teaching, in that it allows for continual interpretation, investigation and reflective conversation with oneself about the problem while employing the information gained from past experiences to inform and guide new actions.

This process of experimentation, reflection and action combined, is cyclically conducted as the problem is continuously framed and reframed and as solutions to complex or ambiguous problems are systematically sought. This approach allows for contextually orientated experimentation in problem solving; it is a way of using past experiences, reflection and action to experimentally problem solve 'on the spot' where the circumstances are confused or unclear. Schon (1983) indicates that understanding new perspectives or views is not enough. He states that '[r]eflection-in-action necessarily involves experiment' (p. 141), indicating that reflection–in-action and the new ideas that evolve as a result must be trialled in a supportive professional arena – the classroom context. In this respect, Schon is acknowledging the experiences of the teacher as a source of knowledge that is valuable in the reflective practice. However, the notion of reflection-in-action requires that teachers have some appropriate, relevant experience upon which to draw and that they have reached a level of teacher competence from which they can reflect and act simultaneously (Hatton and Smith, 1995). This observation, in turn, suggests that teachers are more likely to be able to successfully engage with the cycle that constitutes reflection-in-action as a result of prior engagement in the reflection-in-action process. What remains to be established is what exactly was the circumstance in the relevant experiences that could be usefully drawn upon and what was the content of the reflection and from which perspective or viewpoint was it analysed?

Gore and Zeichner (1991) address these issues. While supporting both Cruickshank's (1985) and Schon's (1983, 1987, 1991) commitment to the development of reflective practitioners, they highlight the importance of both the quality and type of the reflection undertaken: the content of the reflection and the criteria that were considered. They note:

> Neither Cruickshank (1985) nor Schon (1983, 1987, 1988) have much to say about what it is that teachers ought to be reflecting about, the kinds of criteria that should come into play during the process of reflection (e.g. what distinguishes good from unacceptable educational practice) and the degree to which teachers' deliberations should incorporate a critique of the institutional contexts in which they work (V. Richardson, 1990). In some extreme cases, the impression is given that as long as teachers reflect about something, in some manner, whatever they decide to do is acceptable, since they have reflected about it. (Gore and Zeichner, 1991: 120)

Gore and Zeichner (1991) then discuss four 'varieties' of teacher reflective practice, which each have a different focus:

1. an academic version, which focuses on teachers' skills in disseminating the discipline content and presenting in such a way as to maximise its accessibility for their students;
2. a social efficacy version, which is based on research findings and focuses on evidence-based practice;
3. a developmental version, which primarily considers age and developmentally appropriate teaching strategies that focus on students' interests and thinking; and finally
4. the social reconstructionist version, in which reflection is focused on the political and social issues of schooling and on classroom interactions designed to promote greater student equity and justice. (Gore and Zeichner, 1991: 121)

There is considerable value in each of these versions of reflection; however, no one of these alone constitutes adequate, appropriate teacher reflection. While there may be a dominant focal point for reflection, the other foci also need to be considered for good teaching and reflective action to be authentic. Gore and Zeichner (1991) identify the social reconstructionist variety as 'critical reflection' although the term has a number of interpretations. Calderhead (1989) appears to use the term loosely as a general term for self criticism in reflection, while others (e.g. Gore, 1987) use the term consistently to indicate that the reflection is based on a particular set of ideological principles, and the beliefs and assumptions that are embedded in the precise philosophy that is being utilised as a frame of reference.

What Does This Mean for You?

Gore and Zeichner (1991) propose that each of these four types of reflection is important. They indicate four major aspects of your professional work. You need to ask and reflect on pertinent questions about each of these aspects in order to develop a deep understanding of your classroom interactions. These are some suggestions for questions you might think about in order to gain a holistic understanding of your professional work and your role in supporting successful learning by your students. You will be able to add others yourself.

1. *Academic reflection*: Do I know my content really well? Am I using appropriate pedagogical strategies for my students' needs? Am I well-organised and resourced in readiness to teach? Have I sequenced the content suitably for my students' needs and defining characteristics of my discipline? Have I completed the planning cycle with suitable, relevant assessment strategies

to evaluate student learning? Have I been innovative and creative in order to engage and sustain students' interest?

2. *Social efficacy reflection:* Am I implementing what I know from research about teaching this content? Have I considered specific strategies that have proven to increase student academic success? Have I considered any differences in the context and participants used in the research and my cohort and circumstances? Is this evidence-based practice meeting the needs of the students in my class?

3. *Developmental reflection:* Am I providing teaching and learning contexts, tasks and instruction that are suitable and appropriate for the age and stage of my students from a developmental perspective? Have I evaluated my students' skills and thinking to determine the stages at which each of them is able to engage in different learning contexts? Have I planned suitable instructional and task modifications to accommodate the differences in the students' thinking, emotional and physical capacities? Have I designed teaching and learning activities that are interesting for diverse groups of students? Have I taken into account and effectively utilised students' various interests to design lessons and curriculum?

4. *Social reconstructionist (critical) reflection:* What do I believe to be the purpose of education? Do I have specific philosophical beliefs or viewpoints about the values, purposes and functions of education? Have I critically evaluated the statements from my education authorities who articulate the purpose of schooling in my geographical location? Have I considered who determines the curriculum that is designed to meet the nominated purpose of education? Have I considered in what ways the curriculum supports or neglects the learning needs of students from different social, cultural and individual groups? Are there ways in which I can implement the mandatory curricula in my classroom to minimise any disadvantage to particular students or student groups? How can I mitigate any shortcomings in the system to provide more equitable education for all my students? Have I analysed compulsory tests or assessment items to identify bias or prejudice and taken appropriate measures to overcome or to diminish the impact of these where possible?

Different Levels of Reflection

This notion of different levels or types of reflective foci is not new. Van Manen (1977) had earlier developed three levels of reflection based on the work of Habermas as a hierarchical structure. The first level is *technical reflection*. At this level what is considered is the effectiveness and efficiency of achieving predetermined goals. These goals are not the focus of any criticism, modification or change. All that is reflected upon are the competencies and processes that are required to achieve these goals. The second level is *practical reflection*. At this level, the processes or the means by which the goals can be achieved, their underlying rationale and outcomes along with the goals themselves are subject to analysis, examination and assessment. The third level is *critical reflection* which is concerned with informing the practical reflection by incorporating moral and ethical considerations related to the problem into the discussion with the purpose of supporting student equity, justice care and compassion without personal bias. Although both Van Manen's (1977) and Valli's (1997) frameworks (detailed below) have been criticised as hierarchies (Hatton & Smith, 1995), they are certainly useful in that they offer different aspects of reflection practice that are important for teacher consideration.

Valli's (1992) model of reflection incorporates many aspects of Schon's and Van Manen's frameworks. She describes five levels of reflection. The first is *technical reflection*, which is much as described by Van Manen (1977). This is where students match their own competencies to professional standards, graduate competencies, the external goals and competencies of teaching, and continue to work on improving their professional performance in relation to these predetermined benchmarks. The second level, labelled *reflection-in-and-on-action*, is taken directly from Schon (1983) and combines the ongoing engagement with reflection-in-action and reflection-on-action, highlighting the need for ongoing reframing, reconsideration and self discussion of problems, both in the context of teaching itself and as reflection after the event. The third level, *deliberative reflection*, requires teachers to actively seek and consider various viewpoints in relation to pedagogical decision making. It demands that you have a strong research base from which to develop your pedagogical practice and from which to determine how to meet the diverse needs of your learners. The fourth level, *personalistic reflection*, is the development of an awareness of the impact of emotions, intuitions and self knowledge on your own cognition and, in turn, on your relationship with your learners and their personal growth. The final level is *critical reflection*, which follows the understanding of Gore (1987) and others and includes a focus on social, moral, political and ethical issues. It incorporates the development of open-mindedness, rational judgement and creativity. Although a considerable degree of overlap can easily be identified in the levels of reflection discussed, Valli's (1997) framework is the only one that explicitly acknowledges the impact of emotion, feelings and personal attributes on cognition, although others have identified it as a metacognitive activity (Calderhead, 1989; Cruickshank, 1985; Gore and Zeichner, 1991; Jay and Johnson, 2002).

Ultimately, however, while each of the models discussed (and many others that are not) has afforded valuable insights into the reflection for you, the reflective process itself is an intensely personal practice. Reflective practice that is overly dominated by prescription to any ideology, imposed values or academic evaluation is at risk of being less than authentic. Individual, personal reflection has been considered unproductive in the past (Hatton and Smith, 1995), as it has been considered to be prone to be influenced by individual bias and to be unlikely to consider individually held underlying assumptions or to consider different perspectives. However, Vartuli (cited in Heydon and Hibbert, 2010: 796) comments that the research literature confirms that teachers' beliefs are at the heart of their practice. Kinsella (2001) writes that reflective practitioners reflect on themselves, including their assumptions, and use their insights to inform their practice. Mayer (1999) concludes that teacher identities are developed from the individual's personal feelings and how they identify with being a teacher. Although he separates these aspects from teacher function, it is clear that they are, in fact, two sides of the same coin, as one cannot help but impact on another. Habermas (1974), in developing a critical science concept of reflection, regards it as self determined action. Calderhead (1989: 44) comments on this perspective, noting:

> Reflection is viewed as a process of becoming aware of one's context, of the influence of societal and ideological constraints on previously taken-for-granted practices, and gaining control over the direction of these influences.

It appears that all theories acknowledge that teacher reflection is, of necessity, based in experience. Every individual experiences what occurs in their lives differently. It is essentially a very personal interpretation of events which is mediated by several other paradigms, including prior experiences and personal beliefs and values. Given the importance of the individual beliefs, feelings, knowledge of own assumptions, understandings of their individual professional contexts and the responsibility of each of you to be self determined, Valli's (1997) *personalistic reflection* may pave the way for a more authentic, personal, reflective model more closely related to an epistemological perspective. That is, a perspective that reflects what the individual believes about knowledge construction, and their personal definitions of truth and reality. You can see that:

- some levels of reflection are more complex than others
- as student teachers or beginning teachers, you will feel some aspects to be of more urgent consideration that others on occasion (Conway, 2001)
- different situations will often require that you engage in different aspects of reflection and these will become the major focus of your activity.

What is important about the notions of reflection discussed is that, irrespective of your starting point, you do need to engage in each of these aspects of reflection described and you do need to engage with these facets authentically as an individual who recognises and acknowledges the origins and impact of your own belief systems, values and interpretations of what constitutes the role of the professional teacher. Because of your unique experiences, your perspectives in relation to a range of professional considerations will be very personal. One of the difficulties of reflective practices in the past is the perceived importance of being objective. However, the philosophical debate regarding a person's capacity to present a totally objective perspective becomes a moot point in face of the notion that all objectivity is first understood as subjective experience (Nisbett, 2005). As you critically scrutinise the origins, validity and limitations of your personal beliefs, values and principles that help you to understand your experiences, you are able to become more open to other perspectives and interpretations. From this starting point a more realistic approach to reflection practice and its potential to enhance your practice becomes possible; an approach that values the holistic nature of individuals can be developed.

Questions for Reflection

- Q1. Are there any ideas or information in these short overviews which are new for you?
- Q2. Which levels of reflective practice (if any) have you engaged with to date in your teacher preparation course?
- Q3. Are there any ideas here that you would like to discuss or challenge?
- Q4. Have you previously considered the notion of individual objectivity?
- Q5. What do you think the characteristics of an authentic reflection model may look like?
- Q6. Are you able to develop some sample questions that may be useful for supporting reflective practice in each aspect of, for example, Valli's model of reflection?

A Personal Model of Reflection

As reflection is understood to be learning based on experience, it is not surprising that Kolb's (1994) Experiential Learning Cycle provides a framework within which to organise the basic components of a Personal Reflection Model (see Figure 1.1). The first step is to acknowledge the conditions that prompt reflection by identifying an experience upon which to reflect and then describing it. This is the *What?*, which is followed by *So What?*, which requires individuals to analyse the content of the experience in terms of their own understanding of the situation and also in terms of what needs to be discussed, evaluated or challenged. The final phase is *Now What?*, which is conventionally understood to mean what ought to be done or what needs to be done. The final phase of this model as it is currently presented requires action of some sort. This reintroduces the debate regarding the necessity for reflection to result in action being taken in order to be educative and useful to you. There are a number of problems for aspiring and beginning teachers when faced with this requirement for action. These include:

- Who decides what *ought* to be done and whose belief systems and values are being promoted, supported or actioned in this decision?
- There are a number of societal and ideological restraints associated with educational workplaces that mean that these contexts do not readily accommodate the desired action, irrespective of how it may facilitate improvement in the teaching and learning process.
- A third concern focuses on the skills and capacities of the individuals engaged in the reflective cycle to actually execute the action in the event that a consensually agreed action could be determined.

Despite these limitations, however, these basic three phases of reflection are a useful starting point for a personal model of reflection designed to stimulate focused thinking without necessarily having to take action. The model presented for reflection in this instance acknowledges reflective practice as a metacognitive activity. It is an activity where you are asked to think about your own thinking processes, beliefs, values and understandings. It does not separate cognition from personal emotional responses and promotes discussion of the underlying factors that shape individual views, values and beliefs. It utilises both aspects of Gardner's (1993) intrapersonal intelligence domain in order to fully incorporate your own self knowledge and your capacity to use this information to achieve your goals related to developing authentic reflective practice. It incorporates Kolb's (1994) three-part cycle as a means of simply organising the processes embedded in the reflective process itself.

The first consideration is always what exactly needs to be reflected upon. This may be an exceptionally positive, rewarding teaching experience or professional interaction or a matter that you find challenges you in some way and for which you need to think through a satisfactory answer or solution. If rules, guidelines and standards are not to be accepted blindly and acted upon superficially, then there are always experiences that need to be purposefully thought through. The selection of an experience for reflection depends heavily on your individual priorities and how you were prompted by specific aspects of the encounter. You are frequently the person who determines what is significant enough to merit purposeful consideration at a later stage or at the moment of the event. Even at this early, descriptive stage, it is useful for you to bear in mind that the actual recount of the experience, if the situation is reflection-on-action, is an essentially personal version of

Phase (Kolb, 1994)	Questions related to self (Gardner, 1993)
What?	Why have I selected this experience as a focus for reflection? What makes it important for me consciously and purposefully think about this experience at this time?
So What?	What is the focus here as I understand it? Is there more than one level of reflection that I think needs to be considered as a focus for discussion in this experience? In identifying my focus what level(s) am I prioritising in my reflection? Why would that be so? Do my priorities reflect my values and beliefs about the nature of teachers' professional work? Do my priorities reflect anything about how I am developing as a prospective teacher? Do I need to engage at a level of reflection that necessitates engaging with ethical and moral considerations? (critical reflection)
Now What?	Do I need to take action or just think about what action may be appropriate if the circumstances permitted? Do I have the skills, knowledge and strategies to make a well-informed decision about what action may be able to be taken? Can I realistically take action? What personal, social and ideological influences have impacted on the action I would take? How does my proposed action reflect my understanding and personal beliefs regarding what constitutes ethical, professional, effective teaching and the role of the teacher? Are my decisions and proposed actions congruent with my ethical and moral perspectives? Do I have the motivation, perseverance and capacities required to activate my plans successfully?

Figure 1.1   A Personal Model of Reflection

what occurred. While there is certainly no doubt that common understanding does exist between individuals and in society in general, any recount reflects the interpretation of the person compiling it. An experience that may concern or challenge one individual may not present itself as an event or occurrence worth thinking about to you or to others.

The second phase is the analytical stage. It is at this stage that the focus or foci of the experience need to be determined. This usually changes as you gain more experience and gain a greater understanding of contexts of education. For you as aspiring and beginning teachers, reflecting on your own teaching for the first time, the focus could frequently be on the more technical goals related to the profession. It may be a priority to check your own or individual pupils' performances against the levels of the standards or other benchmarks established by others as they are understood by the student teachers at that time. As can be seen in various models already described, there is little discussion or challenge about the actual measures themselves as they are defined for the purpose of gauging professional competencies. The practical implications of these may differ to reflect your relative strengths and limitations when you engage in the next stage. This following stage engages you in the consideration of the ways and means that these goals may be achieved. However, your rather narrow focus, in time and with some experience, needs to expand beyond basic skills and competencies and it is at this stage that you are able to become most acutely aware of your assumptions, belief systems and personal values and the impact that these have on your professional understandings and ideals. It is important to look inward and examine why you hold certain attitudes and perspectives and to challenge personal views and to assess the quality of the veracity and trustworthiness of their foundations. This activity, if engaged with authentically, allows you to examine your assumptions, prejudices, preferences and bias and assess their impact on your professional choices, decisions and practice. It can be argued that it is at this stage that the essence of professionalism comes into play because engaging at the level of critical reflection necessitates the inclusion of moral and ethical beliefs as a crucial part of the reflective process.

The final stage of reflection is the stage when action is planned, options considered and perhaps some intervention or scheme is implemented. However, any prospective action or plans in this stage are significantly determined by the analysis and the level of reflection that was the focus of the preceding stage. The decisions regarding any potential action are guided by available information, your instincts, your previously related experiences and the ethical and moral considerations that guided any critical reflection. In order to plan effectively for decision making, prepare proposed changes to practice or develop a new mindset it is important to be as well-informed as possible. Many professional experiences have the potential to be enhanced, even if reflected upon retrospectively, if sufficient knowledge and understanding are part of the reflective process. Self knowledge is also as important in the final stage as it was in the analytical stage before it, most especially if action actually is to be taken. The *Now What?* should be reflective of your personally held values, perspectives and competencies in relation to the focus of the reflection in order to be authentic. Ideally, the ideologies, social restraints, limitations of context and personal perspectives that are embedded in decision making and potential action should be:

- transparent
- reasoned and founded in fact, ethical considerations and professional values
- open to discussion and alternative perspectives.

However, in many practical situations, the planning for action and decision making components are not complete until they are activated. Because of this, you need to consider if you have the personal capacities to follow through with the planned actions. This is significant, not only to the required knowledge, skills and strategies but also to various personal attributes that will impact on your potential for success. These attributes include motivation, persistence and capacity to persevere when difficulties arise.

Questions for Reflection

- Q1. Are there any aspects of this model that might have helped you determine a course of action while on professional experience?
- Q2. Does this model incorporate the aspects that you nominated as contributing to an authentic model of reflection?
- Q3. Do you think that engaging with professional experiences using this process has the potential to support improved professional practice for you?

Practice in Reflection

Reflection is not always easy. Many professional experiences are challenging in so many ways that it can initially be difficult to conscientiously expend the time and energy required to systemically think through experiences that have proved less than optimal or even those that were serendipitously successful. The most successful approach may be to engage regularly in reflective practice with a small group of peers or with a suitable partner. Interaction of this nature, where individuals can respectfully challenge their own and others' assumptions, can both nurture the habit of engaging in the reflective process and facilitate a deeper understanding of the origins of diverse opinions and perspectives (Burrows, 1995). Additionally, this engagement with others can result in the participants broadening their knowledge base, developing increasingly skilful ways of identifying the focus of reflection and becoming more conscious of the importance of critical, professional reflection.

However, as it is unlikely that any two professional experiences are identical, it may be useful to provide some common focus for the discussions. McGovern (2012) describes the use of carefully chosen objects and literature to facilitate the conversation in the reflection component of his service learning classes; the purpose of which is to help students identify and articulate their own beliefs and values. While a similar purpose can be identified in the use of reflective conversations for student teachers, in this instance, scenarios have been developed to illustrate some of the tensions and conflicts that characterise teaching as a profession. The scenario below and those that are presented for discussion in the following chapters are examples of experiences that can be part of any teacher's professional life. They are useful for reflective practice because there are no 'correct' answers. The diverse responses of individual teachers and students to these situations serve to illustrate both the complexity of teaching as a profession and the need to have a reflective framework from which to unpack, analyse and determine a response, albeit a theoretical response in this context.

The experiences described in the scenarios stem from issues that arise from foundational beliefs or theories about teachers' work, the role of teachers as professionals and current notions of 'best practice' that are commonly used in the development of standards. Frequently, although the standards or benchmarks themselves are not usually the subject of any challenge or change, these measures include assumptions about the commonality of beliefs and value systems and about your degree of understanding and interpretation. As a result, benchmarks and professional teaching standards are often presumed to be interpreted and understood in the same way by all members of the profession, despite their personal diversity. In practice, this is unlikely to be the case, as individuals invariably interpret each construct in terms of their own knowledge and experience. Consequently, many aspects of teaching standards and benchmarks provide fertile ground for discussion, analysis and reflective practice.

Scenario One

James had just completed his teaching degree and was very excited when he was offered his first appointment in a large, local primary school. He had visited for the first time before the summer break for his orientation and to ensure he would be as organised as possible for his first few weeks of 'real' teaching. All was going smoothly and he felt quite comfortable and confident until he entered the staffroom towards the end of the lunch break to wait for the principal, whom he was yet to meet. In the staffroom, several experienced members of staff were discussing the new principal's plans for the upcoming school year. It appeared that he had decided, with encouragement from the local secondary school, to experiment with new class structures for all but the youngest pupils. The other pupils were to be organised in 'performance' groups for literacy and numeracy each day. They were then to be assigned a particular teacher for their group for the year. This meant that the pupils might have as many as three teachers during

(Continued)

(Continued)

the day instead of the usual arrangement of one teacher to one group of pupils identified as their class. If the literacy or numeracy teacher they were assigned happened to be their class teacher, then those pupils experienced less movement and less changes of teachers.

The teachers in the staffroom were debating the proposed changes, when another teacher came in and joined the conversation. She went on to explain that she knew of other information relating to the changes. It appeared that the principal had decided that the most experienced teachers should teach the most needy learners and that the less experienced teachers should teach those who had already demonstrated appropriate competencies in one or other area of learning. Additionally, the groups identified as 'needy' were to be small, with the group size increasing in proportion with the learners' proficiencies. She explained that the groups of needy learners were to be flexible in order to permit them to progress to the other groups as they developed increased competencies. All the restructuring was to be discussed in detail at the staff meeting day at the end of the term.

At this meeting, James was invited to join the other staff members who were reflecting on the implications of the changes. Initially, there were debates and suggestions regarding the supervised movement of pupils from one class to another, the timetable was reorganised to accommodate whole-school literacy and numeracy blocks and a plan for sharing resources was devised. After lunch the teachers were to determine, with the help of the principal, which teachers were to be assigned to the performance groups. Over lunch James listened attentively to the debate about the notion of placing the more experienced teachers with the smaller groups of learners who needed explicit support.

The staff members had obviously taken the time to think the ideas through. They appeared happy with the screening process that had been developed and the idea that flexibility was a key aspect of the programme, but there was some concern about three aspects of the plan. One concerned the provision of appropriate, challenging, teaching and learning tasks for the high achievers if they were in the classes allocated to the less experienced teachers. This was mentioned, they assured James, not because they felt less experienced teachers were not well-prepared but because these learners, when grouped together, needed to be provided for in a variety of ways that were not just extensions of the class activities and they considered that to be a considerable challenge for a beginning teacher. Another concern related to the organisation of the 'flexible' phases when pupils had opportunities to visit and contribute to each other's activities. They agreed that a planned schedule would help them organise that aspect of the restructuring. The third worry concerned the limited range of experience that the newer members of staff would have in supporting the learning of pupils with difficulties in the key areas of numeracy and literacy.

As they left the staffroom on their way to the meeting in the library, James wondered how the principal would respond to the concerns that had been discussed. He was surprised to see as he walked into the library that there was a question written on the whiteboard in large letters. He read 'What is the purpose of education?' He was even more surprised to see the staff laughing and shaking their heads. It was, apparently, a familiar question for these teachers and they began to write their responses on the paper provided. James felt uneasy. It was not the type of 'big picture' question that had been a priority during his teacher preparation, although it had been discussed. He sat, wondering how to respond. What was he going to write on the otherwise blank page that had his name on it?

This scenario presents a predicament explicitly related to professional work. What is the purpose of it all? It illustrates the situation that often arises from the challenges implicit in proposed changes to traditionally held views of schooling. In general, as can be seen in the following chapter, professional standards for teachers generally include statements relating to the requirement for teachers to provide quality education for all learners and to develop the capacities to recognise aspects of diversity and to adapt their practice in order to ensure this goal for all learners is met. What might you consider in order to answer the following questions? Where could you begin your analysis? What important aspects of professional practice might you reflect upon first? In order to facilitate the process, the guiding questions in the Personal Reflection Model described in Figure 1.1 have been customised so they reflect the content of this scenario (see Figure 1.2). As it is often a temptation for students new to the reflective process to try to determine the *Now What?* before engaging in the analytical process that is embedded in the *So What?*, it may be useful to record your answers to each of the questions in the second phase. In this way, the congruence between your analysis and your proposed course of action can remain strong.

Questions for Reflection

- Q1. Are there multiple issues here for reflection? List them.
- Q2. What is the issue for critical reflection?
- Q3. In James' situation, what would you contribute to the discussion?

Phase Kolb, 1994)	Questions related to self (Gardner, 1993)
What?	Would I have selected this experience as a focus for reflection if I were James? What makes it important for me consciously and purposefully think about this experience at this time?
So What?	What are the many foci here as I understand them? What are the levels of reflection (technical, practical and critical or choose from one of the other models that incorporate various types/levels of reflection. Use whichever to help you work through your experience) that I think need to be considered as foci for discussion in this experience? In identifying my focus/foci what level/s am I prioritising in my reflection? Why would that be so? Do my priorities reflect/include consideration of my values and beliefs as a beginning teacher about the nature of teachers' professional work? Do my priorities reflect anything about how I am trying to develop as a beginning teacher? Do I need to engage at a level of reflection that necessitates engaging with my personal ethical and moral considerations (critical reflection) (i) about the purpose and process of education and (ii) my obligation to meet all students' learning needs?
Now What?	What response (action), based on my responses to phase two, would I need to take at the staff meeting when asked to join the discussion about the principal's proposed changes to the organisation and content of lessons in literacy and numeracy? Do I have the skills, knowledge and strategies to make a well-informed decision about the response I may make? If not, does this impact on my response? Can I realistically take action? Is it appropriate of me in this instance to make a response, given that I am the most recent recruit to the school's team of teachers? What personal, social and ideological influences have impacted on the response I would make? How does my proposed action reflect my understanding and personal beliefs regarding what constitutes ethical, professional, effective teaching and the purpose of education? Are my decisions and proposed actions congruent with my ethical and moral perspectives? Do I have the motivation, perseverance and capacities required to activate any ideas I may suggest in my response and to follow them through as successfully as possible?

Figure 1.2   The Personal Reflection Model for Scenario One

Conclusion

This chapter introduces the notion of reflective practice. It provides a brief overview of some of the models of reflection that have been developed over a number of years to support reflective practice in teaching and other professions. Additionally, it discusses some major differences in how the components of reflective practice have been defined and the impact that these variations can have on how you understand and apply strategies in this aspect of your professional work. In addition to identifying some differences, the main phases of reflection, about which there appears to be some consensus, have been discussed. There is also agreement that professional teacher reflection is inextricably linked to professional experiences, whether *in action* or as recounted incidents known as *on action*. Despite a traditional tendency to applaud the attempts of reflective practitioners to be 'objective' in their deliberations, a Personal Reflection Model, based on Gardner's (1993) intrapersonal intelligence domain and utilising Kolb's (1994) three-phase framework, has been developed as a more authentic approach to facilitate improved professional performance in the current climate of increased teacher accountability, newly developed professional standards and changing societal and ideological expectations.

There is also an acknowledgement of the potential for individual interpretations and perspectives on the nature of your work as presented in various professional standards and the need for you, as a prospective teacher, to investigate and to reflect on the concepts and assumptions that underpin your standards, especially if they are presented as mandatory documents. This chapter is developed in such a way as to provide a paradigm for the chapters that follow. There will be discussions of literature, opportunities for you to think about personal knowledge, opinions and perspectives as an ongoing activity and scenarios on which to focus your thinking. This provision of scenarios for discussion provides content for a shared conversation, a means by which you can collegially work together to identify and explore your personally held values and beliefs in relation to your professional work. These conversations also provide opportunities for you to explore some implications of the theoretical and ideological underpinnings that are integral elements of many types of professional standards for teachers. The purpose of engaging authentically with the predicaments and complexities that are conveyed in the scenario recounted in this chapter and those in the chapters that follow, will also serve to provide contexts that allow you to become familiar with, and skilful in, the identification, analysis and planning process that constitute professional reflection for teachers.

How you organise your thinking, record your thoughts and reflections, is really up to you. There are a number of commonly utilised ways of recording which others have found very useful. These include pairing with a carefully selected 'critical friend' for discussion (Burrows, 1995), journalling your own ideas and perspectives in order to develop a deep understanding of yourself (Dinkelman, 2003; Francis, 1995), art making as an expression of self (Grushka, 2005), reflective writing (Hoover, 1994; Nyaumwe and Mtetwa, 2011), action research studies and field-based experiences (Kemmis, 2011; Liston and Zeichner, 1990; Zeichner, 1981), blogging (Killeavy and Moloney,

2010), video making and online discussions (Ozcinar and Deryakulu, 2011), working with the Zen Buddhist notion of 'mindfulness' (Tremmel, 1993), using frameworks and strategies as developed here and elsewhere (Tsangaridou and O'Sullivan, 1994), and developing digital portfolios (Wade and Yarbrough, 1996). The opportunities are endless. In the following chapters you will find discussions of some of the most critical, foundational issues that have the capacity to impact on your thinking, professional perspectives and classroom interactions. You will also find invitations to reflect on these as a means of developing your professional learning.

References

Burrows, D. (1995) The nurse teacher's role in the promotion of reflective practice. *Nurse Education Today*, 15 (5): 346–50.

Calderhead, J. (1989) Reflective teaching and teacher education. *Teaching and Teacher Education*, 5 (1): 43–51.

Conway, P. (2001) Anticipatory reflection while learning to teach: from a temporally truncated to a temporally distributed model of reflection in teacher education. *Teaching and Teacher Education*, 17 (1): 89–106.

Cruickshank, D.R. (1985) Uses and benefits of reflective teaching. *The Phi Delta Kappan*, 66 (10): 704–6.

Dewey, J. (1933) *How We Think: A Restatement of the Relation of Reflective Thinking to the Educative Process*. Boston, MA: DC Heath.

Dinkelman, T. (2003) Self-study in teacher education – a means and ends tool for promoting reflective teaching. *Journal of Teacher Education*, 54 (1): 6–18.

Francis, D. (1995) The reflective journal – a window to preservice teachers practical knowledge. *Teaching and Teacher Education*, 11 (3): 229–41.

Gardner, H. (1993) *Frames of Mind. Tenth Anniversary Edition*. New York: Basic Books.

Gore, J. (1987) Reflecting on reflective teaching. *Journal of Teacher Education*, 38 (2): 33–9.

Gore, J. and Zeichner, K. (1991) Action research and reflective teaching in preservice teacher education – a case study from the United States. *Teaching and Teacher Education*, 7 (2): 119–36.

Grushka, K. (2005) Artists as reflective self-learners and cultural communicators: an exploration of the qualitative aesthetic dimension of knowing self through reflective practice in art-making. *Reflective Practice*, 6 (3): 353–66.

Habermas, J. (1974) *Theory and Practice*. London: Heinemann.

Hatton, N. and Smith, D. (1995) Reflection in teacher education: towards definition and implementation. *Teaching and Teacher Education*, 11 (1): 33–49.

Heydon, R. and Hibbert, K. (2010) 'Relocating the personal' to engender critically reflective practice in pre-service literacy teachers. *Teaching and Teacher Education*, 26 (4): 796–804.

Hoover, L. (1994) Reflective writing as a window on preservice teachers thought processes. *Teaching and Teacher Education*, 10 (1): 83–93.

Jay, J.K. and Johnson, K.L. (2002) Capturing complexity: a typology of reflective practice for teacher education. *Teaching and Teacher Education*, 18 (1): 73–85.

Kemmis, S. (2011) 'A self-reflective practitioner and a new definition of critical participatory action research.' In N. Mockler and J. Sachs (eds), *Rethinking Educational Practice through Reflexive Inquiry*, vol. 7. Dordrecht: Springer Netherlands. pp. 11–29.

Killeavy, M. and Moloney, A. (2010) Reflection in a social space: can blogging support reflective practice for beginning teachers? *Teaching and Teacher Education*, 26 (4): 1070–6.

Kinsella, E. (2001) Reflections on reflective practice. *Canadian Journal of Occupational Therapy*, 68 (3): 195–8.

Kolb, D. (1994) *Experiential Learning: Experience as the Source of Learning and Development.* Engelwoods Cliffs, NJ: Prentice–Hall.

Liston, D.P. and Zeichner, K.M. (1990) Reflective teaching and action research in preservice teacher-education. *Journal of Education for Teaching*, 16 (3): 235–54.

Mayer, D. (1999) Building teaching identities: implications for preservice teacher education. Paper presented at the Australian Association for Research in Education Conference, Melbourne, Australia.

McGovern, D. (2012) Learning serving reflecting. Paper presented at the International Conference Future of Education, Florence.

Nisbett, R. (2005) *The Geography of Thought.* London: Nicholas Brearley.

Noffke, S. and Brennan, M. (1988) The dimensions of reflection: a conceptual and contextual analysis. Paper presented at the American Educational Research Association, New Orleans.

Nyaumwe, L.J. and Mtetwa, D.K. (2011) Developing a cognitive theory from student teachers' post-lesson reflective dialogues on secondary school mathematics. *South African Journal of Education*, 31 (1): 145–59.

Ozcinar, H. and Deryakulu, D. (2011) The effects of reflection points in video-cases and teacher participation in online discussion groups on reflective thinking. *Hacettepe Universitesi Egitim Fakultesi Dergisi-Hacettepe University Journal of Education*, 40: 321–31.

Richardson, V. (1990). *The Evolution of Reflective Teaching and Teacher-Education.* New York: Teachers College Press.

Robins, A., Ashbaker, B., Enriquez, J. and Morgan, J. (2003) Learning to reflect: professional practice for professionals and paraprofessionals. *International Journal of Learning*, 10: 2555–65.

Schon, D. (1983) *The Reflective Practitioner: How Professionals Think in Action.* New York: Basic Books.

Schon, D. (1987) *Educating the Reflective Practitioner.* San Francisco: Jossey Bass.

Schon, D. (1991) *The Reflective Practitioner: How Professionals Think and Act.* Oxford: Avebury.

Tremmel, R. (1993) Zen and the art of reflective practice in teacher-education. *Harvard Educational Review*, 63 (4): 434–58.

Tsangaridou, N. and OSullivan, M. (1994) Using pedagogical reflective strategies to enhance reflection amongst preservice physical education teachers. *Journal of Teaching in Physical Education*, 14 (1): 13–33.

Valli, L. (1992) *Reflective Teacher Education.* Albany, NY: State University of New York Press.

Valli, L. (1997) Listening to other voices: a description of teacher reflection in the United States. *Peabody Journal of Education*, 72 (1): 67–88.

Van Manen, M. (1977) Linking ways of knowing with ways of being practical. *Curriculum inquiry*, 6 (3): 205–28.

Wade, R.C. and Yarbrough, D B. (1996. Portfolios: a tool for reflective thinking in teacher education? *Teaching and Teacher Education*, 12 (1): 63–79.

White, D. (2004) Reflective practice: wishful thinking or a practical leadership tool? *Practising Administrator*, 26 (3): 41–4.

Wieringa, N. (2011) Teachers' educational design as a process of reflection-in-action: the lessons we can learn from Donald Schon's *The Reflective Practitioner* when studying the professional practice of teachers as educational designers. *Curriculum Inquiry*, 41 (1): 167–74.

Zeichner, K. (1981) Reflective teaching and field-based experience in teacher education. *Interchange*, 12 (4): 1–22.

Chapter 2: Teaching as Professional Practice

- Q1. What do think are the characteristics of professional teacher practice?
- Q2. Why do you think you have elected these particular attributes?
- Q3. Have you known any professional practitioners?
- Q4. Do you think that teachers' professional practice has changed over a number of years?
- Q5. Why or why not? Give reasons for your response to Q4.

Introduction

Establishing a definition of 'professional work' in a general sense would be a difficult task at present for you as an aspiring teacher. A glance at advertisements in any of the media will provide a long list of professional builders, professional hairdressers, professional handymen and so forth. It appears that 'profession' has become synonymous with 'occupation' in some aspects of current usage. This situation makes it even more important for you to establish what is meant by professional teaching practice, complex as it may become. Even the idea of professional ethics is now used regularly in connection with a range of occupations, including a removal firm who advertise their drivers as ethical, professional and courteous. In the context of its current usage, it may be difficult for you to decide if you think teaching is a profession or an occupation. The literature discussed in the following section offers some ideas about professionalism, the historical and current implications for you as beginning teachers and student teachers, and critically discusses the frameworks or standards that have been put in place to regulate the profession.

What Does the Literature Say about Teaching as a Profession?

Marsh (2000) offers three perspectives of the characteristics of professions in general. While each of these contains features that may be easily identified with teaching, no single view fully encompasses the unique situation in which teachers currently find themselves. Therefore, a selection of characteristics from each of the models presented by Stinnett and Huggett, Purvis, Travers and Reborc (in Marsh, 2000: 312) provides a useful model from which to start your discussion about teaching as professional practice. You need also to bear in mind that there exists no consensus about the status of teaching as profession and most discourses around this issue are focused on either power or authority, or both (Sachs, 2003a). The selected attributes below are neither comprehensive nor complete and may easily be revised as a result of your own reflection on teaching as a profession. These characteristics are:

- Involves intellectual activities and techniques.
- Has a code of ethics.
- Requires extended specialised preparation.
- Demands continual service and growth.
- Sets its own standards and monitors professional performance with independent judgement.
- Affords a life career within a structure.
- Is a social service.

These traits represent much of what is expected of you as an aspiring teacher and the majority of these provide a number of clear indications of how the current climate relating to professionalism has developed. The significant exception is the notion that you may already have noted, that teachers as professionals set and independently monitor their own performance using independent judgement. Currently this is not the case for many of you. Although many other professional bodies and associations have done this for quite some time and with considerable success (Hinton, 2006; Howie, 2006; Kohler et al., 2006; Paull and Cosgrove, 2003), the general 'one size fits all' standards that are produced for a much wider audience of teachers and those of you who are preparing to teach, are currently developed by individuals who work at some distance from classroom practice. They are likely to be developed by ministerial bodies and others who are advised by teachers or consultants who now work in contexts removed from the realities of classroom environments and who have other, underlying agendas. This other agenda is most often driven by political and market forces. Additionally, these sets of teaching standards tend to be monitored in a supervisory manner using evidence-based portfolios and other 'hard evidence', not independent teacher judgement. These standards are at their most powerful and arguably most dangerous when they are used as the mandatory standards for teacher accreditation. The situation is accentuated when these standards are accompanied by mandated, specific pedagogical models and implemented in the context of compulsory highly regulated curricula. In order to understand how members of your chosen profession have found themselves in the current circumstances with regard to this specific characteristic, it is important to understand the social conditions and political arenas that have facilitated what Groundwater-Smith and Mockler (2009) now identify as the 'age of compliance'.

The change to the traditionally held notions of the purpose of education came to Westernised countries in the 1980s. In England, policy documents related to teaching were developed specifically for the purpose of changing the nature of your work as a teacher (Friedson, 1994; Furlong et al., 2000). With societal values changing, a world recession looming, technology advancing rapidly and the constant redefining of the workforce, governments began to reassess educational aims and purposes in terms of the economy and global market forces. Educational endeavour, which had previously been focused on the promotion of social equity and on preparing young people for work in societies that retained many of the characteristics of the Industrial Era, became increasingly viewed as a means by which national economic viability and social stability could be sustained (Brown and Lauder, 1996). These circumstances resulted in massive changes in approaches to educational governance which subsequently impacted as changed professional practice. Formerly a relatively autonomous profession, with agency to implement various basic curricula through any number of personally meaningful pedagogical practices, teachers and student teachers now found themselves in a culture of unprecedented and increasingly intensive external audit and supervision.

The transformation in education has included the development of common policy and management agendas (new managerialism), a shift of financial responsibility to more localised levels of authority accompanied by rigid accountability structures and a commitment to a particular type of 'audit' approach to 'school effectiveness', the results of which are publicly advertised and often negatively compared (Angus, 2007). As a result, teachers then became publicly responsible for poor school outcomes, as measured on the standardised testing that was introduced (Kelly, 2009) for entire nations of school pupils. These tests were designed and planned to be implemented in a rigorously organised fashion, irrespective of the diverse contexts in which teachers worked and of the teaching and learning needs of their various groups of clientele. In turn, any poor school results were attributed to lack of teacher competency and teaching, as the profession suffered a collapse of public confidence. This chain of events contributed to the erosion of teacher professionalism (Parr, 2004) as it was previously understood. Day and his colleague (Day and Smethem, 2009), acknowledge that professionalism is culturally and geographically subject to interpretation (Helsby, 1996). As a result, ideas defining what it is to be professional are socially constructed and historically mediated (Holroyd, 2000). This leads to influences from social, economic and political factors (Sachs, 2003a). Day et al. (2006) summarise the changes in this way:

> Although reforms in schools are different in every country in their content, direction and pace, they have five common factors.
>
> (i) They are proposed because governments believe that by intervening to change the conditions under which students learn, they can accelerate improvements, raise standards of achievement and somehow increase economic competitiveness.
>
> (ii) They address implicit worries of governments concerning a perceived fragmentation of personal and social values in society.
>
> (iii) They challenge teachers' existing practices, resulting in periods of at least temporary destabilisation.
>
> (iv) They result in an increased work load for teachers; and
>
> (v) They do not always pay attention to teachers' identities – arguably central to motivation efficacy, commitment, job satisfaction and effectiveness. (Day et al., 2006: 603)

Bloomfield (2006) noted these similar trends had appeared in Australian policy documents and remarked that, as a result, a particular type of teacher and teaching was being promoted, following the general trend that was being experienced by teachers across Britain and North America. Conformity to standards, increased levels of accountability and the notion of 'professional objectivity' (Groundwater-Smith and Mockler, 2009: 8), were endorsed as a means to promote and sustain 'quality' in educational contexts. It was anticipated that these measures would then flow into the general community as increased social and economic stability. It is these three aspects of teachers' professional lives and the associated consequences of these that have created the most disquiet and concern among discerning academics who have specialised interests in teachers and teaching. That is not to say that the introduction of teaching standards or the standards themselves are universally criticised. Indeed, they are being welcomed and promoted by various sections of the teaching community (Cheers, 2001; Cosgrove, 2007; Draper et al., 2007; Emmett and Paull, 2003; Ingvarson, 1995, 2002a, 2002b, 2010; Ingvarson and Kleinhenz, 2003; Ius and Emmett, 2006; Paull, 2001; Ramsey et al., 2006) who agree that standards are a means by which teacher professionalism will be improved and teacher standing in the community enhanced. Others are appraising the standards more cautiously (Apple, 2001; Darling-Hammond, 1999; Evans, 2008; Groundwater-Smith and Mockler, 2009; Sachs, 2003b; Schuck et al., 2008; Thiessen, 2000), some acknowledging the potential of standards to open up opportunities for professional discourse, ensure quality in content knowledge and other basic competencies, others voicing significant areas of concern.

Darling-Hammond's (1999: 39) much-quoted comment sums up the concerns of many that the standards may be interpreted as a panacea for all problems related to teachers and to education in general. She writes, 'Teaching standards are not a magic bullet'. Any sets of professional standards that are presented or interpreted in such a way that limits diversity, pose professional risks. School staffs, professions or associations are made up of a number of diverse individuals. It is this strength in diversity that has the potential to ensure the profession remains strong, innovative and inventive in pursuit of its common goals (Kincheloe, 1998) and the lack of allowance for diversity in any 'one size fits all' paradigm that is problematic. Among the identified problems there are concerns that teachers will not have the freedom to develop specific work-related attributes. The curtailing of professional teacher judgement is one that is causing concern and is a major contributor to the perceived lack of confidence in this particular teacher attribute (Groundwater-Smith and Mockler, 2009). The reality that teachers are no longer relied upon to assess the progress of their students in the foundational areas of numeracy and literacy is a considerable blow to the notion of teachers as professionals. While not an advertised, integral part of teaching standards themselves, the introduction of standards for students is certainly related to the big picture of standardising the profession as testing student academic outcomes is perceived as providing the 'proof' (or otherwise) of increased teacher competencies. The rise in popularity of compulsory, 'one size fits all' standardised testing of students' basic competencies (and other purposes) as indicated by the set, mandatory curricula has added to teachers' workloads by increasing their administrative duties (Groundwater-Smith and Mockler, 2009: 9). In addition, the results of one study indicated that teachers' feelings about standardised testing was in direct relation to their perceptions of the degree of negative impact these measures have on their efforts to provide for their students' needs (Darling-Hammond and Wise, 1985).

This situation, in turn, raises another potential problem. Standards for teachers and students have the potential to deny educators the opportunities they need to develop their personal pedagogies, which are the product of ongoing efforts to marry content and strategies together in a manner that is personally meaningful and productive for both teacher and students. Shulman (1983) comments on the nature of the teaching and learning process itself, noting that teaching is an interactive activity: teachers make decisions and commit to actions in response to their students' responses and actions. As a result, he remarks (Shulman, 1983: 488) that it is 'ludicrous' to try to dictate how teachers should best respond when policy and practice are so often the antithesis of each other. Indeed, creative and effective ways of responding to students' needs is often to be found by engaging in critical professional discourse, the capacity for which is an essential component of transformative education (Armstrong, 2006; Barth, 2006; Beck, 2008; Grady et al., 2008; Groundwater-Smith and Mockler, 2009). 'One size fits all' standards, by their very nature, tend not to promote either critical discourse or transformative education. Transformative education in this context is understood as educational practices that trigger the learners to challenge or question personally held perspectives and assumptions, which necessitate reflection and discussion and which have the capacity to allow the learners to reconceptualise previously held convictions or beliefs.

What Does This Mean for You?

There are several implications of the introduction of professional standards, mandatory curriculum documents, compulsory pedagogies and standardised testing for you as an aspiring teacher. You must be well-informed regarding which documents are mandatory and which are recommended. Indeed, you need to know which *parts* of various documents are mandated and which are not. You need to become aware of several features of your work that will impact on you personally in your professional context. These include:

- There may be no choice about what to teach, despite the diversity of your students, their geographical locations and their cultural expectations.
- Planning for teaching may need a significant amount of detail. Some education authorities mandate exactly how many minutes a week are spent teaching

(Continued)

(Continued)

different subject content and you may have to identify the required varied subject matter in your integrated units of work.

- There may be restrictive pedagogical approaches and frameworks within which you will have to be creative and innovative in order to successfully meet the learning needs of your students.
- The standardised testing regime may be counterproductive in terms of your usual pedagogical approaches and may not provide the opportunities for a range of students to demonstrate what they know about the material being examined.
- There may exist some personal conflict if the standardised testing results show a disparity between your professional judgement of a child's capabilities and what they could achieve on the test day.
- Many standards are minimum standards only. They describe the most essential competencies that are expected to be demonstrated. They are rarely a complete inventory of all the skills, capacities and professional attributes that need to be demonstrated by you as a teacher. Irrespective of how well-developed they are in detail, they are open to personal interpretation and degrees of achievement.
- As a result, you will need to engage in professional conversation and reflection in order to develop your personal understanding of teaching as a profession, remain motivated, experience job satisfaction and develop your identity as a teacher.
- While teaching standards may be highly important in your preservice education and beyond, Darling-Hammond's cautionary comment about them not being a magic bullet should not be forgotten. There are many issues that will necessitate that you use your professional judgement, despite all the compulsory documents and mandated standards.
- You will still have to develop considerable skills in planning for diagnostic, formative (ongoing) and summative assessment in order to guide your planning for teaching and inform your practice to meet students' diverse needs.
- You will need to develop an understanding of the differences between testing and assessing, the strengths and limitations of each and the ways in which the results can be interpreted.

Day and Smethem (2009) argue that the 'heart' of the matter for teachers has not been adequately considered. They suggested that the reforms are challenging teachers both emotionally and cognitively. They appreciate that the response of teachers who are gradually losing control of long-held personal principles and pedagogies may be expressed as a range of negative emotions. These may be expressed as a loss of professional identity and moral integrity and a subsequent reduction of the altruistic motivators that lead individuals to initially select teaching as a profession. This becomes the most significant impact of the reforms that seek to improve the teaching profession. The very nature of various 'one size fits all' schemes, models or assessments is countercultural to a healthy school ethos that celebrates the diversity of their students. They may even be counterproductive and detrimental to the very personal nature of teachers' work and to many of the reasons teachers remain engaged in the profession. Day and Smethem (2009), in their discussion of teacher identity, stress the importance of self knowledge, arguing that strong, accurate self knowledge facilitates teachers' engagement with the moral agency that characterises the teaching profession. In acknowledging teaching as a caring profession, in which individual values and beliefs are of paramount importance and an integral part of everyday work, Day and Smethem (2009) recognise the challenge for teachers as individuals to retain a positive sense of teacher identity in the face of measures that increasingly regulate every aspect of their professional lives. Teachers need to be able to know that they have capacity to make a difference in students' lives and that they have the autonomy to act on their personal values and beliefs in order to ensure the best possible outcomes for their students in a holistic manner.

Day et al. (2006: 601) note that:

> If identity is a key influencing factor on teachers' sense of purpose, self-efficacy, motivation, commitment, job satisfaction and effectiveness, then investigation of those factors which influence positively and negatively, the contexts in which these occur and the consequences for practice, is essential.

Malm (2009) also proposes that the contexts in which teachers currently work necessitate consideration of personal dispositions. She suggests that teacher preparation programmes should include components that promote development in personal attributes, including self awareness, as they play a critical role in the development of individual understandings of what it is to be a teacher. Mockler (2011) contends that professional teacher identities, formed and reformed over a career, are infinitely more valuable to the profession itself than the functionalist 'role' of teachers which is presented in the standards. She goes further and argues that they are also a more powerful political tool than the type of teacher identity that is promoted by the standards and other mandatory professional constraints. As teachers appear to be bearing much of the responsibility for social and economic reform and sustainability, it may appear, paradoxically, that they are both powerful and powerless. It may be that Sachs (in Groundwater-Smith and Mockler, 2009: 6), in calling for teachers to be more active in their own profession and to work towards a professionalism that is characterised by 'democratic principles, negotiated and collaborative roles, is socially critical, future orientated and strategic and tactical', has provided a model of the teaching profession that is diametrically opposed to the 'managerial' model that is represented by mandatory standards, prescribed curricula and external testing. Sachs (2001) believes that the professionalism that is currently emerging from teachers themselves is characterised by more democratic principles and collaboratively negotiated roles and is a new 'democratic professionalism'. However, the degree to which teachers are able to promote and sustain a new 'democratic professionalism' will depend largely on their capacities to know themselves as professionals and understand how their values and beliefs about their work can be sustained in their diverse professional contexts and under the increasing pressure of standardisation of the profession.

Questions for Reflection

- Q1. What do you think about professional teaching standards?
- Q2. Do you think that they have the potential to improve the public perception of teachers as professionals and raise the standard of educational outcomes? Give your reasons.
- Q3. What do the standards mean to you?
- Q4. What sort of identity would you like to develop as a beginning teacher?
- Q5. Why did you choose teaching as a profession?
- Q6. What do you think of a notion of 'democratic professionalism'?
- Q7. What ways are there, if any, to promote this idea of 'democratic professionalism'?
- Q8. Do you think that self awareness is an important aspect of being a teacher? Validate your answer.
- Q9. What do you think of the concept that teacher identity is modelled and remodelled several times during a career? Give some reasons.
- Q10. Why do you think that researchers and others are concerned about teacher identity in the 'age of compliance'?
- Q11. How exactly do you think your emotions, beliefs and values will impact on your professional work?
- Q12. Why do you think there is so much to reflect upon in this section of Chapter Two?

Professional Ethics

- What are ethics?
- Who needs them?

- Do you think codes of conduct, professional standards and competencies and the current managerial structure found in education systems have made personal, ethical decision making obsolete?

Make a note of your thoughts in response to these questions. We will return to them later.

Amidst all the discussion about compliance to standards, the audit society, mandatory curricula and predetermined pedagogical models, there may easily be questions raised regarding the role of professional ethics. Are they still important? Are there still decisions for teachers to make and situations to be resolved that require to be thought through in terms of justice, fidelity and other professional values? The answer is yes. The daily interaction of teachers and students in classrooms cannot be standardised and it is because of this reciprocal relationship and the uncertainly and dilemmas that result, that professional ethics may be considered to be even more important than ever before. Becoming a member of a profession such as teaching is more than just to meet a set of professional standards. It is a commitment to a profession that is regulated by laws relating to practices, duties and responsibilities. Teaching is a value-laden, moral activity. It is a personal, interactive activity situated in educational contexts where there exists a considerably disproportionate balance of power. Unfortunately, as Campbell (2007) notes, because of this and a number of other factors, teachers sometimes become desensitised to behaviours that they would certainly consider inappropriate in other circumstances. These behaviours may include engaging in actions that are unfair, patronising, bullying or arrogant and those considered to be basically immoral. The ways in which you interact with your students, make decisions and act in response to moral and ethical situations and dilemmas reflects your understanding of the complexity of teachers' work and indicates how you have chosen to express your perception of your teacher identity in relation to your personally held moral principles, values and codes.

The concepts of duty, obligation and responsibility in relation to teachers' work make it even more vital for teachers to deliberate about the possible options for decision making and problem solving, to act in an informed manner and to behave in ways that reflect their ethical and moral values and those of their profession because they are in position of extreme trust. Among the many decisions that teachers make in their daily professional work, there are always going to be some that have no easy answer, no obviously 'right' solution. Frequently, the 'right' course of action to take is obvious, but taking that action is problematic. In some scenarios, there are no actions that will impact positively on the participants or bring about an entirely satisfactory solution; there are frequent ethical dilemmas, and no sets of rules, standards or codes of conduct are entirely acceptable (Terhart, 1998) or even useful substitutes for personal ethical analysis. This may be especially pertinent in situations where it becomes apparent that what is ethical is not always legal and what is legal is not always ethical. It is because there are no 'recipes' for this type of problem solving or guidelines for actions to be taken, that understanding of the role of ethics in the professional work of teachers remains critical. Basic to this understanding are the concepts of autonomy, non-maleficence, beneficence, justice and fidelity (Newman and Pollnitz, 2002: 7–8).

Autonomy is the individual's right to choose a course of action. However, it presumes that the individual has the capability to make a decision that does not infringe on the rights of others and that protects the rights of those who are not able to make autonomous decisions themselves, and that the professional is able to make the decision independently. Non-maleficence means basically 'do no harm'. This is frequently the first principle that you may have to call to mind when making autonomous decisions. Decisions and actions taken, whether intentionally or unintentionally, should do no physical, mental or emotional harm. Newman and Pollnitz (2002: 8–9) note that this principle may involve comparing 'the level of potential harm that may caused by a decision with the level of potential good that might come from a decision'. Beneficence is acting to impact positively on others. As in the cases of non-maleficence, individual cases often have to be considered in their own specific contexts and circumstances and a decision made regarding the potential good and the potential harm that may be done. Justice is the concept of fairness.

Justice is a much debated issue as it is one of the most difficult for teachers, causing as it often does a tension between the ethic of care and the ethic of justice. Campbell (2007: 33–34) discusses the dilemma of teachers who acknowledge that the needs of students are different and who seek to respond to these appropriately. While treating children differently in response to their needs may be regarded as reasonably fair, widely different treatment may be considered unjust, irrespective of the teacher's motive. She writes:

> On one hand, a focus on the just application of impartial and consistent standards is criticised for potentially ignoring human differences in ways that negate genuine sensitivity to the needs of others. On the other hand, the goal of caring in its responsiveness to the shifting relational and situational demands of others may be seen as gross unfairness by being neither impartial nor equal. (Campbell, 2007: 33)

Katz (in Campbell, 2007) agrees that this is always a tension for teachers. Newman and Pollnitz (2002: 9) also indicate that justice involves being fair to others and acting in the common good, indicating that 'justice depends on the benefits and disadvantages of decisions being spread to others equitably on the basis of effort or merit, including references to issues about diversity and disadvantage in the community'. However, Strike (in Campbell, 2007: 33) disagrees, criticising the notion of the tensions between the ethic of care and the ethic of justice, indicating that he advocates a 'moral pluralism' which involves a wide range of moral characteristics, not just those of justice and care. He indicates that he views these 'interwoven virtues' as characterising moral life, both when the virtues conflict and when they are compatible. In other words, the notion of caring itself and the notion of justice both incorporate many other virtues, irrespective of whether they are considered in situations when they work harmoniously together or in situations of apparent conflict. Campbell (2007: 33) comments, in relation to the ethic of care, that care involves 'kindness, compassion, sensitivity, empathy, gentleness and understanding'.

Fidelity is about keeping promises, being loyal, avoiding deception and being honest (Newman and Pollnitz, 2002: 9). It is also one of the moral principles upon which trust is developed (Sockett in Campbell, 2007: 104). The other virtues associated with trust are identified as veracity, friendliness and care. In many ways it can be argued that a cornerstone of the teaching profession is trust. The trust of the public is vital for teachers. This is because parents and guardians, who delegate much of the responsibility for the formal, compulsory education of children and youth to teachers, have with a deep understanding of the inequitable power relations that exist in classrooms and place their trust in the individual teacher's professionalism. The public trust that teachers will act in ways that benefit their students, and not exploit their students or abuse their considerable power over them. Individuals who are perceived by the public as trustworthy have, in turn, a greater degree of responsibility to exhibit 'higher moral standards' (Dellatre in Campbell, 2007: 105) in both their professional and private lives. As professionals, teachers are subjected to sanctions related to immoral or illegal acts in a way that other citizens may not be. A breach of the trust that is invested in them by the public, individually or collectively, is referred to in legal terms as a breach of 'fiduciary duty'. Teachers have a responsibility to respect and respond to the trust placed in them by the public in general, the school community and the students themselves, even though finding the balance in professional and private relationships may be problematic (Aultman et al., 2009). Arguably, teaching is itself an act of trust (Thompson, in Campbell, 2007: 104) and requires adherence to the highest moral and ethical codes and principles.

What Does This Mean for You?

There are many occasions when you will have to rely on your ethical judgement to make work-based decisions. These are concerned with the non-technical aspects of your work.

- **In your classroom.** For example, you have thirty 6-year-old learners in your class and one has a medical problem that requires you to be aware of specific symptoms and call medical assistance quickly. How much extra attention can you give to that child on a daily basis without being unfair to the others? The notion of fairness presents difficulties with any age or stage of students. If you are aware of individuals with emotional or learning difficulties do you spend more time attending to their needs? Do you persevere with their disruptive or unproductive classroom behaviours and comment on these less often than you would with learners who have the same behaviours but are not considered disadvantaged? Do you allow the students to pass comment on one another's personality, capabilities, or attributes that, even if true, are negative? Do you systematically give less attention but more rewards to those who work quietly, complete work promptly and ask fewer questions? How do you use your teacher power?
- **With your professional colleagues.** For example, one of your students is the son of another teacher at the school. She asks often about his progress and behaviour. While you are happy to discuss the student's progress, are there concerns about doing this more frequently and less formally than you interact professionally with other parents? When the staffroom conversation focuses on students and/or their families, are you acutely aware that the nature of the information may raise ethical issues, even if no one discusses this outside of school?
- **In your interaction with parents and caregivers.** For example, you have a child in your class who has separation anxiety every morning and the parents ask that the child spends every morning until school commences with you as you prepare your classroom. The other children are not allowed in the classroom and remain on the playground until school starts. Do you point out the inequitable situation for the other children or do you allow the child to be with you every morning?
- **In the school community.** For example, there are a limited number of school awards. One student has won two awards at prize-giving already and has scored equally well with another student in public speaking. How do you decide who gets the award? Do you give the award to the student who has won none, in an effort to be fair, or do you have other options?

- **In the wider community.** For example, when you attend a Saturday sporting event with your child or school-aged relative, the coach of the most skilful team approaches you and enquires about the behaviour and temperament of one of your students. As it is clear that the coach is considering the student for inclusion in the elite team, do you oblige or do you indicate that there are confidentiality and trust issues to be considered and refuse to respond?

So how do teachers and other professionals reflectively find their way to make sound moral judgements and ethically considered statements? Certainly, individuals always have instinct, values, beliefs and perspectives that may provide good, general guidelines but more informed decisions and statements may be made by understanding where these personal attributes can be placed in terms of ethical theory. Ethical and moral statements are often made as the result of deciding the 'rightness' or 'wrongness' of an action in terms of two, traditional, major types of theories: those that consider the consequences of the action in the decision making process and those that do not. People who believe and act on consequentialist theories (think about the possible consequences of their actions and decisions) have a desire to generate results that produce the most good for the maximum number of people. The rights of individuals are often sacrificed in this ethical model. This is also identified as 'ends-based thinking' (Newman and Pollnitz, 2002) or utilitarianism and is a frequently used model in school decision making. Included in the theories that do not consider consequences are those that are rule-based. Rule-based thinking does not take into account any possible consequences of the action when making a decision. This type of decision making is frequently based on adherence to the law, or to strict societal or moral codes and is implemented out of a sense of duty. Rules-based thinking is associated with making the principle upon which it is based the rule or the law for everyone in all future situations of that nature. Other non-consequential theories that are important for teachers to be introduced to include those identified as virtue ethics, ethics of care and postmodern ethics.

Knowing what is best to do is a perennial problem for most teachers. However, the very experience of not being able to decide what to do is the start of engaging with ethical reflection. Most individuals utilise more than one ethical perspective in their professional work. While each of you will have different preferences and perspectives in ethical and moral matters, Haynes (1998) suggests that the three aspects of her taxonomy of ethics are all necessary to consider when determining ethical action in educational contexts. These three aspects draw on the traditional rule-based ethics, the utilitarian model in consequences-based ethics and the ethic of care, which Haynes interprets as the function of responsibility. Consequently, the triadic taxonomy of ethics comprises consistency, consequences and care. Using Kohlberg's levels and stages of moral development (Haynes, 1998: 13), she explains that individuals move through this (Kohlberg's) rational developmental model in order to develop a personal understanding and coherence of rules and values. In this rational consistency view, if, for example, lying is considered to be wrong, then lying in all contexts, in all situations, for all people must also be wrong. This may often be heard in the reasoning of younger children who may insist that certain behaviours are 'not allowed' irrespective of the context or circumstances. The rule is generalised to include all future situations of a similar nature. This deliberate and subjective aspect of the taxonomy is termed 'consistency'. The second aspect of the taxonomy of ethics presented by Haynes (1998) requires you to be more objective and to consider consequences and causes. In this view, while lying may be considered generally wrong, there are occasions when it would be the right thing to do, depending on the context and circumstances.

The third aspect is the ethic of 'care', which requires a more personal, immediate response than either of the other two theoretical views. The ethic of care, or the ethic of responsibility, is based on responding to others' concerns, not out of duty or from an analytical, theoretical perspective but from a perspective that views responsibility as the act of responding to others in a holistic manner. This in turn is based on situational and contextual factors and is orientated towards maintaining or establishing justice or fairness as the outcome. Haynes (1998: 26) uses the interlocking circles of the Borromean knot, similar to the Olympic rings, to illustrate the interdependence of these three aspects of the taxonomy and to provide an adequate basis for ethical decision making. The Borromean knot is constructed so that the breaking or removal of one of the circles results in the collapse of the remaining two. In this way the interconnected, intertwined nature of the theoretical, ethical model that she is proposing is highlighted and the inadequacy of two of the three aspects alone is practically demonstrated. While cautioning that using any single approach or framework for determining what to do in response to ethical and moral dilemmas may be counterproductive, simply because ethical analysis is so complex, both Campbell (2007) and Newman and Pollnitz (2002) have offered some suggestions regarding the questions that you might ask yourself in order to become

Newman and Pollnitz (2002: 13) Sequential steps	Campbell (2007: 136-7) Practical suggestions
Legal aspects. If there are no laws governing the issue in question, go to the next step.	Identify core principles relevant to the situation and ask if they are being upheld (honesty, fairness kindness).
Professional considerations (policies and guidelines, codes of conduct) If there is no helpful information in these documents, continue to the ethical principles.	Listen to your conscience. Ask yourself why you have reacted in that way, don't be pressured into taking action you think is wrong.
Ethical principles (e.g. autonomy, beneficence, non-maleficence, justice and fidelity). If a solution is not apparent after considering these guiding principles, then proceed to consider the ethical theories with which you are familiar.	Reflect and anticipate. (If I do this, could this happen?)
Ethical theories (rule based, utilitarian, care based). If you are still undecided, then proceed to the next step that could be termed your professional conscience.	Put the students first (individually and collectively).
Informed inclination (professional disposition, knowledge, expertise and extended experience). Here you have an opportunity to stop and consider what you think is the right thing to do.	Remember your professional status. You are publically and personally accountable. Think carefully about addressing controversial issues and indoctrination in classrooms. If your issue is political, is the classroom the place to air it?
Negotiation (alternative options, the action to be considered and the follow up). Once you have decided what should be done, consider all possible actions and determine the best one. Validate your decision by going to the next step and indicating the reasoning behind your decision and the subsequent action.	Don't compromise your moral principals in the way you speak (tell intimate stories, humor expressed, use of language) or act in order to appear part of the peer culture. You are not part of it.
Make the judgement (that is, the outcome of reasoning, can be justified, is the ethical basis for action).	Be familiar with the school rules and policies and know how to access legal information if needed.
Take action.	Seek advice and help from colleagues and executive staff and consider what they offer.
Document the process. This is an important part of professional learning as it can be revisited for reflection and may prove to useful in contentious issue.	Do not say, do or condone anything you would not want to be made public (integrity).
Critically evaluate the outcome, the efficacy of the response cycle and own self development. This is also an informative part of the process so is best documented.	

Figure 2.1   Two Approaches for Guiding your Ethical Decision Making

more skilful and develop greater depth in your reflections about ethical solutions in two professional contexts (see Figure 2.1).

Questions for Reflection

- Q1. Would you now reconsider any of the answers that you recorded at the beginning of the ethics section?
- Q2. Do you think that reflection is part of ethical analysis, decision making and action?
- Q3. Which of the ethical models do you feel reflects your personal way of doing the 'right thing'?
- Q4. What do you think of the triadic taxonomy of ethics? Might this model help you make an ethical decision?
- Q5. In Figure 2.1 did you find any common themes between the suggestions for everyday practice and the elements of working through an ethical dilemma?
- Q6. In your opinion, is teaching an act of trust? Give your reasons.

Terhart (1998: 434) comments that professional ethics can be seen as a 'controlling and balancing element' to teacher autonomy. With reference to the control of teachers, he observes that there are two solutions to the problem of 'controlling the uncontrollable'. The first is by 'moralising' student teachers and teachers into a classical idea of the ideal teacher, which results in a search for professional perfection and the accompanying sense of guilt when individuals realise that they are not professionally flawless and they need to keep on working on various aspects of their professional work through their careers. The second solution, he observes, is to standardise their work, thus removing much of their autonomy. In the current circumstances it may appear that, although opposite perspectives, both solutions are currently being put in place simultaneously. The paradoxes that constitute teachers' work certainly require much reflection! One of the questions that may be investigated might easily be 'What priorities should I have (or could I have) to be the best teacher I can be?' (not a perfect teacher, nor a slave to the standards). A suggestion of some important priorities for you to think about is presented in Figure 2.2. Respectfully entitled the 'Holy Trinity for Teachers', it may be interpreted as an attempt at a holistic view of teacher attributes or a proposal for a summary of attributes that are of considerable importance in the unique circumstances in which teachers work.

Component	Ways in which this might realistically be achieved
Know yourself and how this self knowledge impacts on your professional self.	Have a good understanding of your personal values, attitudes and belief systems. Be aware of your level of understanding of moral and ethical matters and decision making strategies. Have sound accurate knowledge of your relative strengths and limitations on an ongoing, changeable basis. Identify the characteristics that you would associate with your personal teacher identity and be prepared to develop, change and remodel in response to changing contexts and circumstances. Be aware of your profile in the public view as a representative of your profession. Be critically reflective …
Know your content and how to teach it.	Have sound basic knowledge of what you are teaching and be prepared to build on it by accessing further new or more complex notions. Know the pedagogical approaches associated with your content areas. Be prepared to be flexible and to adapt or adopt a alternative, appropriate pedagogical approach to suit changing circumstances or contexts. Know how to teach your content to groups of diverse students (culturally, socially and individually diverse). Keep up to date with technology and how to use it effectively to enhance students' learning in your content areas.
Know your students and how they learn.	Know your students' learning preferences, their relative strengths and limitations on an ongoing changeable basis. Know how to assess each of them to allow them to demonstrate what they actually know and where they would like/need to go next in their development and learning. Know the interests of your students and their families as they relate to your professional work. Know their communities and their family beliefs, values and preferences as they relate to your professional work. Engage systematically with each student on an individual basis to discuss their learning. Allow students to express their point of view. Understand their choices and why they made them.

Figure 2.2   The 'Holy Trinity for Teachers'

Questions for Reflection

- Q1. What do you think of the Holy Trinity for Teachers? Do you have any suggestions of what might be added or what is less important and could therefore be deleted?
- Q2. Do you agree that teaching is an act of trust? Give your reasons.
- Q3. Do you think that reflection is an essential, ethical aspect of being a teaching professional?
- Q4. What do you think of the solutions that are reportedly suggestions for balancing teacher autonomy?

Scenario Two

Sally had just started her final professional experience with her colleague teacher and her class of 11- and 12-year-olds. She was looking forward to it immensely as she had developed good relationships with the pupils in the classes of her previous professional experiences. She was fortunate in that she had developed an instant appreciation for her colleague teacher's friendly but firm attitude to the class and had decided to try to establish the same type of classroom culture in her relationships with the pupils when she was teaching independently. At present she was teaching with her colleague teacher and performing the usual duties that comprised a school day. These duties included playground duty. One morning, slightly bored with shadowing her teacher, she decided to join in a game with her pupils. As they were laughing and joking about who was in and who was out, Sally caught sight of her colleague teacher watching her. She did not look especially pleased. As she had done nothing wrong that she could think of, Sally continued to play with the pupils until it was time for school to commence. At lunchtime, however, her colleague teacher had a quiet word with her after the pupils had left the room. She explained kindly that it was very difficult to 'wear two hats' when building a relationships with pupils and indicated that she thought it would be better in the future if Sally did not join in the playground games with the older pupils. She was hoping that Sally would be teaching independently in the next few days and felt that it would be easier for Sally to maintain a professional, friendly relationship with the pupils if she was not so familiar with them outside the classroom. Sally spent the rest of the day feeling a little annoyed about the conversation. She had interacted on the playground with her younger pupils on her previous professional experiences and no comment had been made. She had not read anything about this being unprofessional in the school policies she had studied in preparation for her time at the school. She realised that her colleague teacher was anxious to support and mentor her, but was she missing an opportunity to get to know her pupils in a way that could support her classroom practice?

Questions for Reflection

- Q1. What are the issues here?
- Q2. What might be bothering Sally?
- Q3. What might she be able to do about her dilemma?
- Q4. What might your personal response as a pre-service teacher be to this situation?

- Q5. If this had happened at the end of the professional experience, would your response differ in any way? Why would that be so?
- Q6. Can you utilise any of the information in Figure 2.1, in addition to the Personal Reflection Model, to help you think what Sally might do?
- Q7. Is there anything else in this chapter that may help you to decide on a response after some reflection?

Conclusion

This chapter investigated some of the complexity of teaching as professional practice. Evaluating different perspectives of compulsory standards and the impact on teachers, collectively and individually, may be initially confusing or confrontational for beginning teachers and for you at the moment, but as part of the current culture in the teaching profession the impacts of increasing standardisation do merit some consideration on your part. Ethics are an integral part of any professional's responsibility and the contexts in which educators work demand a high level of commitment to sound ethical practice and decision making. The current circumstances in which teachers undertake their work may afford them very little opportunity for professional decision making in many aspects of their work but at the same time, it demands that their ethical judgements and actions are beyond individual and collective public reproach.

References

Angus, L. (2007) 'Globalisation and the reshaping of teacher professional culture : do we train competent technicians or informed players in the policy process?' In T. Townsend & R. Iates (eds), *Handbook of Teacher Education: Globalisation, Professionalism and Standards in Times of Change*. Dordrecht, The Netherlands: Springer. pp. 141–156.

Apple, M. (2001) Markets, standards, teaching, and teacher education. *Journal of Teacher Education*, 52 (3): 182–96.

Armstrong, D. (2006) Dreaming our future: developing democratic professional practice? *Australian Educational Researcher*, 33 (3): 1–11.

Aultman, L., Williams-Johnson, M. and Schutz, P. (2009) Boundary dilemmas in teacher–student relationships: struggling with 'the line'. *Teaching and Teacher Education*, 25 (5): 636–46.

Barth, R. (2006) Cooperate: improving professional relationships. *Teacher*, 171: 22–6.

Beck, J. (2008) Govermental professionalism: re-professionaling or de-professionalising teachers in England? *British Journal of Educational Studies*, 56 (2): 119–43.

Bloomfield, D. (2006) A new discourse for teacher professionalism: Ramsey, standards and accountability. Paper presented at the Australian Association for Research in Education Conference, Adelaide.

Brown, P. and Lauder, H. (1996) Education, globalization and economic development. *Journal of Education Policy*, 11 (1): 1–25.

Campbell, E. (2007) *The Ethical Teacher*. New York: Open University Press.

Cheers, S. (2001) Issues of professionalism, quality and professionalisation. *Primary Educator*, 4: 15–17.

Cosgrove, F. (2007) Standards of professional practice: supporting effective teacher learning in Victoria. In Centre for Strategic Eduction Occasional Paper no. 100. Jolimont, VIC: Centre for Strategic Education.

Darling-Hammond, L. (1999) *Reshaping Teacher Policy, Preparation and Practice: Influences on the National Board for Teaching Professional Standards*. Washington, DC: AACTE Publications.

Darling-Hammond, L. and Wise, A. (1985) Beyond standardization: state standards and school improvement. *The Elementary School Journal*, 85 (3): 315–36.

Day, C., Alison, K., Gordon, S. and Sammons, P. (2006) The personal and professional selves of teachers: stable and unstable identities. *British Educational Research Journal*, 32 (4): 601–16.

Day, C. and Smethem, L. (2009) The effects of reform: have teachers really lost their sense of professionalism? *Journal of Educational Change*, 10 (2): 141–57.

Draper, J., Christie, F., and O'Brien, J. (2007) 'Meeting the standard? The new teacher education induction scheme in Scotland.' In T. Townsend & R. Iates (eds), *Handbook of Teacher Education: Globalisation, Professionalism and Standards in Times of Change*. Dordrecht, The Netherlands: Springer. pp. 391–406.

Emmett, G. and Paull, R. (2003) Taking the plunge: implementing teaching standards. *Professional Educator*, 2 (2): 10–11.

Evans, L. (2008) Professionalism, professionality and the development of education professionals. *British Journal of Educational Studies*, 56 (1): 20–38.

Friedson, E. (1994). *Professionalism Reborn: Theory, Prophesy and Policy*. Chicago: University of Chicago Press.

Furlong, J., Barton, L., Miles, S., Whiting, C., & Whitty, G. (2000). *Teacher Education in Transition: Reforming Professionalism?* Buckingham: Open University Press.

Grady, M., Helbling, K. and Lubeck, D. (2008) Teacher professionalism since *A Nation at Risk*. *Phi Delta Kappan*, 89 (8): 603–9.

Groundwater-Smith, S. and Mockler, N. (2009) *Teacher Professional Learning in an Age of Compliance: Mind the Gap*. Dordrecht: Springer Netherlands.

Haynes, F. (1998) *The Ethical School*. London: Routledge.

Helsby, G. (1996) Defining and developing professionalism in English secondary schools. *Journal of Education for Teaching*, 22 (2): 135–48.

Hinton, F. (2006) By the profession, for the profession. *Teacher*, 171: 28–31.

Holroyd, C. (2000) Are assessors professional? Student assessment and the professionalism of academics. *Active Learning in Higher Education*, 1 (1): 28–44.

Howie, M. (2006) Some reflections on quality teaching, teaching standards, professional learning and teacher accreditation. *English in Australia*, 41 (2): 69–72.

Ingvarson, L. (1995) *Professioanl Credentials: Standards for Primary and Secondary Science Teachers in Australia*. Canberra: Australian Science Teachers Association.

Ingvarson, L. (2002a) *Development of a National Standards Framework for the Teaching Profession*. Alexandria, NSW: ACER.

Ingvarson, L. (2002b) *Strengthening the Profession? A Comparison of Recent Reforms in the UK and USA*. Melbourne: ACER.

Ingvarson, L. (2010) Recognising accomplished teachers in Australia: Where have we been? Where are we heading? *Australian Journal of Education*, 51 (4): 46–71.

Ingvarson, L. and Kleinhenz, E. (2003) *A Review of Standards of Practice for Beginning Teaching*. Alexandria, NSW: ACER.

Ius, A. and Emmett, G. (2006) Standards of professional practice: strengthening teaching. *EQ Australia*, Autumn: 11–13.

Kelly, A. (2009) Globalisation and education: a review of conflicting perspectives and their effect on policy and professional practice in the UK *Globalisation, Societies and Education*, 7 (1): 51–68.

Kincheloe, J. L. (1998) 'Pinar's currere and identity in hyperreality: grounding the post-formal notion of intrapersonal intelligence.' In W. F. Pinar (ed.), *Curriculum: Towards New Idenities*. New York: Garlanf Publishing. pp. 342–352.

Kohler, M., Harbon, L., Fischmann, V., McLaughlin, M. and Liddicoat, A.J. (2006) Quality teaching: views from the profession. *Babel*, 40 (3): 23–30, 38.

Malm, B. (2009) Towards a new professionalism: enhancing personal and professional development in teacher education. *Journal of Education for Teaching*, 35 (1): 77–91.

Marsh, C. (2000) *Handbook for Beginning Teachers*, 2nd edn. Frenchs Forest, NSW: Pearson.

Mockler, N. (2011) Beyond 'what works': understanding teacher identity as a practical and political tool. *Teachers and Teaching*, 17 (5): 517–28.

Newman, L. and Pollnitz, L. (2002) *Ethics in Action: Introducing the Ethical Response Cycle*. Watson, ACT: Australian Early Childhood Association.

Parr, G. (2004) Professional learning, professional knowledge and professional identity: a bleak view, but oh the possibilities. *English Teaching: Practice and Critique*, 3 (2): 21–47.

Paull, R. (2001) The Victorian Institute of Teaching: an opportunity too extraordinary to miss. *AEU News*, 7 (5): 8–9.

Paull, R., & Cosgrove, F. (2003). Conversactions : conversation and action : developing standards of professional practice in schools. Paper presented at the Conference of Australian Curriculum Studies Association, Adelaide, SA. Retrieved from www.acsainc.com.au/content/paull___cosgrove-_conversactions.pdf

Ramsey, G., Blair, A., Gazis, S., Dow, K.L., Lewis, J., McGrath, P. and Tumak, A. (2006) Our profession: our future. *Australian Educational Leader*, 28 (3): 40–1.

Sachs, J. (2001) Teacher professional identity: competing discourses, competing outcomes. *Journal of Education Policy*, 16 (2): 149–61.

Sachs, J. (2003a) *The Activist Teaching Profession*. Buckingham: Open University Press.

Sachs, J. (2003b) Teacher Professional Standards: controlling or developing teaching? *Teachers and Teaching*, 9 (2): 175–86.

Schuck, S., Gordon, S. and Buchanan, J. (2008) What are we missing here? Problematising wisdoms on teaching quality and professionalism in higher education. *Teaching in Higher Education*, 13 (5): 537–47.

Shulman, L. (1983) 'Autonomy and obligation.' In L. Shulman and G. Sykes (eds), *Handbook of Teaching and Policy*. New York: Longman. pp. 370–391.

Terhart, E. (1998) Formalised codes of ethics for teachers: between professional autonomy and administrative control. *European Journal of Education*, 33 (4): 433–44.

Thiessen, D. (2000) A skillful start to a teaching career: a matter of developing impactful behaviors, reflective practices, or professional knowledge? *International Journal of Educational Research*, 33 (5): 515–37.

Chapter 3: Education in the Twenty-First Century

- Q1. What are some of the major societal changes that impact on education?
- Q2. What may be some future occupations for the students who are in schools now?
- Q3. What is a 'quality' teacher and does it matter?
- Q4. Does quality come with teaching experience?
- Q5. What does reflection contribute to become a quality teacher?
- Q6. Do you think it is possible to plan to educate for the twenty-first century given the current education system and conditions for teachers?

Introduction: Looking to the Future

Throughout the last chapter there was considerable discussion about the implementation of mandatory standards, the educational reform agenda and the role of you, the teacher, under these new conditions. There was dialogue and mandates and the increasing importance of teachers developing their self knowledge. It was suggested that you will need to have deep self knowledge and an understanding of how to use this to improve your practice and know yourself better. The strategies that were identified as plausible means by which to achieve this were discussion, reflection and individual engagement with ethical issues, decisions and actions. The notion of forming and reforming teacher identity, which is integral to each person's sense of self as a teacher, was discussed. To illustrate the need to do this on a continual basis, this chapter discusses some of the demands of educationalists that will undoubtedly arise as the decades of this century slip by. In the previous chapter, Day et al., (2009: 603) summarised the reasons for the educational reforms, the first of which was that governments had decided that by changing the conditions under which young people and children learn, they were introducing teaching and learning environments that had the potential to raise educational standards, improve student achievement and somehow ensure improved economic stability. This emphasis on improving the national financial status in a global market, which appears to have been originally among the main motivators for reforming education, places a considerable responsibility on educators to prepare learners for the workforce of the future. While this may be a rather narrow view of the purpose of education currently, it certainly is a major focus.

The questions that arise, however, as a result of the changing demands on educational systems and educators, are difficult to answer. The questions that you may ask as you prepare for a career in teaching and that are discussed most frequently in the literature may include:

- What does the workforce of the future look like? What skills, strategies and knowledge will young people need to develop at school in order to be suitably prepared to make a meaningful contribution to their society in, perhaps, twenty years time?
- What will teachers need to do in order to ensure they are themselves fully prepared with a clear focus and appropriate knowledge, attitudes and skills to facilitate a suitable education? Is this an ever-increasing anxiety for teachers as their options to develop professional identity, autonomy and judgement become increasingly limited by mandatory coherence to a range of professional restraints?
- Are education systems currently structured, managed and resourced to meet the learning needs of young people in the future? Are teachers empowered, for example, with the resources of time, professional development, skills and strategies, to make critically informed decisions about the use of research findings in their everyday classroom interactions?

There are perhaps no satisfactory answers to these types of question. This does not mean that they should not be the focus of some discussion and reflective thinking. It is assumed that the workforce of the future will be a development of the current Information Era and will be driven by increasingly advanced technology and a paucity of employment opportunities that do not require technological skills, problem solving strategies and creative solutions to hitherto unseen challenges. While it may be suggested that technology may even replace teachers in the future, it would be realistic to assume, as you read in the previous chapter, that educationalists are still making decisions in their professional role at some level of the teaching and learning interaction, although this may not be in the ways that are currently witnessed in classrooms. That teachers have been identified as the major determinant of student academic success would be a significant consideration for those wishing to advocate for totally technological teaching and learning contexts. How teachers continue to develop their professional skills and to stay current with research findings in a number of disciplines related to teaching remains to be seen. This will be especially pertinent if mandatory professional learning schemes become part of the accreditation standards as the content and processes may also be designed as a 'one size fits all' programme and would not able to be accessed in response to your individual professional needs and preferences. Further discussion of this issue can be found in Chapter 12, as can an evaluation of the 'goodness of fit' between the requirements of the mandatory standards and their associated consequences and the realities of the situated nature of teachers' work. At present it may be useful to review some of the relevant literature that focuses on the perceived societal needs of the future and the implications for educators, and on the role of the teachers themselves in promoting and supporting effective student outcomes.

What Does the Literature Say about Looking to the Future?

The concerns educators and others have about preparing learners for the future are not entirely new, but have been the topic of much discussion in the past four decades (Gidley and Hampson, 2005). Despite some comment on the tardiness of education to change anything (Doyle, 2012), this has intensified in light of the recent standardisation of many aspects of education. The additional demands and expectations of the teaching profession (Brown and Lauder, 1996) can be more fully realised when the sheer scale of the expectations about to be placed on teachers is expressed in this way:

> The education revolution is profoundly transforming postindustrial culture, creating new human talent; a new workplace and conception of jobs; and new styles of parenting, political mobilisation, and reach of mass religion. At the same time, educational achievement, degree attainment, and credentials have come to dominate social stratification and social mobility, superseding and delegitimizing all non educational forms of status attainment. Four decades of sociological research points to a future society where education performance will be the singular dominant factor in social status attainment, and education will be one of the most transforming of social institutions for individuals and other social institutions. (Baker, 2011: 1)

If teachers and education systems are going to be able live up to this huge responsibility, then they will need strong leadership support (Dinham et al., 2011), flexible educational curricula (Nyburg and Egan, 1981) and appropriate pedagogies (Gidley and Hampson, 2008). Broadly speaking, two main perspectives are strongly represented in this discourse about the nature of education for the future. Those who subscribe to the notion that future education studies are driven by economies, technologies and associated political agendas such as students working smarter in order to enter the workforce and make a meaningful contribution (e.g. Samet, 2010), and those who are concerned with the nature and integrity of education and the futures of young people (e.g. Spring, 2008). Sparks (2012), in a review of the deliberations of an expert panel of American academics, reports that American educational systems should be preparing students for their future as global citizens by developing skills in three areas of competence: cognitive skilling to promote increased critical thinking and analytical reasoning, interpersonal skilling to ensure they know how to work effectively with others, and intrapersonal skilling so that they develop resilience and conscientiousness. American educationalists, in defining future skills in this manner, demonstrate their understanding of the need for educational change even though they are at the forefront of globalisation. Indeed, in stating that globalisation is actually the 'Americanisation' of the rest of the world, Gidley (2008: 257) considers that 'One of the greatest obstacles to creating learning societies for the future is the model of Western culture – and by default, the model of education – being promoted by globalisation'. In her philosophical discussion of this perspective, Gidley (2008) considers the advantages of an educational approach that utilises diverse learning processes and that provides an alternative to the 'industrial factory model of education as schooling' (Gidley, 2008: 257).

Gidley (2008) considers that aims and pedagogies of Steiner schooling are a more appropriate approach to developing a transformed society. Steiner schooling is characterised by its focus on developing the innate potential in every child. This is often achieved by the development of a curriculum that is centred on the development of students' creativity, individual expression and exploration. Gidley (2008) proposes that an education that rediscovers the educational ideologies of Steiner and Dewey and perceives educating for wisdom as a fundamental tenet would transform society. This perspective may indeed be a productive education for students in the future; as Lanning (1994) points out, many of the writers who have speculated on the future of education have been concerned with the impact of relatively 'value free' rapid technological change when what is more realistic is a change of ideology (Lanning, 1994: 467). Sellars (2008) also supports a more holistic approach to education, nominating three components of a 'new pedagogy'. These comprise a new notion of the nature of intelligence, the importance of the quality of the learning environments and the negotiated nature of the curriculum that is based on the relative strengths of each student. Zhao (2011), for example, also enthusiastically embraces Hargreaves and Shirley's (2009) 'Fourth Way', in which it is proposed that the students are partners in driving educational change and have a voice in the preparation that they need to operate successfully as global citizens. As the inevitability of globalisation is realised (Mok, 2005; Rupérez, 2003), there are a number of questions still being asked, both about the purpose and responsibilities of education (Kelly, 2009; McLaren and Farahmandpur, 2001) and the nature of the skills that will best prepare students to become these 'global citizens' (Agbaria, 2011). Much of the discussion has been focused on the means by which students can be encouraged to know themselves as learners and develop increased competencies in the cognitive skills that are identified as higher-order thinking skills and to become flexible thinkers in response to rapid ongoing change.

What Does This Mean for You?

There are several important implications for you regarding teaching for your students' future needs. These may involve challenging some of the notions you have previously held about teachers' work, the way you implement the curriculum, the curriculum itself and the roles that teacher and learner have traditionally played in formal educational contexts. They may be focused more explicitly on some precise areas of professional practice and on the technological and other changes associated with developing global citizens. The specific areas that may be most challenging may include the following:

- The need to negotiate both curriculum and practice with learners themselves in order to facilitate their metacognitive and other self knowledge.
- The inevitable, rapid change in curriculum documents.
- The capacity to recognise that all students are capable of successful learning, irrespective of their diversity and differences.
- The importance of allowing students to explore, discover and explain their knowledge and thinking strategies, and share with others.
- The overarching value of teaching appropriate higher-order thinking strategies and skills from a very young age and continuing throughout schooling and beyond.
- The value of students' thinking skills and how best to develop these in individual students.
- The importance of the learning environment, its relationships, its rules and its compromises.

- The acceptance and promotion of your own and your students' wisdom and insights into learning and its procedures and strategies.
- The roles that you and your students must undertake in order to promote successful thinking.
- The necessity for flexibility and extreme organisation.
- The motivation and competencies to stay current with technological advances and use these to enrich and enhance the learning experiences in your classrooms.
- An appreciation that no discipline or content area exists in a vacuum and that most learning can be linked with, or is somewhat dependent on, other areas of skills and knowledge.
- That individual physical health and characteristics are vital, as are interests, creativity and motivation in educational endeavours designed to maximise the potential of learners.

Burchsted (2003), for example, urges managers and policy makers for schools and systems to 'study the future' in an effort to equip school students with the skills, strategies and perspectives that will enhance their abilities to succeed in the face of challenges and changes in the twenty-first century. She proposes five 'elements' that characterise this ongoing process of 'studying the future'. This process requires students to develop considerable competencies in skills such as identifying, monitoring, exploring and describing various aspects of society, in addition to planning and implementing goals, and Burchsted (2003) indicates she is confident that students and their teachers have the capacities to effect these changes in the educational process. Henderson (2002) also creates a positive image of the future. She imagines what life would be like for a student in 2050 and presents a picture of a world that has risen to meet the multiple challenges inherited from the previous century, concluding with giving notice that 'a paradigm shift to map these changes was required and the curricula of all schools and universities have changed accordingly' (Henderson, 2002: 12). What exactly constitutes this 'paradigm shift' and how it may be implemented are questions that are left unanswered.

Dickenson (2002) offers more guidance in these areas, tracing the key principles that are impacting positively on teaching, learning and assessment. These include an understanding that all students are capable of learning and are indeed capable of learning more effectively than may have originally been understood (Dickenson, 2000). Beare (2003) identifies seven 'radical differences' that will characterise schools of the future. One of these may be particularly pertinent to teachers currently: the re-conceptualisation of the curriculum. Beare (2003) envisages a new curriculum that necessitates:

- Working collaboratively in the search for new information and learning.
- Multi-level thinking and increasingly complex questions and answers.
- This future curriculum would integrate disciplines and areas of knowledge formerly studied in isolation from each other.
- It would not necessarily be age-related, as the curriculum has been in the past and remains currently.
- Perhaps the most interesting aspect of Beare's (2003) proposal is that students would be able to respond to this new concept of teaching and learning in terms of their own individual interests, needs and competencies.

Lepani (1995: 1–2) was one of the first educationalists to examine future educational trends and she concluded nearly twenty years ago that minor reforms to the existing educational system were not going to be substantial enough to guarantee success for all learners. She gathers together current educational theory relating to educating for the future and proposes eight principles on which to develop a 'mind-ware industry', upon which to enhance the learning capacity of the human mind in order to cope with the increasing demands of the society of the future. She places great importance on the capacity of educational systems to provide experiences and learning contexts that facilitate the foundations for lifelong learning. She further qualifies her interpretation of these foundations. She identifies them as students' enjoyment of the learning process and their knowledge or understanding of the learning process itself. She recognises that the major component of an individual's capacity to develop knowledge of the learning process is how capably one can identify one's own learning preferences. This is the basis on which individual students can develop their own learning strategies that support personal, successful learning.

In order to facilitate this process, Lepani (1995) agrees with Beare (2003) that curriculum practices and content need to be reexamined and implemented from a different perspective than that identified as traditional education. Lepani (1995) suggests some ways in which this may be achieved. These include:

- Global learning resources and materials, for example, must be made more relevant for students by being customised to accommodate the cultural, physical and intellectual differences of the learners. It is not enough to provide only learning tasks that are 'one size fits all' or a curriculum that is not genuinely culturally inclusive (see Chapter 10).
- The learners themselves must have a greater stake in determining the learning strategies they will use to facilitate learning, in consultation with their teachers. A single approach does not reach all the students so learning strategies must be differentiated in order to provide multiple opportunities to develop understanding in any concept or knowledge domain (see Chapter 11).

- The actual curriculum materials provided, content examined and practices implemented in educational settings must be designed to promote students' capacities to challenge and change their belief systems and behaviour patterns, allowing the educational process to become a principal player in societal transformation and renewal. Different perspectives must be provided in the resources and materials utilised to support learning. These may challenge or support students' own beliefs or behaviours. In each case their opinions and perspectives must be validated by reasoned reflection and critical examination of the sources of their belief systems.

- Student learning needs to be relevant and valid: that is, based in experience where students are given opportunities to develop their knowledge and understanding through applying their learning. This may be in real-life contexts such as cooking, making, gardening and designing for younger students. Building on these, apprentice-type experiences for older students in addition to school-based opportunities to continue their previous applications of knowledge in specialised school-based contexts such as laboratories, kitchens, gardens, interaction with non-English-speaking members of the community or visitors, industry-based school partners and other professionals.

- Lepani envisages that much of this learning will be explored and consolidated through student engagement in collaborative and cooperative learning contexts where students explore and investigate knowledge, concepts and skills as part of a team of students. Learning will be complex and the resultant problem solving will necessitate the skills of several students who will each have the unique knowledge and strategies to contribute to the final solution or product. There is a great stress here on interpersonal and intrapersonal capacities as this is essential to team building and to collaborative problem solving. In these contexts the linkages of one discipline knowledge and context with that of others will also become increasingly apparent and the need for this to be recognised will be important in the process of learning.

- The final defining characteristic of Lepani's (1995) vision of education for the future serves to summarise her re-conceptualisation of education. She states that students must be provided with basic skills and knowledge, including those relating to information, communication and learning technologies, so that they are able to access information and construct knowledge when and where they need it. Students will rely on technological aids to access pertinent, current information around which to organise their thinking. All students will need access to current technological resources and to teachers who are competent and confident in their capacities to integrate and use technological tools to inform and enhance their teaching (see Chapter 11). They will also individually need the well-developed skills and strategies that are necessary to investigate, manipulate, analyse and reformulate their findings in response to the requirements of their tasks.

Gardner (2006a) also looks to the future in what he terms an 'ambitious, even grandiose' scheme of cultivating five minds for the future (Gardner, 2006a: 153). In addition to the disciplined mind (Gardner, 2000), Gardner explores the development of synthesising, creating, respectful and ethical minds as a means of coping with future changes and challenges. This perspective is presented also by Greenberg et al. (2003), who view education as holistic and supporting not only the students' academic needs but also their social–emotional competence, character, health and civic engagement (Greenberg et al., 2003: 466), by Hare (2004), who discusses Dewey's notion of open mindedness, and by Schecter (2011). Gardner provides two 'legitimate' reasons (2006a: 10–11) for changes in educational practice.

Firstly, Gardner argues that current educational practices are not actually working in facilitating student learning, and secondly, he argues that the consequences of significant changes in the world may demand that educational endeavours are refashioned to 'stretch' the minds of learners in ways that have not previously been considered as important educational goals, capacities or competencies. In an interview (Unknown, 2004) to discuss a previous work, *Changing Minds* (Gardner, 2006b), he gives some firm indications of two processes that may facilitate change in the sphere of education. He lists these as:

- multiple representations of knowledge and skills (see Chapter 11)
- challenging basic ideas and misconceptions (see Chapter 7 and Chapter 8).

The notion of presenting knowledge and facilitating skills in a number a different ways is the practice of differentiating the curriculum in both content and cognitive processes (see Chapter 11). The idea of challenging ideas and beliefs that are held by students is more complex. Student beliefs and misconceptions may be held in relation to any topic or idea, but arguably the most pressing one for most educators may be the beliefs that are held by school students, their parents and whole-school communities that relate to the nature of effective education and the roles that should be assumed by teachers and students (see Chapters 7, 8 and 9).

Although these writers offer differing perspectives and definitions of the skills and competencies that will be required for individuals to live comfortably in the future, there is a common theme throughout; people will have to improve their thinking skills to cope with the complexity of life in the twenty-first century. Effective cognition in some specific domains will be the currency of the future and this will bring considerable challenges for everyone involved in educational policy making, leadership and practice, given the degree of diversity that exists in any group of learners. Henderson (2002) notes that presently most humans use approximately 10% of their brains, although it is important to note that this claim is challenged by others (e.g. Sellars, 2008). Henderson (2002) would argue that the development of cognitive skills is well within the grasp of most people, but how exactly will this development be facilitated? Smyre (2000: 5) poses the question 'how do we introduce into educational curricula the need to think about future trends as well as transforming underlying assumptions?' Some educationalists (e.g. Warner, 2006) have already been considering these questions for several years. However, the answer may lie in the two processes suggested by Gardner (2006b), both of which depend on an acceptance of the uniqueness of the process by which individual learners construct knowledge and the need to challenge assumptions that limit students' thinking (see Chapter 11 for strategies in differentiation, Chapters 7 and 8 for strategies for developing respectful communities of learners, and Chapter 9 for understanding difference).

Questions for Reflection

- Q1. What do you think of the idea of all schools implementing strategies like the Steiner schools' child-centred pedagogies (which have a heavy emphasis on developing learners' own creativity and imagination through the arts) as education for the future?
- Q2. How do you think students can be prepared adequately for the future? Which of the ideas presented could you develop into an appropriate framework for educating students in your class?
- Q3. Do you think that the standardisation of many aspects of teachers' work is helpful or harmful to your ideas about educating students for the future? Give your reasons?
- Q4. How might you involve students as partners in determining what they need to learn?
- Q5. What you think is the purpose of education?
- Q6. What misconceptions do you think parents, teachers and students may hold regarding the nature of effective education?
- Q7. How do you think you might go about changing people's minds?

The Importance of Teacher Quality

Within the frameworks of policies and systems, as previously noted, much of the responsibility for supporting the development of the selected future-orientated skills will lie with classroom teachers. Restructuring the curriculum necessitates restructuring teachers' roles and redefining teachers' work. Teachers are currently being asked to face the challenges of developing and implementing pedagogies that support learning for all students, being mindful of their individual differences, provide realistic opportunities for successful learning and encourage appropriate, educational risk taking. Latham et al. (2006: 135) define teachers who are willing to engage in and develop an understanding of such demanding pedagogies as 'courageous teachers'. These are the teachers who acknowledge the challenges and difficulties that surround theories and pedagogies that cater for the learning of all students, rather than just a few. The importance of the beliefs, understandings and theoretical foundations that individual teachers identify as their personal pedagogical approaches to their work cannot be overstated. The discussions of the previous chapter indicated that although 'teaching is framed as a value-free technological activity' (Armstrong, 2006: 4), in the many standards and aspects of compliance, the reality is very different. Certainly, teachers need to know the content they are teaching and a variety of pedagogical strategies with which to teach it. This is simply because the models of education suggested as those that can support student learning for the twenty-first century cannot be realised without teachers who have the capacity to make them a reality in everyday classrooms. Lovat and Smith (2003: 11) present the popularly accepted view of the causal relationship between student learning outcomes and the quality of their teachers when he states,

> Teacher quality is the single greatest factor in explaining student achievement more important than classroom related issues such as resources, curriculum guidelines and assessment practices or the broader school environment such as school culture and organisation.

However, it needs to be noted that, in an analysis of the research purporting to support the connection between improved student learning outcomes and teacher characteristics, Hanushek and his colleagues (Hanushek et al., 2004) determined that not all of the information that would be required to support these research claims could ever be made available for consideration. These variables would include such factors as social and financial status of parents and caregivers, size of classrooms, student numbers and levels of resourcing, and student attitudes and behaviours.

Nevertheless, some general conclusions can be drawn about teacher characteristics and their capacity to provide conditions in which students and their learning thrive. For students to be able to benefit from the reconstructed curriculum and renewed pedagogical perspectives mentioned, they would, of necessity, have to operate in rich, supportive, learning environments (Noble and McGrath, 2008) that provide students with the opportunities to 'stretch' their minds as individual learners and these can only be provided by positive teachers who are morally and ethically invested in their work (see Chapter 8). Strong teacher beliefs are important because rich environments are those that are achieved in an atmosphere of constant positivity and critical thinking. Brennan (2007) cautions against the negative consequences of anger, for example, on student learning. Learning in a positive environment can be achieved only under the guidance of an appropriate mentor. These 'appropriate mentors' are the 'courageous' teachers (Latham et al., 2006: 135) who demonstrate specific characteristics such as:

creativity and flexibility (see also Brady and Scully, 2005)

academic optimism regarding their capacities to 'make a difference' to their students' lives (see also Woolfolk, 2004; Woolfolk and Margetts, 2007)

recognise the need to provide intellectually challenging and socially supportive learning environments for all their students (see also Noble and McGrath, 2008; Stefanou et al., 2004; Stipek, 2002)

who understand that learning to be an effective teacher is an ongoing journey and not an end state (see also Aspland et al., 2002)

accept that some knowledge and expertise is only learned through experience (see also Bromme et al., 2001).

Many of the most important characteristics of effective teachers are described in Hattie's (2009) model of visible learning. In asserting that what teachers do in classrooms does matter, he perceives that these teachers:

intervene when they observe that students are not learning successfully. They intervene in very specific, meaningful ways to redirect the focus of the learning in order to ensure that students are able to attain their learning goals.

offer multiple opportunities for students to develop their learning strategies in different ways and they promote both surface and deep understandings of the content knowledge and conceptual skills that are embedded in the learning

match their students to appropriately challenging learning goals

most importantly, join their students and engage in a personal learning journey alongside them

recognise that in order to achieve this, clear learning outcomes must be kept in mind

know their students' capacities to cognitively engage with their learning tasks and the degree to which they are learning successfully

have the skills and knowledge to intervene when appropriate and to withdraw when students are progressing satisfactorily with their learning by working independently

provide students with learning environments that are rich in ideas and socially comfortable, supportive and safe (see also Burgh et al., 2006).

The safety of these classrooms is not concerned exclusively with physical health and safety. It is also primarily concerned with providing students with an environment in which:

- students can be intellectually challenged, make mistakes and learn from them
- the teacher develops a personal pedagogy that is dominated by the desire to facilitate the learning needs of the students
- the teacher allows students to engage in such a way as to enjoy their learning challenges, to overcome their inevitable frustrations and to develop a passion for learning.

Hattie (2009: 24) observes that:

> teachers who are students of their own efforts are the teachers who are most influential in raising student achievement. Seeking positive effects on student learning … should be a constant theme and challenge for teachers. As this does not occur by serendipity or accident, then the excellent teacher must be vigilant to what is working and *not* working in the classroom.

Hattie (2009) perceives effective teachers who promote visible learning are those who:

- are instigators of change and innovation in their classrooms
- are in control of the learning and manage it directly but do not monopolise classroom talk
- are not primarily curriculum driven
- do not use teacher power in a manner which is didactic and overly authoritarian.

He summarises his perceptions very simply in saying 'Effective teaching is not the drilling and trilling to the less than willing' (Hattie, 2009: 25). Additionally, he comments on the power of effective feedback to students as part of the teaching and learning cycle (Hattie and Timperley, 2007).

The teachers to whom these various writers refer (Hattie, 2009; Latham, et al., 2006; Lovat and Smith, 2003) have other characteristics in common. These teachers value high standards and expectations; not just for themselves, but also for their students. This is a particularly important teacher trait for successful teaching and learning. Weis and Fine (2003) found that low teacher expectations regarding students' capacities had a powerful, negative influence on student achievement, as did environments where teachers focus on the social aspects of interaction and neglect dimensions of intellectual challenge. In order for students to experience changes in school curricula, teachers must seek, identify and engage with pedagogies that both strengthen these productive teacher characteristics and facilitate the development of students as increasingly complex thinkers. What needs to be explored, therefore, are ways to develop such pedagogies within the limitations of present educational systems and restraints and within the context of the characteristics of the learners. The answer must ultimately lie in the planning and implementation of appropriate, differentiated learning programmes (Dempsey and Arthur-Kelly, 2007; McGrath and Noble, 1995a, 1995b, 1998; 2005; Tomlinson, 1999, 2000a, 2000b) and the provision of opportunities for students to develop an understanding of, and responsibility for, their own thinking and learning.

What Does This Mean for You?

There are many characteristics mentioned here that are considered overall to indicate 'good practice'. However, the same themes are continued into teaching for the future. The most important of these relate to the Holy Trinity for Teachers in these ways:

- Knowing your content and how to teach it. This relates to being able to think of alternative ways of teaching content so that students have multiple representations of one idea. It means you have to develop your creativity and be innovative with your knowledge in order to teach it to your diverse students. You have to identify links with other disciplines and content, which means you have to have wider knowledge than the specific outcomes you are preparing to teach and the strategies to help students make appropriate associations. You also need to be extremely well prepared and thoroughly organised in regard to content and effective teaching strategies.
- Knowing your students and how they learn. This necessitates having high standards for all students and knowing exactly how to develop activities so that they might learn effectively. It means you have to know how your students like to learn so you can intervene effectively when they are in difficulty. It means that you can perhaps anticipate areas of potential difficulty for individual students and support them in ways that are meaningful for them. Tasks and learning that is most effective is that with which the students have some interest or is significant for some reason. It is important that you know what this is for your students.
- Knowing yourself and your values and belief systems. This relates to your beliefs about teaching and the value of being a learner alongside your students. It requires you to use your teacher power to support your students.

(Continued)

(Continued)

You need to have an interest in your students individually for themselves and not just their academic achievements so you are not simply or solely curriculum driven. It means that you have the capacity to acknowledge and respect the creativity of others while modelling innovation and creativity in your classrooms. The degree to which you are able to allow students to dominate or dictate classroom discussion while still managing it effectively depends entirely on your perspective of teachers' work, the purpose of education, your interpersonal skills, how safe you feel in a classroom and how you have developed your classroom and other school-based relationships. A vital aspect of self knowledge is an accurate understanding of your capacity to remain positive about your students and your professional work while trying to hone your skills and juggle all the demands that are placed upon you in a classroom context.

There are a number of pedagogical models that address the importance of the 'technical' qualities and competencies that characterise effective teachers. The Quality Teaching model (Professional Support and Curriculum Directorate, 2003) mandated in New South Wales schools, like the Productive Pedagogies Model mandated in government schools in Queensland, and Hattie's (2009) work, brings together many of the aspects of effective teaching that have been researched over a number of years. The Quality Teaching model expands on and defines three critical dimensions of teaching, namely:

- pedagogies that promote high levels of intellectual quality
- quality learning environments
- the significance of their work for the students.

Similar findings can be located in other studies (e.g. Askew et al., 1997) that have specifically investigated student success in one specific area of the curriculum. Askew et al. (1997) investigated teaching and learning of numeracy in primary settings and found that teachers had three dominant pedagogical models. These were connectionist, transmission and discovery. They found that the connectionist teachers were the most successful in terms of student learning outcomes. They explicitly linked the mathematics concepts, skills and strategies that they were teaching to the learners' own lives and experiences in addition to linking them to other content matter in the curriculum. While this may not always be appropriate, especially in secondary schools, some linkages are always practical and useful to learners who are developing their own understandings and knowledge.

Within the current educational context, however, the required exploration may be severely hampered for some teachers. They may not have the opportunities or experience to develop successful supportive strategies for working with their students. Hattie (2009) suggests that teachers need to be students of their own efforts and identify what works and what does not for student learning. While it is very important that teachers constantly reflect upon and learn from their classroom interactions, it may also be useful to note one major theme that arises in much of the literature about the most effective teachers. Anders and her colleagues (Anders et al., 2008) found that teachers could make a difference to their students' lives through 'values' education. Dally (2010) also found that 'values' education had a positive impact on the students in her study, most particularly in the ways they became more inclusive of their peers, more honest and more responsible for their actions. Lovat (2007) argues that the most important aspects of teaching, namely due care, mutual respect, fairness and appropriate modelling, are concerned with teacher values and beliefs.

Lovat (2010) goes further and indicates that 'values' education is the missing link in the Quality Teaching model (Professional Support and Curriculum Directorate, 2003) mentioned earlier, which is the mandatory pedagogical model in New South Wales public schools and that the implicit values dimension is a characteristic of quality teachers. This emphasis on teacher beliefs and values certainly supports Burgh and his colleagues' (Burgh, et al., 2006) discussion of the benefits of developing mutually respectful interaction in the classroom, particularly in circumstances where students have different opinions or perspectives. In the discussion of how teachers might develop 'a community of enquiry' in their classrooms, no one perspective is considered 'correct' or more appropriate. All students learn to respect that there are diverse opinions and that all may be equally valid. This type of classroom interaction is based on trust. Students trust that they will be heard impartially and they trust that they will not be ridiculed or criticised for their contribution, however different it may be to the prevailing perspectives. In this way, ethically sensitive teachers can facilitate learning from peers that is not confrontational or threatening. It appears that the teacher qualities that make the most difference are the ones that are not actually articulated in the mandated aspects of the teaching profession, although reflective practice is certainly mentioned in all of these diverse sets of standards and is identified as a means by which teachers become increasingly effective in terms of their students' learning outcomes (Brookfield, 1995; Lester, 2004; Robins, et al., 2003).

Questions for Reflection

- Q1. Do you think that teacher quality is the single most important factor in determining student learning outcomes? Give some reasons.
- Q2. There are three major themes around which the Quality Teaching model and other similar models are developed, and the significance of the learning for students is one of these. Do you think that making the learning of significance to students may be a matter of values?
- Q3. Do you think that teachers' ethical and other values and beliefs are the most important characteristics of quality teachers? Why?
- Q4. What sort of strategies do you have to help students become more responsible for their own learning?
- Q5. How might you develop a culture of high social support and high expectations for all the learners in your class, despite the student diversity?
- Q6. How would you view your particular set of teacher standards? Are they all to do with technical competencies and codes of 'acceptable' behaviour or not? Give your reasons for your answers.
- Q7. Hattie suggests that teachers who promote 'visible learning' in the classrooms are instigators of change and innovation. Do you think that your mandatory documents have enough flexibility for teachers to develop their own ideas that promote change and innovation in their teaching and learning?

Scenario Three

Jasmine was on a professional experience placement in a large inner city school. Her teacher taught several classes of different ages throughout each week. In each of these classes, Jasmine observed that Mrs Green, her teacher, appeared to be relaxed about the ways in which she introduced her lessons. On occasion she would start with a video clip, a piece of literature or narrative or even a piece of music and then invite comment from the class about the theme of the introductory presentation. At other times she simply stated what was being introduced in the lesson and sought out prior knowledge and perspectives. Jasmine was rather confused at first because Mrs Green was supposed to teach science and mathematics and Jasmine thought that it may be less confusing for the students to just be taught exactly what they had to learn. Over the first week, however, she began to develop a better understanding of Mrs Green's pedagogy. Often the introductory presentations were designed initially to engage and interest the students. In the discussions that followed, however, if the students did not appear to be making the connections between the content matter and the music or video, for example, she would skilfully draw on what she knew about each of them to help them make the associations that she had planned. This process intrigued Jasmine, as she noticed Mrs Green did not explicitly tell the students what to think; she did not even take a prominent part in the discussion. She did manage the discussion well, however, and the students did not miss out on any part of her planned learning experiences related to the content. During the week the students picked up the threads from one lesson to another and really appeared to enjoy the discussions about the relevance of the mathematics topics or the potential and possibilities for the practical science experiments. Jasmine also noticed several interesting things happening. The students had often established what they needed to know about before attempting new learning, especially in practical contexts; they had accepted the ideas of others with respect and often lots of humour; they worked really well at supporting each other and often introduced novel concepts or ideas to the discussion that she herself would not have thought of. Mrs Green, while she was always interested in her students and friendly towards them, seemed to have developed the knack of being in the place where a student might need her help or affirmation. As all the students were not necessarily engaged in the same task, Jasmine wondered how she could possibly do that! She also worked out very quickly that the more specific directed lessons were often planned for the senior students who already had developed an interest in these specific areas and were keen to get ahead and learn the next part of the curriculum. These senior students were exceedingly competent in their chosen areas and frequently initiated the discussions themselves as Mrs Green managed the learning and frequently requested validations or proof for the proposals that arose in relation to problem solving.

Jasmine was very excited about teaching the following week and began to think of ways that she could be creative in engaging her students in what Mrs Green had termed 'joining the dots'. Science and mathematics as creative subjects at school, she thought. What an interesting time she could have!

Questions for Reflection

- Q1. What are the aspects for discussion and reflection here?
- Q2. Are the perspectives of the teacher what you might term 'quality teaching?'
- Q3. What are the difficulties that might arise for Jasmine and how might she manage these?

(Continued)

(Continued)

- Q4. What ethical perspectives are embedded in this pedagogical practice?
- Q5. Is there anything in the chapter that you have read that would indicate why a teacher would develop pedagogies such as this?
- Q6. Do you think Mrs Green was an experienced teacher or do you think that, with the right disposition and skills, any teacher or aspiring teacher could develop and implement these strategies?
- Q7. Do you think you would find promoting learning for the future a challenge? Validate your answer.
- Q8. Have you known teachers who use similar strategies to Mrs Green to promote increased learning outcomes for students?
- Q9. Would you think that Mrs Green knew her content and how to teach it? What about the other two aspects of the Holy Trinity for Teachers; do you think she was aware of these?

Conclusion

This chapter has introduced the notion of teaching students the skills, knowledge and cognitive capacities they will need to be prepared for a rapidly changing environment in the future. It has explored various perspectives related to perceived student capacities and suggestions have been made regarding pedagogical practices that can best support the effective development of these competencies. Among the strategies were several that challenged the traditional roles of teachers and learners, suggesting instead that collaboration, negotiation and respectful conversation were more likely to effectively prepare students for a lifetime of learning. It was suggested that the purpose of education is changing and a new perspective needs to be developed so that students can perceive themselves as global citizens in an ever-changing, increasingly complex world where personal values and belief systems become increasingly important. In order to meet these challenges, teachers must have a clear understanding of the ways in which students learn most efficiently and can achieve academic success that reflects their optimal potential. The following chapters introduce some of the many factors that impact on teachers' work and on students' capacities to develop and learn holistically.

References

Agbaria, A.K. (2011) The social studies education discourse community on globalization: exploring the agenda of preparing citizens for the global age. *Journal of Studies in International Education*, 15 (1): 57–74.

Anders, D., Moni, K. and Gitsaki, C. (2008) The classroom teacher: making a difference through values education. *The Social Educator*, 26 (2): 11–18.

Armstrong, D. (2006) Dreaming our future: developing democratic professional practice? *Australian Educational Researcher*, 33 (3): 1–11.

Askew, M., Brown, M., Rhodes, V., Wiliam, D., and Johnson, D. (1997) Effective teachers of numeracy in primary schools: teachers' beliefs, practices and pupils' learning. Paper presented at the British Educational Research Association Annual Conference University of York.

Aspland, T., Brooker, R., Macpherson, I., & Cuskelly, E. (2002). Professional practice research: conversations about the uncertainties. Paper presented at the AARE: Problematic futures: educational research in an era of uncertainty Brisbane. http://www.aare.edu.au/02pap/mac02279.htm 9th July 2013

Baker, D.P. (2011) 'The future of the schooled society: the transforming culture of education in postindustrial society.' In M.T. Hallinan (ed.), *Frontiers in Sociology of Education*, vol. 1. Dordrecht: Springer Netherlands. pp. 11–34.

Beare, H. (2003) The future school. *Prime Focus*, 32: 2–6.

Brady, L. and Scully, A. (2005) *Engagement: Inclusive Classroom Management*. Frenchs Forest, NSW: Pearson Education Australia.

Brennan, B. (2007) Don't get angry, get even tempered. *Teacher*, 178: 42–3.

Bromme, R., Neil, J. and Paul, B. (2001) Teacher expertise. *International Encyclopedia of the Social and Behavioral Sciences*. Oxford: Pergamon. pp. 15459–65.

Brookfield, S. (1995) *Becoming a Critically Reflective Teacher.* San Francisco: Jossey Bass

Brown, P. and Lauder, H. (1996) Education, globalization and economic development. *Journal of Education Policy*, 11 (1): 1–25.

Burchsted, S. (2003) Future studies: preparing learners for success in the 21st century. *New Horizons*, February. pp. 3–6.

Burgh, G., Field, T. and Freakley, M. (2006) *Ethics and the Community of Enquiry: Education for Deliberative Democracy*. South Melbourne: Cengage.

Dally, K. (2010) 'A teacher's duty: an examination of the short-term impact of values education on Australian Primary school teachers and students.' In T. Lovat, R. Toomey and N. Clement (eds), *International Research Handbook on Values Education and Student Wellbeing*. Dordrecht: Springer Netherlands. pp. 503–20.

Day, C. and Smetham, L. (2009) The effects of reform: have teachers really lost their sense of professionalism? *Journal of Educational Change*, 10 (2): 141–57.

Dempsey, I. and Arthur-Kelly, M. (2007) *Maximising Learning Outcomes in Diverse Classrooms*. South Melbourne: Thomson.

Dickenson, D. (2000) Learning society of the future. *New Horizons for Learning*. www.newhorizons.org (accessed 24 July 2006).

Dickenson, D. (2002) Positive trends in learning: meeting the needs of a rapidly changing world. *New Horizons*. pp. 12–16.

Dinham, S., Anderson, M., Caldwell, B. and Weldon, P. (2011) Breakthroughs in school leadership development in Australia. *School Leadership and Management*, 31 (2): 139–54.

Doyle, C. (2012) Let's stop forecasting 21st century skills. *Education Week*, 31 (36): 8. Retrieved 12th August 2012 from www.edweek.org/ew/articles/2012/07/18/36deeper.h31.html?tkn=O MLFyJ5UVWqtTE5UXEoDn9DVO%2FwjH%2FiqdEnIandcmp=ENL-CM-NEWS2.

Gardner, H. (2000) *The Disciplined Mind: Beyond Facts and Standardised Tests, the K–12 Education Every Child Deserves*. New York: Penguin Books.

Gardner, H. (2006a) *Five Minds for the Future*. Boston, MA: Harvard Business School Press.

Gardner, H. (2006b) *Changing Minds*. Boston, MA: Harvard Business School Press.

Gidley, J. (2008) 'Beyond homogenisation of global education: do alternative pedagogies such as Steiner education have anything to offer an emergent global/ising world?' In

S. Inayatullah, M. Bussey and I. Milojevic (eds), *Alternative Educational Futures: Pedagogies for an Emergent World*. Rotterdam: Sense Publications. pp. 253–68.

Gidley, J. and Hampson, G. (2005) The evolution of futures in school education. *Futures*, 37 (4): 255–71.

Gidley, J. and Hampson, G. (2008) 'Integral perspectives on school educational futures'. In M. Bussey, S. Inayatullah and I. Milojevic (eds), *Alternative Educational Futures: Pedagogies for an Emergent World*. Rotterdam: Sense Publications. pp. 253–68.

Greenberg, M., Weissberg, R., O'Brien, M., Zins, J., Fredericks, L., Resnik, H. and Elias, M. (2003) Enhancing school-based prevention and youth development through coordinated social, emotional and academic learning. *American Psychologist*, 58 (6/7): 466–74.

Hanushek, E., Rivkin, S., Rothstein, R. and Podgursky, M. (2004) How to improve the supply of high-quality teachers. *Brookings Papers on Education Policy*, 7: 7–44.

Hare, W. (2004) Education for an unsettled world: Dewey's conception of open-mindedness. *Journal of Thought*, 39 (3): 111–27.

Hargreaves, A. and Shirley, D. (2009) *The Fourth Way: The Inspiring Future for Educational Change*. London: Corwin.

Hattie, J. (2009) *Visible Learning: A Synthesis of over 800 Meta-analyses Relating to Achievement*. Abingdon: Routledge.

Hattie, J. and Timperley, H. (2007) The power of feedback. *Review of Educational Research*, 77 (1): 81–112.

Henderson, H. (2002) Education for the third millennium. Paper presented at the Education for the Third Millennium Conference, Catamarca, Argentina.

HGSE News, June. Retrieved from http://www.gse.harvard.edu/news/features/gardner 06012004.html 9th July 2103

Kelly, A. (2009) Globalisation and education: a review of conflicting perspectives and their effect on policy and professional practice in the UK. *Globalisation, Societies and Education*, 7 (1): 51–68.

Lanning, R. (1994) Education and everyday life: an argument against 'educational futures'. *Canadian Journal of Education/Revue canadienne de l'éducation*, 19 (4): 464–78.

Latham, G., Blaise, M., Dole, S., Faulkner, J., Lang, J. and Malone, K. (2006) *Learning to Teach: New Times, New Practices*. South Melbourne: Oxford University Press.

Lepani, B. (1995) Implications for change in a learning culture: meeting the challenges of the knowledge economy. Paper presented at the International Confederation of Principals Second World Convention, Sydney.

Lester, N (2004) 'Professional learning through reflection on practice'. In B. Bartlett, F. Bayer & D. Roebuck (eds), *Educating: Weaving Research into Practice* (Vol. 2). Nathan QLD: Griffith University, School of Cognition, Language and Special Education. pp. 214–21.

Lovat, T., & Smith, D. (2003) *Curriculum: Action on Reflection*. Tuggerah, NSW: Social Science Press.

Lovat, T. (2007) *Values Education: The Missing Link in Quality Teaching and Effective Learning*. Paper presented at the Values Education and Lifelong Learning: Principles. Policies and Programmes: Berlin.

Lovat, T. (2010) Synergies and balance between values education and quality teaching. *Educational Philosophy and Theory*, 42 (4): 489–500.

McGrath, H. and Noble, T. (1995a) *Seven Ways at Once. Classroom Strategies Based on the Seven Intelligences*, Book 1. Melbourne: Longman Australia.

McGrath, H. and Noble, T. (1995b) *Seven Ways at Once. Units of Work Based on the Seven Intelligences*, Book 2. Melbourne: Longman Australia.

McGrath, H. and Noble, T. (1998) *Seven Ways at Once. More Classroom Strategies and Units of Work Based on the Seven Intelligences*, Book 3. Melbourne: Longman Australia.

McGrath, H. and Noble, T. (2005) *Eight Ways at Once*, Vol. 1. Frenchs Forest, NSW: Pearson Education Australia.

McLaren, P. and Farahmandpur, R. (2001) Teaching against globalization and the new imperialism: toward a revolutionary pedagogy. *Journal of Teacher Education*, 52 (2): 136–50.

Mok, K.H. (2005) Globalisation and governance: educational policy instruments and regulatory arrangements. *International Review of Education*, 51 (4): 289–311.

Noble, T. and McGrath, H. (2008) The positive educational practices framework: a tool for facilitating the work of educational psychologists in promoting pupil wellbeing. *Educational and Child Psychology*, 25 (2): 119–34.

Nyburg, D. and Egan, K. (1981) *The Erosion of Education: Socialization and the Schools*. New York: Teachers College Press.

Professional Support and Curriculum Directorate (2003) *Quality Teaching in NSW Public Schools*. Sydney: New South Wales Department of Education and Training.

Robins, A., Ashbaker, B., Enriquez, J. and Morgan, J. (2003) Learning to reflect: professional practice for professionals and paraprofessionals. *International Journal of Learning*, 10: 2555–65.

Rupérez, F. (2003) Globalization and education. *Prospects*, 33 (3): 249–61.

Samet, R. (2010) Futurists and their schools: a response to Ziauddin Sardar's 'the namesake'. *Futures*, 42 (8): 895–900.

Schecter, B. (2011) 'Development as an aim of education': a reconsideration of Dewey's vision. *Curriculum Inquiry*, 41 (2): 250–66.

Sellars, M. (2008) Education for the 21st century: three components of a new pedagogy. *International Journal of the Humanities*, 6 (2): 27–34.

Smyre, R. (2000) Transforming the 20th century mind. *New Horizons*, 1–8.

Sparks, S. (2012) Panel of scholars define 21st century skills. *Education Week*, 31 (36): 7.

Spring, J. (2008) Research on globalization and education. *Review of Educational Research*, 78 (2): 330–63.

Stefanou, C., Perencevich, K., DiCinto, M. and Turner, J. (2004) Supporting autonomy in the classroom: ways teachers encourage student decision making and ownership. *Educational Phychologist*, 39 (2): 97–110.

Stipek, D. (2002) *Motivation to Learn: Integrating Theory and Practice*. Boston: Allyn and Bacon.

Tomlinson, C.A. (1999) Mapping a route towards differentiated instruction. *Educational Leadership*, 57 (1): 12–16.

Tomlinson, C.A. (2000a) Differentiation of instruction in the Elementary grades. *ERIC Digest*. Retrieved from www.eric.ed.gov (29 April 2005).

Tomlinson, C.A. (2000b) Reconcilable differences? *Educational Leadership*, 58 (1): 6–11.

Tomlinson, P. (1995) *Understanding Mentoring: Reflective Strategies for School-Based Teacher Preparation*. Buckingham and Philadelphia: Open University Press.

Unknown. (2004) *Changing Minds: The Art and Science of Changing Our Own and Other People's Minds*. An Interview with Hobbs Professor Howard Gardner

Warner, D. (2006) *Schooling for the Knowledge Era*. Camberwell, VIC: Australian Council for Education Research Press.

Weis, L., and Fine, M. (2009) 'Working method: research and social justice'. In P. Burch (ed.), *Hidden Markets: The New Education Privatization* New York: Routledge.

Woolfolk, A. (2004) *Educational Psychology*. Boston, MA: Pearson Education.

Woolfolk, A. and Margetts, K. (2007) *Educational Psychology*. Frenchs Forest, NSW: Pearson Education.

Zhao, Y. (2011) Students as change partners: a proposal for educational change in the age of globalization. *Journal of Educational Change*, 12 (2): 267–79.

Chapter 4: The Learning Process

- Q1. What do you know about the learning process?
- Q2. In what ways can you help students with their learning?
- Q3. Are all students basically the same?
- Q4. Where does learning take place and what do you know about it that is useful in preparing you to teach?
- Q5. Can you enrich the learning of your students by understanding some basic knowledge about what goes on in the brain?

Introduction

While it is really informative to know what good quality teachers do, it is also important to understand a little about why these strategies, attitudes and pedagogies enhance student learning and have the potential to improve their academic outcomes. The emotional impact that interested, welcoming teachers can have on their students' motivation to learn and be part of a learning community may be easily understood. You may have read about the power of effective feedback (Hattie and Timperley, 2007) and the impact of perceptive, well-informed teachers who learn with their students by constantly reflecting on their professional practice with a specific focus on what works for their students and what does not (Weis and Fine, 2003). You may question, however, why specific pedagogies are more successful in promoting learning than others. One such strategy was mentioned in the last chapter. Askew et al. (1997) found in their research that the teachers they identified as the 'connectionist' teachers were the most successful at improving their students' numeracy outcomes. Why do you think this could be? The answer can be found in some basic explanations of how the brain works.

The same technological developments that have created a new focus and model of professionalism for teachers are also responsible for the technology that medical sciences are currently utilising to explore and explain how the brain functions in the learning process. You may consider that the challenges of the new teacher role are compensated for, to some degree, by the explosion of information that is the result of medical research on the human brain. A consideration of the nature of the brain in the learning process is not currently an automatic response for many teachers when they are planning to meet their students' learning needs. You may think that it is neither imperative nor practical for you to try to understand the ways in which the brain works in the construction of knowledge, as beginning teachers already have several other means by which to identify students' learning preferences and have a strong focus on getting the more technical aspects of teaching well-established. However, as the brain is the site of all cognition (the ability to acquire knowledge by using reasoning, perception and other mental faculties), it is an important aspect of knowing how your students learn best and how you can effectively prepare and implement appropriate learning tasks in your classroom, despite the fact that only a tiny percentage of brain research is relevant in educational contexts (Guilford, 1967). It is also useful for you to have some general knowledge about the brain. It needs, for example, like other parts of the body, to be kept healthy through adequate nutrition. Sleep deprivation can have a severe negative impact on the brain and learning as it interferes with cognition, decision making, reasoning and innovative thinking (Sellars, 2008). It seems that, during sleep, the brain reactivates the regions that are used for learning during the day. This serves to positively reinforce the learning and to support the memory, which is important to know for your longer-term planning. Factoring in your knowledge of brain structure and functions will help you with the technical, ethical and moral aspects of the profession, such as planning for learning, organising materials, balancing active and quiet activities and understanding student differences more comprehensively.

What Does the Literature Say about How the Brain Works?

The human brain is designed to be educated (Blakemore and Frith, 2005). Sometimes this appears to happen instinctively and with little apparent effort. This may be why, as yet, studies into the workings of the brain are not making a significant impact on educational systems, learning environments or curriculum development. Another reason may be that the entire picture of how learning takes place is not yet available (Guilford, 1967). Despite this, findings from neuroscience have been used to contribute to significant advances in the teaching of academic skills in mathematics and reading and to establish the interdependence of emotion and cognition (McCombs, 2004). It is known that from the very first cell division in the womb there is an intricate balance between genetic inheritances and environment. The brain is literally created by experiences. All types of sensory experiences, visual, auditory, tactile, physical, gustatory and olfactory, create imprints on the brain which are represented as a series of images (*The Jossey Bass Reader on the Brain and Learning* 2008). The brain even starts life with a capacity for emotional responses, which can later be educated to respond appropriately to moral and ethical challenges. These emotions and feelings have images that are based in the body itself as opposed to the responses elicited by outside stimuli: 'Images are the currency of the mind' (*The Jossey Bass Reader on the Brain and Learning* 2008) and the owner, interpreter and comprehender of the mind is the 'self'. When individuals are awake, there is awareness of the mind itself and also of the 'self'. The human mind employs the physical structure of the brain as an indispensible medium for the brain. The capacity of the brain to generate images depends on its ability to process sensory experiences as a chain of events that come together as coherent perceptual maps of the stimuli experienced. These neural experiences encountered by the brain are then transformed into learning by an incredibly complex process (Zins et al., 2004).

A very simple explanation of the key features of the brain is provided for you here so that you are able to reflect on the impact these might have on learning tasks and conditions that you provide for your students. Firstly, babies are born with all the brain cells they will have for life, with the exception of those in the regions of the hippocampus and the cerebellum. These brain cells increase dramatically in the first years of life (Barlow, 2000; Sellars, 2008). These millions of nerve cells, known as neurons, are arranged in circuits in the brain. The word 'circuit' is not used arbitrarily but because it helps you to imagine what actually occurs in the brain. This is because it conjures up the notion of actual electrical wiring and the different paths that it may take, for example, to different parts of a home, each with an array of light switches, power points and electrical appliances. The cells are organised in these circuits so that two neurons can make contact with each other as the result of electrochemical processes.

This contact is called a synapse, and when this happens, learning occurs on that specific pathway. There are 'trillions' (Zins et al., 2004: 61) of synapses in the brain which are associated with memory, learning, emotions and feelings, reasoning and so forth. When this learning happens, the specific neuron pathway or circuit with which it is associated becomes easier to 'travel' (Zins et al., 2004: 65) because of the facilitation of these synaptic occurrences and the brain changes to accommodate new learning (Arnold, 2005). These synapses are always instigated as responses to experiences. The willingness of the brain to constantly change and accommodate new learning is termed brain plasticity (Sellars, 2008; Zins et al., 2004). To add to the complexity, every individual's brain is 'wired' differently (Christenson and Havsy, 2004; Johnson and Johnson, 2004). These 'wiring' differences are rendered additionally complicated in a teaching and learning environment as they are also influenced by learning related to personal values and belief systems, social modelling and cultural complexity. However, each brain, though wired differently, responds to stimuli in the same manner:

> The brain changes its physical structures as a result of learning taking place.
>
> These changes in physical structures alter the functional organisation of the brain.
>
> Different parts of the brain exhibit a 'readiness to learn' at different times, supporting the theories of developmental psychologists. (see also Lopes and Salovey, 2004)

Not only does the brain structure change after learning takes place, but the functional, organisational changes that take place are as individual as the brain wiring itself. It is important for you, as aspiring teachers, to be aware that individuals with a lot of learning in specific content areas (experts) organise their learning differently to those individuals (novices or students) who have sparsely populated organisations of knowledge, or 'schemata' as they are identified in cognitive science. As all individuals are wired differently, this means that experts organise differently to one another and so do the novices. There are clear implications here for how you might structure your instruction for learning.

What Does This Mean for You?

While the brain is very complex and is still being investigated, there are some clear implications for professional practice. These include:

- An understanding that all experiences, good or otherwise, are part of creating the brain. Successful learning experiences and those that are not successful have equal impact.
- The brain can learn ideas and strategies that are incorrect as readily as it learns correct ideas and strategies, so knowing your content and how to teach it is vital.
- As different parts of the brain exhibit a readiness to learn at different times, it is important that learners are encouraged to undertake appropriate tasks. It also means that tasks that appear too difficult are reserved until the part of the brain that facilitates this learning is ready to be active in the learning

(Continued)

(Continued)

process. Students need to be encouraged to believe that they will achieve various tasks when they are ready and not to suppose that they will never be good at the area that they are finding difficult at any moment in time.

- Relating new ideas to previous knowledge is very important in the learning process. Learning occurs all the time, so learning outside the classroom context is an important source of reference on which to base related, new learning as the synaptic occurrences make the learning easier on that pathway.
- Sequencing is important. In order to give students the best opportunity of learning successfully, ideas and knowledge, strategies and procedures should be taught in as logical, ordered a fashion as possible.
- It is often necessary to teach the same concept in different ways because novices' brains are organised differently one from another and from their teacher's!
- The brain changes in response to learning. However, as everyone is 'wired' differently, it is safe to assume that none of your students will experience exactly the same changes in organisational structures, despite the common attribute known as 'brain plasticity'.
- Given (2002) proposes that the brain is organised into five learning systems, each of which impacts on and interacts with each other. She names these as the emotional, social, cognitive, physical and reflective systems. Teaching to promote increased social and emotional competency is discussed further in Chapter 7 in relation to emotional intelligence in addition to the content of this chapter in which Vygotsky's understanding of learning in a social context is explored. The cognitive system is discussed below in terms of which areas of the brain are utilised for different types of thinking. The need for learning by 'doing' is recognised as a significant part of learners' experiences and is explored in Chapter 11, which discusses differentiation and below. The notion of a reflective or monitoring system may be not significantly represented in a number of educational contexts, despite its importance. However, it is this system of learning; reflecting and self monitoring that is discussed in Chapter 9 as executive function skills and in the context of metacognition.

Brain Facts

There are four lobes in the brain: the temporal, frontal, parietal and occipital. The outermost layer of the brain is called the cerebral cortex and covers the cerebrum, the front part of the brain (Sellars, 2008). The cerebral cortex is often termed 'the grey matter' and is the most highly developed part of the brain. It is the critical component in the learning process. It is divided into left and right hemispheres. There is, as yet, no complete understanding of the precise function of each of the two hemispheres of the cerebral cortex, which are joined by clusters of nerve fibres known as the corpus callosum and the anterior commissure, which also facilitate communication between the two hemispheres. However, it is known that different parts of the brain are used, either independently or more usually in coordination with other parts of the brain, for different types of learning (Gardner, 1993). For example, the hippocampal system, which is located in the temporal lobe, is concerned primarily with learning facts. The cerebellum and the basal ganglia, which can both be found under the cerebral cortex are the locations responsible for the development of skills (Zins et al., 2004). It appears that 90% of individuals have language in the left hemisphere of the brain but, inexplicably, 10% have language in the right side of the brain, which is interesting as an individual's language hemisphere determines the dominant hemisphere. Blakemore and Frith (2005: 78) indicate that the learning required for reading- and writing-related skills are located in three areas of the brain.

Various areas in the temporal lobe facilitate the storage and retrieval of whole words, the decoding of language and the processing of the spelling, sound and meaning of words. An area of the frontal lobe is responsible for the production of spoken language. A specific region of the parietal lobe has many functions, one of the most important of which is to establish the association between spoken and seen words. Semantic processing uses both hemispheres of the brain, irrespective of the developmental or life stage in which it is learned. In contrast there appears to be a critically responsive stage for the efficient learning of grammar. If an individual learns English as a child, then the grammatical processing activity is wholly in the left hemisphere as a rule (Gardner, 1993). However, the older the individual is introduced to the language the more extensively both hemispheres are used to process the grammar, which indicates they are using different, less proficient strategies. Neville (in Sellars, 2008: 47) indicates that after the age of 13 years grammar is more difficult to learn because individuals are using less efficient strategies. She also suggests that the earlier grammar is learned, the easier it is for the individual child.

Very young children have also been proven to possess innate number sense. The difficulty is, however, harnessing that potential. As Devlin (2010: 163) comments:

Mathematics teachers – at all education levels – face two significant obstacles:

We know almost nothing about how people do mathematics. We know almost nothing about how people learn mathematics.

What is known is the human brain has number sense, concepts of discrete whole numbers, the capacity to distinguish a correct from an incorrect answer when the scenario involves arithmetic and small whole numbers, and that numbers and arithmetic beyond three require the use of language (Lopes & Salovey, 2004: 164)

Although there is no one area of the brain that is responsible for all the different types and components of learning and processing in mathematics, the parietal lobe is the lobe associated with spatial representations, sense of direction, locating objects in time and space and with numbers and their relationships. Exact calculations also appear to be processed in this area of the left hemisphere but the capacity to process approximation of number appears to be located in a different area of the brain altogether, which is in the right hemisphere. Although the brain actively seeks and recognises patterns, and both hemispheres are able to compare numbers, only the left hemisphere can add and multiply. Interestingly, there still exist some difficulties in locating the exact sites of some other learning. For example, theorists present some differences in their understandings of where the skills of reading music are located. Jensen (2005) indicates that reading music activates both sides of the brain. Blakemore and Frith (2005), however, report the findings of a study that located these skills in the same area of the parietal lobe that facilitates spacial awareness.

There, are, of course, as in any other emerging field of enquiry, some contentious issues. One of these must be that adults have been the participants in most brain research that contributes to the facts known about the brain and specific areas of learning. This is despite a number of studies with children and babies that indicate the brain's innate potential to learn effectively at various developmental stages (Sellars, 2008). The reason that children are not included in studies of the brain that require neurological imaging is simply because of the requirement for the participants to stay absolutely still throughout the process. The slightest movement could easily cause the imaging to be misinterpreted and the findings misrepresented. Other concerns for teachers are popular notions about the brain that impact negatively on their efforts to provide holistic education for all their students. One such concern centres on the degree of physical difference in the actual construction of male and female brains and how important this may be in educational concerns. There appears to be a consensus (McCombs, 2004; Sellars, 2008) that there are gender differences in both the construction and function of male and female brains, but that these are generally very subtle and it is believed that it is more important for educators to be aware of the individual differences, rather than focus on male or female brains as stereotypes.

Similarly, identifying students as predominantly left-brained or right-brained learners is discredited (McCombs, 2004) as research findings indicate that both hemispheres are important for learning. Much learning depends on the brain's capacity to integrate and orchestrate activity in many parts of the brain to perform even simple tasks. The two hemispheres of the brain are constantly and instantly in communication with each other via the nerve clusters of the corpus callosum and the anterior commissure and so to attempt to classify students as right- or left-brained learners is erroneous, despite students' individual learning preferences. The most important consideration, however, may be the confirmation of the significant impact that emotions have on learning; confirmation of the knowledge that the brain cannot function effectively or efficiently unless it 'feels safe' (Christenson and Havsy, 2004; McCombs, 2004).

What Does This Mean for You?

Although some general implications for teaching are discussed below, it might be useful for you to have specific notions about the brain in your mind to inform your professional practice. These include:

- Only one part of the brain is utilised when learning is about learning facts. This means that other types of learning are important in any lesson plan.
- Parts of the brain usually coordinate with each other during the learning process.
- Many different locations in the brain deal with language, indicating that talking and listening and a range of appropriate literacy skills are important in the learning process in all content areas.
- Not all learners have language in the right side of the brain and the site of language determines the dominant hemisphere for each individual. There are differences in learning for these students that need to be accommodated by your pedagogy.
- Young children have the best propensity for learning grammar. As students get to secondary schools they have more difficulty with new grammatical concepts as their strategies are less efficient. This can be a very important consideration for students who are learning English as an additional language.
- Students cannot always explain how they know various aspects of mathematical understanding as number sense is part of the brain's function.
- There is no specific knowledge relating to how individuals learn or do mathematics, making the work of the mathematics teacher less informed in terms of how the brain functions exactly in their area of knowledge.
- Perhaps the most important overall finding of neuroscience is the need for the brain to be emotionally safe for cognition to occur. This knowledge informs both the nature of the optimum learning environment and the quality and nature of classroom interactions and teacher–student relationships. The less stress and anxiety that students experience, the more able their brain is to learn, so being positive is important.
- The entire body is involved in learning. Physical activity is significant in the learning process, as are the ample, appropriate provision for sensory experiences.

(Continued)

(Continued)

- Students who are not well-nourished, are sleep-deprived or afraid, distressed, anxious or otherwise unhappy are unlikely to be able to learn as effectively as those who have nutritious diets, adequate sleep and feel safe in the learning environment. It is difficult for them to fulfil their full learning potential, even if they are otherwise motivated to learn.
- Creativity is important for effective learning as it coordinates parts of the brain not utilised together in more ordered, convergent thinking.

Implications for Teaching

There are several ways in which you can use the emerging information about the brain to impact positively on your professional practice. The brain's plasticity and its capacity for change make it receptive to learning from poor teaching practices as well as those that are sound (McCombs, 2004). There are several general aspects that you are able to reflect upon in relation to your own professional practice. These include:

- The ways in which you model activities, provide a variety of explanations and accept students' thinking as valuable and useful provide evidence of your acknowledgement of individuals' unique brain 'wiring' and information structuring.
- The provision of learning activities that are carefully planned to provide a range of sensory experiences indicates your understanding of how knowledge is created, how physical activity and movement have the capacity to enhance learning and the role of emotions in creativity and the learning process.
- The means by which you are able to build on prior knowledge and experiences and introduce new learning opportunities effectively by explicitly exploring links to other knowledge signify the importance you place on the fact that the brain is biologically designed to actively seek connections in order to organise associated learning.
- The opportunities that you create to nurture the innate emotional capacities of your students to respond to ethical and moral issues both in the school environment and in the wider community, reflect your own understanding of your professional work as an ethical undertaking and your commitment to the school and wider community.
- Your degree of sensitivity related to the impact of poor nutrition and sleep on a student's capacity to learn or to perform tasks proficiently can guide your expectations and inform your ethic of care.

- Even the learning environment and classroom culture you develop are significant as they signify the degree of respect and appreciation you have for the importance of the findings from social and emotional neuroscience regarding the brain's need to feel emotionally safe in order work effectively.

So how might you plan to teach with the brain in mind? Several suggestions from experienced educators are presented and discussed here, but you will also find, in the following chapters, many other topics for reflection and debate that can inform and support your efforts to incorporate your professional practice as a beginning teacher. Perhaps the first things that you need to remember are the ethical guidelines for developing communities of enquiry in your classroom (Burgh, et al., 2006) and the brain's capacity for responding emotionally to ethical and moral challenges. You need to be open to different opinions, various perspectives and ideas and to explore these in a mutually respectful way with students in a manner that allows them to identify and acknowledge the sources of their beliefs systems. By engaging with students and their ideas in a non-dismissive, non-judgemental manner, you allow individuals to hold different viewpoints and express diverse attitudes while still exposing them to the beliefs and perceptions of others, which may, in turn, prompt them to critically evaluate their views.

Planning for sensory experiences is too frequently interpreted as being the exclusive province of those who teach young students. However, you may experience yourself, or be aware of others who have to 'do' things themselves in order to learn effectively. This may be particularly so for the learning of new ideas, concepts, skills or procedures. It is not surprising, then, that Sousa (2010) indicates that movement has been shown to enhance learning capacity and memory. Springer (2002) believes that individuals develop learning preferences as the result of positive experiences. Individuals, once they recognise the quickest and easiest way that they can solve problems, continue to use that neural pathway, which in turn strengthens that specific modality. The strengthening occurs as the repeated use of these neurons makes the connections stronger. Jensen (1998) agrees, indicating that students who are learning at an unsatisfactory rate should be re-taught using their preferred learning modality. This has implications for classroom practice, especially as there are only approximately 20% of learners in any class group whose learning preferences would be auditory (Fleming & Bay, 2004). Sousa (2010) reported findings that even those individuals who had auditory learning preferences tuned out mentally after 15–20 minutes of lecturing. Obviously younger listeners would have difficulty sustaining mental alertness and listening for a shorter period of time than this. Springer (2002) indicates that auditory learners do not necessarily need visual materials, they learn easily from discussions and debates but cannot listen for too long without having some input themselves.

Visual learners find accessing information easier if organised in charts, diagrams, pictures and other visual displays, including mental models (Fleming and Bay, 2004). Visual information is processed in the fourth brain lobe, the occipital lobe and these learners often prefer models that are non-linguistic. As the brain stores and processes information and memories as pictures, it is not really surprising that the majority of students in any class would be visual learners. Tileston (2004: 23) indicates that visual learners may:

- have difficulty understanding oral instructions
- have difficulty remembering names
- enjoy looking at books or drawing pictures
- watch the speaker's face
- like to work puzzles
- notice small details
- like the teacher to use visuals when talking
- like to use non-linguistic organisers.

The third category of learners prefer to learn by doing. These are the kinaesthetic learners who store new information in the motor cortex and then in the cerebellum (Guilford, 1967). These are the students who always need hands-on activities to learn efficiently. They need opportunities for movement, manipulation of materials and appreciate opportunities to be learning in an outside environment that provides enough room for physical activity to be engaged with comfortably. The reason that movement has the impact it does on potential learning is simply that as students move around they increase the flow of blood and fluids to the brain and this facilitates more effective learning. These students also tend to be physically fitter and access their long term memories more easily. Exercise is also strongly correlated to increased brain mass and cell production and improved mood and cognition (McCombs, 2004: 15). The impact of movement and exercise on mood is important for learners. The research from social and affective neuroscience confirms what you may already have experienced in classrooms. Your experiences may have already led you to recognise the negative impact of stress and anxiety and the positive impact of emotionally and physically safe environments for learning. The planned, conscientious development of and expectations of a community of learners (Connella, 1999) is one way that you can provide and manage an emotionally and socially safe environment for your students. Another is to simply appreciate the enormous impact that emotions have on cognition and how it is impossible to separate one from the other, although reasoning and rational thinking can inform and modify emotional thoughts (Seligman et al., 2009). The foundations of the Personal Reflection Model that you are using throughout the text are built on this understanding.

Creativity is often thought of as a special quality that individuals possess, not as a capacity that can be developed (Dupré and O'Neill, 1998). Creativity uses parts of the brain that are not ordinarily strongly connected in other, more convergent thinking. The divergent thinking that characterises creative minds is mediated by the frontal lobes and comprises a high degree of specialised knowledge and frontal lobe processes such as ready access to working memory and sustained attention. However, as far as it can be established, there is no one part of the brain that specialises in creative thinking, although a loss of inhibition has been found to link to high levels of creativity (Dupré and O'Neill, 1998). Improvisation has also been shown to contribute positively to creative capacity. Deasy (in Dupré and O'Neill, 1998: 233) identified some positive learning behaviours that could be fostered by students engaging in the arts. These included:

- persistence in sustaining concentrated attention to a task
- symbolic understanding by using multiple modes to communicate
- resilience in overcoming frustration and failure
- engaged learning through absorption in content
- collaborative learning as a member of group processes for acquiring and manifesting knowledge.

Winner and Hetland (in Dupré and O'Neill, 1998: 233) identified the mental habits that students learned as a result of being engaged with the arts as 'studio habits of mind'. These included persistence and other qualities identified by Deasy, but included also a focus on the self. They indicated that the arts scaffolded students' capacities to express their personal voice, to engage with evaluative self reflection in order to analyse, judge and revise their work and to create mental images in order to think about things in new and unusual ways. In keeping with the brain's predisposition to seek out patterns and relationships, Hardiman (2010: 239) also stresses the ability to find and understand 'relationships between relationships' as one of the most important skills for students to learn in the twenty-first century.

Finding these relationships and exploring connections have been found to impact positively on student learning outcomes (Askew et al. 1997). Certainly relating new knowledge, concepts and skills to what students have already learned is commonly found in the strategies that are implemented as the introductory sections to lessons. It is worth carefully planning these activities and revisiting the connections during the in-task discussions you have with your students because, although the brain actively seeks connections, some may not be as obvious to the students as they are to you (Seligman, 2002). The connections that are made by students between prior knowledge and new knowledge is known as transfer (Seligman, 2002). Two factors are important in successful transfer:

- the impact of the new learning on prior learning
- the degree to which the new learning is considered to be useful.

When new learning is in progress, there can be positive or negative transfer depending on the ways in which the new learning in the working memory supports or challenges the prior knowledge that is stored in the long term memory (Sousa, 1995). The process of retrieving the prior knowledge can be supported by your actions in the learning process. Tileston (2004: 28)

Association	This refers to events, actions or feelings that are learned together. These are personal associations and are the most frequently used types of prompts that are used by teachers. They often refer to previous lesson content and, because the brain associates with strong emotions and these strong emotions actually takes priority over everything else in the brain, students are more likely to recall events or learning with which they have strong emotional ties. This process of association creates ownership of the learning. Depending on the age of the students, prompts or hints about what is about to be engaged with in the learning process may be given prior to the actual learning itself to allow for retrieval time. It is also important that any misinformation that student may have about the learning so that it does not become stored in the long term memory. This type of prompting is useful for promoting cross-disciplinary links in addition to links within one subject area. The questions that might trigger memory retrieval of association may start with 'Do you remember when ...?' for recalling events.
Similarity	As the name suggests, this technique involves transferring skills and knowledge from one situation to another which is very similar. This could be a similar environment, or you can relate new information to experiences or understandings that you know your students are already personally familiar with. The questions that might trigger memory retrieval of association may start with 'Do you remember how ...?' for recalling how skills where used before in a different context
Critical attributes	This method of prompting effective memory retrieval depends on identifying the main characteristics of the information or idea that make the idea unique. The brain, in its constant searching for patterns, can readily identify the patterns that it has already stored in the long term memory by their unique characteristics. The questions that might trigger memory retrieval of association may start with 'Do you remember what exactly ...?' to recall what distinguished that idea from others
The content and degree of original learning	If the original learning was robust or well-understood and accurate, then building in that knowledge by adding new knowledge will not only be easier but will be more successful for the students. This factor places great stress on the need for students to have time to fully engage with new learning, to build on their existing knowledge structures and to explore the new information fully in the context of what they already know. The questions that might trigger memory retrieval of association may start with 'What do you remember about ...?' to recall as broadly as possible everything that was previously learned

Figure 4.1   Factors that Can Influence the Rate and Degree of Student Retrieval (after Sousa, 1995, in Tileston, 2005)

discusses Sousa's four factors (McCombs, 2002, 2004) that can make the retrieval process easier for students and, in turn, make the connections to new learning more successful. These are detailed in Figure 4.1. Making the connections for and with students as they learn is the core of the learning process, as you will see in the discussion of the cognitive science perspective of learning detailed below, and is one of the most significant attributes demonstrated by effective teachers, as you read in the previous chapter. In this discussion, the focus of teaching and learning is to establish accurate information in the long term memory where it can be readily accessed and form a firm foundation for further learning.

Questions for Reflection

- Q1. Did you read anything of interest or of relevance to you as you are developing your own professional practice? It may be useful to list some points that you would find helpful to remember in your planning.
- Q2. Do you think that you have read anything that may explain what you have witnessed in a classroom during your professional experiences?
- Q3. Do you recall which type of 'memory joggers' you have heard used or have used yourself to support students' recall? How powerful were they? Are there other ideas you would like to incorporate into your usual routine in the classroom?
- Q4. If you do not exclusively teach the arts or other discipline areas that involve a degree of movement, how might you integrate some of the benefits of these content areas into your planning and practice?
- Q5. Does the overriding impact of emotion on cognition encourage you to reconsider the cultural climate that best promotes effective learning?
- Q.6 Do you think that the research on the brain and how it learns is relevant for your practice? Validate your answer.
- Q.7 Why do you think that research from neuroscience is not widely impacting on educational contexts at present?
- Q8. Do you think it should? Validate your answer.

The Cognitive Science Perspective of Learning

One perspective that explains how all these processes work together and construct knowledge is the cognitive science perspective of learning (Fleming and Bay, 2004; Fredrickson, 2001; Reese, 1998). This model explains how some learning is robust, well-understood, integrated with prior learning, and easily connected and connectible to new information

(Bernstein and Waber, 2007). It also examines how other information is not integrated, despite being well-learned and is only available in the specific context in which it is learned. Stimuli are received by the brain from the senses. This information is then held in the cortex. From there it is either dismissed as not relevant or useful, or proceeds to either the working memory or to the long term memory. Once learning has been accomplished, it moves to the temporary memory, which comprises an aspect of the sensual register and the short term memory, and then to the working memory for processing (Seligman, 2002). Information only remains in the short term memory for long enough to be of instant use, about 30 seconds, and then the decision is made about whether to disregard the information or send it to the working memory for processing. The working memory can only process a few pieces of information at one time; exactly how much can be processed simultaneously depends on the age of the child. How long information is held in the working memory depends also on the development of the individual, but it is agreed that the duration increases as students get older. It does appear that after 20 minutes, if something is not done with the information, then it is discarded. If the information needs to be retrieved at a later date, then it must be stored in the long term memory. There are several ways in which information can be stored in the long term memory but each of these relies on the information to be learned being of interest and relevance to the learner. It also requires that information be presented in ways that support and scaffold learning and in the context of an emotionally safe environment.

It is not really known in how many different ways the brain stores and organises information in the long term memory. Jensen (2011) identifies three memory storage systems, Tileston (2004: 39) discusses five:

- Semantic. As you would expect, the semantic memory holds information learned from words themselves. For semantic information to be established in the long term memory, it must either have found connections with which to associate or be repeatedly rehearsed so that it is remembered. The two connections that are most useful in retrieving information from the semantic memory are relevance and prior knowledge. The former gives meaning to the information being learned, the latter helps the student make sense of the information as they already have something to build on. The semantic memory is frequently found to be the most difficult from which to retrieve stored information.
- Episodic. Episodic memory stores the information about the time and place new information was learned. Students in the same learning space can often visualise where information was displayed long after the display

itself has been discarded or replaced. They can do this using their episodic memory.

- Procedural. Procedural memory, however, is quite dependent on repeated rehearsal. If students are required to demonstrate something, they must practise often enough to have the procedural elements stored in their procedural memories. Procedural memory can be enhanced by the provision of hands-on activities, manipulating concrete materials and performance such as role-play and drama. This part of the long term memory is particularly important for correcting behaviours as negative actions and thinking can be replaced by repeated positive actions and thinking. Because this storage system is the easiest from which to recall information, movement is often considered to enhance learning.

- Automatic. Automatic memories are stored in the long term memory. The most frequently used example of automatic memory is the capacity to read, but not of course the ability to understand what is read as that would be stored in the semantic memory. Once the information relating to actual decoding and whole sight words is processed, gradually accumulated and becomes readily available information that is not consciously engaged with during the process of reading, it belongs in the automatic memory.

- Emotional. The emotional memory is the most powerful. As you have read previously, the brain remembers things to which it has attached emotion. Obviously, in the case of learning, if you are eliciting strong emotional responses to support learning and the retrieval from the long term emotional memory, these emotions need to be positive emotions; otherwise the brain cannot function effectively. While positive emotion is best for learning, all emotional responses relating to the best and the worst experiences are located in the emotional memory.

As you have seen from the factors that enhance memory retrieval, various types of hints, cues, prompts and signals are utilised to support students' memory retrieval from all of these systems located in the long term memory. Consequently, it is as important to help students to recall information as it is to teach with an explicit goal of developing learning that is relevant and interesting for each student. In this way, the information proceeds as a matter of course to the long term memory and does not get discarded along the way. When you consider how many sensory stimuli are competing for students' attention in every classroom, on a daily basis, it is not difficult to understand the powerful nature of individual teachers' strategies and techniques in establishing professional practice. The best professional practice is characterised by a safe learning environment, by relevant and interesting learning tasks and by assessment procedures that provide students with adequate prompts for successful recall and reflection.

Questions for Reflection

- Q1. What do think about the sample planner in Figure 4.2?
- Q2. Could you use it to plan more effectively?
- Q3. Are there any components stressed in the sample planner (Figure 4.2) that are not specific features of your current lesson/unit planners?
- Q4. Can you identify what purpose each suggestion in the sample planner (Figure 4.2) has in planning the lesson and relate it to the cognitive science perspective of learning?
- Q5. How could you effectively assess if learning had taken place for each student and knowledge was filed in their long term memory?

Outcomes/Indicators/Objectives/Links to Curriculum Documents
Memory Retrieval
Hints/Cues/Prompts/Signals   **Association/Similarity/Critical**
Attributes

Links with home knowledge
Links with outside school learning
Links with prior learning in discipline content ideas and processes
Links with other prior learning in other discipline content ideas and processes

Differentiated Learning Tasks and Assessment Details

Interest
Usefulness
Relevance
Movement/Action/Manipulation of Materials

Personal Reflection (for students and teachers)

Figure 4.2   Sample Lesson Planner Based on the Cognitive Science Perspective of Cognition

Scenario Four

Andrew had just arrived in Mr Watson's classroom to begin his observations prior to his professional experience. He had been happy to learn that Mr Watson was not too much older than himself and that they had lots in common in their leisure activities. The students in the classroom were chatting about something they had just been constructing. They each had their water bottles on the desk, were moving around freely in the classroom and appeared to be really comfortable and confident in their classroom community. Mr Watson asked everyone to come to the front and settle ready for some discussion. They did not all obey instantly and Andrew was surprised to see that Mr Watson was not concerned. Instead he asked brightly was anyone ready to start explaining the difficulties they had experienced in their construction teams. One student answered that they would not be too long and another answered that his team still needed to talk quietly for a minute or so. However, there was one team who were ready to start and so Mr Watson asked the unprepared teams to send a team representative to participate in the discussion and share ideas later with their teams. This worked very well and eventually all teams had reported on their construction, discussed suggestions with their peers and were working on their constructions once again. Mr Watson had picked up from the discussion that one or two teams had some considerable difficulty solving the construction problem and so he went to support their work. He offered explicit, precise strategies to the teams in question and asked them to consider which they thought might work best in their context. Andrew noticed that as he made these suggestions, Mr Watson drew little diagrams to accompany the notes he had made for them. He also asked lots of questions, prompting students to recall when, how and what exactly they could recall about a task that had some similar demands before specifically asking what they remembered about certain skills, knowledge, strategies and procedures that they had learned previously. To complete the 'conference' Mr Watson made some quick annotations on his notepad and moved along to the next group he wanted to talk to about their work. Andrew watched as the students chatted and tried out their ideas. Andrew was interested to listen to the conferencing as he realised that Mr Watson was actually getting the students to think in certain ways to retrieve the information they had learned and was not just telling them exactly what to do next. He was also noticing that Mr Watson was managing the learning by being aware of all the discussions at one time and intervening when the team was at a standstill. He just seemed to know and anticipate who might need what advice and when. After a while Mr Watson indicated that the students could take a break if they needed to and have a walk around and look at the other teams' work and chat.

(Continued)

(Continued)

In their meeting after school Andrew learned a little more about Mr Watson's pedagogical practice. He was interested in working in any ways that gave his students opportunities to learn to their best potential. He insisted that all the students had tasks planned for them with a focus on extending their learning by a manageable amount. He also indicated that he expected Andrew to conference with the students in the ways that he usually did and explained why he felt that the talking and listening was so important. He told Andrew that he was aware of some of the implications of the findings of neuroscience and attempted always to make sure that there was enough variety of verbal, visual and kinaesthetic activity in a day. It was also important to him to give the students enough cues when supporting them in their learning so they were able to rely on their robust knowledge more readily and so that he could continually assess what they had retained as robust knowledge. Andrew understood immediately and asked Mr Watson if he was recording the students' progress and limitations in his personal code in his notebook after the discourse. Mr Watson affirmed he was doing that and by completing this simple task he was getting to know how his students used their strategies, how they worked out problems and how they generally thought about the tasks. The breaks were always suggested if the session was lengthy. There was a lot of class discussion, when he also took notes in his code, and the class group was encouraged to work and interact collaboratively and respectfully. He had high expectations of all his students and of Andrew. He asked him to plan for individuals, for groups and teams. and find common areas where the entire class could interact together. He also expected that Andrew would make the notes for the formative assessment as he taught and facilitated. However, Andrew could make his own code if he wished as it was understood that individuals make meaning in their own ways. Mr Watson also indicated that Andrew could do things differently as long as these basic pedagogical practices remained. He explained that consistency was important and the degrees of apparent freedom that Andrew had witnessed were actually negotiated with students and had helped them to improve their levels of academic success.

Questions for Reflection

- Q1. What would you do differently from Mr Watson?
- Q2. Do you think that Mr Watson should have been less demanding of James? Validate your answer.

- Q3. Can you identify any of the teacher attributes with Mr Watson's pedagogies?
- Q4. Would you want to have professional practice like Mr Watson's? Give your reasons.
- Q5. Which parts of Mr Watson's pedagogies would you find the most difficult? Why?
- Q6. Are there any questions around ethical practice, professionalism or standards here?
- Q7. Could you think of any ways in which Mr Watson could support James in similar ways to the ways he supports his students?
- Q8. Do you think there are any issues here to discuss?
- Q9. What do you think will be the most demanding aspect of James' professional experience

Conclusion

This chapter has presented and discussed the findings of neuroscience that are relevant for teachers. Although not a consideration by everyone involved in educational endeavours at present, these findings have the potential to positively inform classroom practice. As the scientific investigation invariably progresses, it may contribute to making learning not only easier for some students, but also more productive. The information that is known can already help you to understand how to prepare lessons for your students more effectively, and to help them to make connections with prior learning more readily. It helps you to explicitly teach with a focus on supporting your students' efforts to engage with the mental processes known as memory. Various other considerations about the brain have perhaps been elevated to new status; most especially the role of emotion in learning. Another contribution is the significant understanding that the brain is a social brain (Bernstein and Waber, 2007). The brain is constantly seeking stimuli from the world around it and interacting with these experiences in order to make sense of the world, to establish personal meaning and to place the 'self' in relation to the world it inhabits. Further exploration and research may be able to establish ways in which the individual brain patterns not only language, but values and concepts.

While the brain could not be studied in the past in the way it can be currently, due to advances in technological imaging, some of the notions that have been confirmed by neuroscience have, in part, already been explored by theorists wishing to explain the learning process. Despite the limited technological supports, theorists have investigated and attempted to explain various aspects of learning. These include:

- the developmental differences in the brain's capacity to understand and to learn concepts at different stages throughout human life
- the impact of learning in social contexts
- the degree to which emotional factors impact on cognition.

A discussion of some of these theories in the following chapter may help you not only to realise how insightful these scholars were in developing their models or theories of learning, but also to create a personal understanding of why specific strategies have been identified as supporting improved learning outcomes. All of this occurred long before educationalists considered that teaching may be an interdisciplinary endeavour.

References

Arnold, R. (2005) *Empathical Intelligence: Teaching, Learning and Relating*. Sydney: University of New South Wales Press Ltd.

Askew, M., Brown, M., Rhodes, V., Wiliam, D. and Johnson, D. (1997) Effective teachers of numeracy in primary schools: teachers' beliefs, practices and pupils' learning. Paper presented at the British Educational Research Association Annual Conference, University of York.

Barlow, C. (2000) *Guildford Structure of the Intellect*. Retrived on 12th September 2009 from www.cocreativity.com/handout/guildford.pdf

Bernstein, J. and Waber, D. (2007) 'Executive capacities from a developmental perspective.' In L. Meltzer (ed.), *Executive Function in Education: From Therory to Practice*. New York: The Guildford Press. pp. 39–55.

Blakemore, S. and Frith, U. (2005) *The Learning Brain: Lessons for Education*. Oxford: Blackwell.

Burgh, G., Field, T. and Freakley, M. (2005) *Ethics and the Community of Enquiry: An Approach to Ethics Education*. Melbourne: Thomson Social Science Press.

Burgh, G., Field, T. and Freakley, M. (2006) *Ethics and the Community of Enquiry: Education for Deliberative Democracy*. South Melbourne: Cengage.

Christenson, S., and Havsy, L. (2004) 'Family-school-peer relationships: significance for social, emotional and academic learning.' In J. Zins, R. Weissberg, M. Wang & H. Walberg (eds.), *Building Academic Success on Social and Emotional Learning*. New York: Teachers College Pree. pp. 59–75.

Connella, G. (1999) 'Postformal though as critique: Re-conceptualization and possibility for teacher education reform.' In J. Kinchelon, S. Steinberg and L. Villaverde (eds.), *Rethinking Intelligence*. New York: Routledge. pp. 145–164.

Devlin, K. (2010) 'The mathematical brain.' In D. Sousa (ed.), *Mind, Brain and Education: Neuroscience Implications for the Classroom*. Bloomington, IN: Solution Tree Press. pp. 163–78.

Dupré, J. and O'Neill, J. (1998) Against reductionist explanations of human behaviour. *Proceedings of the Aristotelian Society, Supplementary Volumes*, 72: 153–71, 73–88.

Fleming, J., and Bay, M. (2004) 'Social and emotional learning in teacher preparation standards.' In J. Zins, R. Weissberg, M. Wang and H. Walberg (eds.), *Building Academic Success on Social and Emotional Learning*. New York: Teachers College Press. pp. 94–111.

Fredrickson, B. (2001) The role of positive emotions in positive psychology. *American Psychologist*, March, 56 (3): 218–26.

Gardner, H. (1993) *Frames of Mind. Tenth Anniversary Edition*. New York: Basic Books.

Given, B. (2002) *Teaching to the Brain's Natural Learning Systems*. Alexandria, VA: Association for Supervision and Curriculum Development.

Guilford, J. (1967) *The Nature of Human Intelligence*. New York: McGraw–Hill.

Hardiman, M. (2010) 'The creative-artistic brain.' In D. Sousa (ed.), *Mind, Brain and Education: Neuroscience Implications for the Classroom*. Bloomington, IN: Solution Tree Press. pp. 227–28.

Hattie, J. and Timperley, H. (2007) The power of feedback. *Review of Educational Research*, 77 (1): 81–112.

Jensen, E. (1998) *Introduction to Brain Compatible Learning*. Del Mar CA: Turning Point.

Jensen, E. (2005) *Teaching with the Brain in Mind*. Alexandria: Association for Supervision and Curriculum Development.

Jensen, E. (2011) *Brain Based Learning*. Retrieved from www.youtube.com/watch?v=HyYhoCqo58w (accesed 9 July 2013).

Johnson, D. and Johnson, R. (2004) 'The three Cs of promoting social and emotional learning.' In J. Zins, R. Weissberg, M. Wang and H. Walberg (eds.), *Building Academic Success on Social and Emotional Learning*. New York: Teachers College Press. pp. 40–58.

The Jossey Bass Reader on the Brain and Learning (2008) San Francisco: Jossey Bass.

Lopes, P. and Salovey, P. (2004) 'Toward broader education: social, emotional and practical skills.' In J. Zins, R. Weissberg, M. Wang and H. Walberg (eds.), *Building Academic Success on Social and Emotional Learning*. New York: Teachers College Press. pp. 76–93.

McCombs, B. (2004) 'The learner-centered psychological principles: a framework for balancing academic-achievement and social-emotional learning outcomes.' In J. Zins, R. Weissberg, M. Wang and H. Walberg (eds.), *Building Academic Success on Social and Emotional Learning*. New York: Teachers College Record Press. pp. 23–39.

Reese, A. (1998) Implications of results from cognitive science research for medical education. *Medical Education Online*, 3 (1). Retrieved from www.utmb.edu/meo/ 30 August 2013.

Seligman, M. (2002) *Authenic Happiness: Using the New Positive Psychology to Realize Your Potential for Lasting Fulfillment*. New York: Free Press.

Seligman, M. (2004) Can Happiness be Taught? *Daedalus*, 133 (2): 80–7.

Seligman, M., Park, N. and Peterson, C. (2005) Positive psychology progress: Empirical validation of interventions. *American Psychologist*, 60 (5): 410–21.

Seligman, M., Einst, R., Gillham, J., Reivich, K. and Linkins, M. (2009) Positive education: Positive psychology and classroom interventions. *Oxford Review of Education*, 35 (3): 293–311.

Seligman, M. (2011) *Flourish: A Visionary New Understanding of Happiness and Well-being*. New York: Free Press.

Sellars, M. (2008) Education for the 21st centuary: three components of a new pedagogy. *International Journal of the Humanities*, 6 (2): 27–34.

Sousa, D. (1995) *How the Brain Learns*. Reston, VIC: National Association of Secondary Principals.

Sousa, D. (2010) 'How science met pedagogy.' In D. Sousa (ed.), *Mind, Brain and Education: Neuroscience Implications for the Classroom*. Bloomington, IN: Solution Tree Press. pp. 9–26.

Springer, M. (2002) *Becoming a 'Wiz' at Brain Based Learning*. Thousand Oaks, CA: Corwin Press.

Tileston, D. (2004) *What Every Teacher Should Know about Diverse Learners*. Thousand Oaks: Corwin Press.

Tileston, D. (2005) *10 Best Teaching Practices*. Thousand Oaks, CA: Corwin Press.

Weis, L. and Fine, M. (2003) *Silenced Voices and Extraordinary Conversations: Re Imaging Schools*. New York: Teachers College Press.

Zins, J., Bloodworth, M., Weissberg, R. and Walberg, H. (2004) 'The scientific base linking social and emotional learning to school success.' In J. Zins, R.Weissberg, M. Wang & H. Walberg (eds.), *Building Social and Emotional Success on Academic Learning*. New York: Teachers College Press. pp. 3–22.

Chapter 5: Teaching for Learning

- Q1. What teaching strategies are most successful in your experience?
- Q2. What do the terms constructivism, social constructivism and behaviourism mean to you?
- Q3. Do you think there is a 'recipe' for effective teaching, or that classroom, school and system dynamics change what needs to be in place?
- Q4. What do you think are the most important considerations when you are planning to teach?

Introduction

In the previous chapter you read about the brain and how the findings from neuroscience can support teachers in their professional work. While this is really informative and useful, knowing all this does not actually guarantee that all the students in your class will automatically learn what it is you have to teach in the way of mandatory curriculum. Nor does it mean that learning in school will be robust in that it will be well-connected and transferable. There have been many theories about how cognition, the process by which learning occurs, actually happens and how students can be taught effectively. The notion of 'effective teaching' is not static and has changed substantially over the last few decades in response to a changing world. This is demonstrated in the four major philosophical approaches to education that can be seen in current teaching practice. A very brief description of the major tenets of each of these perspectives is detailed below. You may have experienced some degree of each of these in what you have already observed in classrooms. By the time you reach the conclusion of this chapter, you may be able to identify the major philosophical thinking that underpins your mandatory standards.

- Perennialism. This approach seeks to ensure students engage with the all-time truths and wisdoms of the Western world. These truths and wisdoms are considered to be the principles that are consistently important for all people throughout the passage of time. Much of this approach is taught through the writing of great thinkers who have influenced the course of Western history. The development of the human mind is at the centre of this educational approach, which celebrates rationality, logic and dialogue. The curriculum of Educational Perennialism, for example, would be a general, non-specific agenda in which explicit teaching would cover the 'basics' of reading, mathematics, natural science philosophy and fine arts with an overall view to developing an appreciation for the great thinkers in the Western world and using this appreciation as a basis for self development.
- Essentialism. In contrast, this approach focuses on ensuring that a bank of important knowledge is transmitted to students in a very structured, ordered manner. The 'basics' are important as it preparing students to become useful members of society. Much of the taught curriculum is vocationally orientated. It acknowledges that curricula can change and stresses hard work, discipline and respect for authority.
- Progressivism. This approach celebrates the whole child and, in contrast to the previous two perspectives, understands that students learn through experience and are active participants in their own learning, and experienced in their own social and cultural settings. A leading advocate for this type of education was Dewey.
- Social reconstructivism and Critical Theory. These approaches stress a curriculum that focuses on social issues with a view to promoting democracy and a more equitable society through education and schooling. Students engage with an enquiry process; discussion, multiple perspectives and bringing the real world into the classroom are prominent features of this approach. A prominent contributor to this educational perspective is Freire.

What Does the Literature Say about Learning?

A key challenge you face today is how to ensure that all the students for whom you are responsible are moved beyond the experiences that they bring to your classroom, while engaging with these experiences as a basis for new learning. One of the most significant understandings you can have as a teacher is that children, long before they arrive at school, have already formed some sense of the world with which they have interacted (Darling-Kuria, 2010). They have already given meaning to their experiences by the connections and relationships they have constructed for themselves as individuals. This does not necessarily mean that children construct meanings alone; it simply means that no one else can construct meaning for any individual, irrespective of their chronological age. Bearing this in mind, do you think it is possible to offer students a curriculum that is individually meaningful, and 'intellectually, emotionally, ethically and aesthetically rich' (Robertson and Gerber, 2000: 67), and to offer it to them at exactly the time they want and need it? There are numerous questions that spring to every educator's mind when confronted with ideas around effective teaching for all students. This discussion about construction, constructing knowledge and the uniqueness of construction for each individual mind itself prompts many questions. These include, 'Is there any room in teaching today for explicit instruction?' and 'How and why do students develop unconnected pieces of knowledge known as "inert knowledge" which is not integrated or linked to other knowledge and is therefore discarded or of little value?' A discussion of the most frequently implemented pedagogical model in current educational settings (McCarty and Schwandt, 2000) – constructivism – may inform your thinking and give you an opportunity for reflection.

Overview of Constructivism

The first component of the cognitive science perspective of learning, which is connected to progressivism, reflects the understanding that learners need to be active in their own knowledge construction. One of the means by which this may be achieved is found in the basics foundations of constructivist theory (Hacker et al., 1998; Hein, 1991). All constructivists propose that individual learners must actively construct knowledge (at times, not without a struggle) in a personally meaningful way. They must also be able to attribute meaning to their learning while engaging in dynamic personal and social processes. The first attribute reflects an understanding that learners need to be active in their own learning. They propose that individual learners must actively construct knowledge (at times, not without a struggle) in a personally meaningful way and they must be able to attribute meaning to their learning while engaging in dynamic personal and social processes. This is an important insight for those involved in the practical implementation of these policies. Based on the work of Piaget (Gruber and Voneche, 1977), Dewey (1933; 1958, 1966a, 1966b), Vygotsky and others (Hacker, et al., 1998; Prawat, 1999), this view of learning impacts on both learning theory and epistemology – which is the branch of philosophy that studies the actual nature of knowledge itself – in that the nature of knowledge is personally mediated (Hein, 1991).

Howe and Berv (2000: 30–1) distinguish between constructivist pedagogies and constructivist learning theories. In support of the Deweyan notion of constructive epistemology, they comment that Deweyan pedagogy starts with what students know, value and are interested in, but does not finish there. Although acknowledged by Dewey himself to be a more difficult teaching approach to the more traditional authoritarian strategies, it avoids the criticisms of other constructive models discussed below. In successful learning experiences, according to Deweyan pedagogy, students complete their learning opportunities with the shared meanings particular to their community. They do this as the result of exploration, deep thinking and reflection, all of which are completed in the context of shared dialogue. This avoids what Howe and Berv (2000: 38) describe as leaving 'knowledge ultimately stranded on private constructions'.

Howe and Berv (2000), in their discussion of pedagogical models in education, propose that constructivist learning theories have two foundational principles:

- Learning takes as its starting point the knowledge, attitudes and interests students bring to the learning situation.
- Learning results from the interaction between these characteristics and experience in such a way that the learners construct their own understanding, from the inside, as it were.

As a result, constructivist pedagogy has two 'parallel' foundational ideas:

- Instruction must take as its starting point the knowledge, attitudes and interests students bring to the learning situation.
- Instruction must be designed so as to provide experiences that effectively interact with these characteristics of students so that they may construct their own understanding.

What Does This Mean for You?

If constructivists understand learning to be constructed in the context of what is already known, the attitude the learner has to specific tasks or learning in general and has a heavy reliance on the individual's interests, then teaching and learning tasks must reflect this. You can see this easily in the two foundational ideas of constructivist pedagogy. Specifically it means that:

(Continued)

(Continued)

- It is very difficult to plan for learning if you do not know your students. You may get to know some aspects of their capabilities by implementing carefully constructed open-ended tasks or diagnostic assessment for a short period of time.
- You must be able to understand your students' attitudes to specific content or to learning as a whole. Discussion, reflection and attention to student evaluations of the materials used and pedagogies implemented help you to understand their perspectives and work towards what is the optimum for each student.
- You need to know your students in order to accommodate their interests in the learning situation. It is important to talk to students about the work in class and their pastimes outside of the classroom in a friendly, accepting manner that shows your professional interest in each of them as individuals.
- These three considerations need to dominate your planning for learning at any stage of schooling. You need to develop the skills and knowledge, the disposition and motivation, and the professional perspective that best facilitates your decision making in this aspect of professional practice.
- The students are at the heart of the meaning making in this pedagogical model. You must plan to facilitate their learning and then extend this into the wider class community to create shared understandings and meaning in that specific learning context.

Abbott and Ryan (1999: 67) explain, 'Constructivist learning is an intensely subjective, personal process and structure that each person constantly and actively modifies in light of new experiences'. A further challenge is that constructivism can take many forms, the majority of which include explicit instruction in learning skills and strategies. These are designed to support students' construction of knowledge and are appropriate to the specific learning needs of the students. Matthews, for example (in Richardson, 2003), identified eighteen different forms of educational constructivism, the major differences being between models of social constructivism and those of psychological constructivism, which are detailed in Figure 5.1. This may be because, as Howe and Berv (2000: 32) have noted,

A general constructivist pedagogy includes (1) embracing a constructivist learning theory and (2) mixing ostensibly constructivist and non-constructivist teaching techniques as appropriate.

However, at its most basic, behaviourism and constructivism represent the difference between learning by remembering what has been explicitly taught and accumulated, which is what Freire criticises as the banking model (Parr, 2004; Stevens, 2010), and learning by understanding. Much of behaviourist teaching is based in the stages of Gagne's Model of Instruction, which stresses a highly structured linear progression of teaching and learning, as indicated in Figure 5.1. In addition to the linear development of students' skills and knowledge, behaviourist pedagogy is also, of necessity, teacher-directed. It is focused on the acquisition of knowledge and skills. It shows little evidence of any investment in the individual students' interests, their thinking and ideas or their understandings of the material they have learned. It also relies heavily on the cognitive capacities of the students' memories, rather than on more complex thinking skills, including understanding and the higher-order thinking skills of Bloom's Revised Taxonomy (Anderson and Krathwohl, 2000). Behaviourist pedagogies are often used in training contexts, where the objectives are very clearly defined and not open to personal negotiation of meaning (Anderson and Dron, 2011). The means of assessing learning in these contexts usually consists of testing in order to ascertain if the material had been recalled in the format in which it was originally taught.

Students need opportunities to develop robust knowledge – knowledge that has links to previous knowledge and is transferable to other contexts and problems where appropriate. The skills and knowledge students learn in reproductive learning are not able to be transferred as easily into other learning tasks or disciplines because they are not necessarily understood, although they are remembered. They are most frequently retained as inert knowledge or unattached skills and knowledge that are context-specific, as opposed to the robust knowledge. Robust learning is more readily built into existing knowledge and can be adapted to new learning situations and tasks. Splitter (2009), in his discussion of authentic education, supports dialogue as a key priority as a means by which students can see and understand themselves as one among others. He suggests that in classrooms where communities of enquiry are supported, students can engage in authentic personal development in addition to learning about genuine enquiry processes. This perspective does not fit comfortably with predominantly behaviourist pedagogy, as you can observe from Figure 5.1. However, an important aspect of the constructivist perspective is that it is open-ended and has no boundaries. In this respect, it mirrors what is actually known about the neural structure of the brain, as this is also open-ended (Posner, 2005), in addition to supporting Splitter's (2009) notion of authentic education, which honours the inner, subjective self as an active learner in the educational process in the manner proposed by Dewey (1903).

Get student attention
Tell students of the lesson objectives so they are aware of what to expect
Recall previous learning using working
Present the lesson, modelling or demonstration
Check the students understand the lesson focus
Elicit student response
Reinforce or correct student responses
Assess the students' work
Encourage memorisation and practical usage

Figure 5.1   Gagne's Model of Instruction (Adapted from Anderson and Dron, 2011)

Dewey (1903) argued at the beginning of the twentieth century for an education that provided active experiences for students. He listed equipment and facilities that he felt were important for every classroom and encouraged teachers to be innovative and creative in their teaching and in the design of the activities with which students were asked to engage as learning experiences. While Dewey in this instance was advocating manual construction as part of the formal learning environment to support cognition, it was not too long before he was writing more specifically about the lived experience and its impact on how individuals think (Dewey, 1910). Dewey's (1910) notion of social constructivism necessitates learners to engage with and expand on real-life experience. He believed that teaching needed to include quality activities that required the learners to explore, think deeply and reflect. He proposed that quality learning environments were necessary for learning. The ways and conditions in which Dewey envisioned that learning was able to take place, has been confirmed by the work of neuroscientists. You will find that a detailed account of Dewey's theory actually reflects how the brain works to create knowledge. Dewey emphasised the holistic nature of the experience and the individual engaged in the content of the experience in contrast to some of his peers. He also took a holistic view of the curriculum, believing that all subjects should be integrated and taught with an overreaching common goal of developing a truly democratic community, not just in classrooms but in the wider community (Boyles, 2006). Dewey's work focused on the learner's own experiences, which were guided by an experienced mentor. This view of constructivism is unique to Dewey as, although the model is correctly named, it is not the same as other models and theories of constructivism, which concentrate on the intellectual developmental stages of young students (Rowe and Berv, 2000).

These major, developmental, constructivist theories were proposed by Piaget (Gruber and Voneche, 1977; Piaget, 1964), who developed psychological constructivism, and Vygotsky (Dixon-Krauss, 1996; Gordon, 1995; Speaker, 1999; van der Heijden, n.d.; Vygotsky, 1968; Waite, 2003), who developed the notion of social constructivism. While some theorists have attempted to combine the salient features of each of these two quite different theories,

Askew et al. (1997) Piaget's theory of psychological constructivism:	Askew et al. (1997) Vygotsky's theory of social constructivism:
Came from a liberalistic, and in some aspects individualistic philosophical tradition.	Came from a socialist tradition.
Focused heavily on the organic and biological aspects of human life and development.	Focused on the socio-cultural aspects of human life and development.
Was influenced by the writings of Plato, Descartes, Rousseau and particularly Kant.	Was influenced by the writings of Marx, Engels and Lenin.
Proposed that development started from an individual ego and gradually became more socialised.	Proposed that development was based on firstly being a social being who relied on interpersonal interaction to gradually become more individual.
Explained first speech as egocentric speech that was an external indication of thinking. This declines as individuals become less egocentric. Development was seen to be from egocentricity to socialisation.	Explained first speech as social and interpersonal communication. Believed this was not an external indicator of thinking but it was, in fact, thinking as it developed into inner speech, then verbal thinking. It was an individual expression of the social function of speech and the child used this in a self regulatory manner, in much the same way as the parents and community had modelled in their directed speech to the child to control and direct actions.
Proposed that the motivator for cognition was an intrinsic, biological need to maintain 'equilibrium' in cognition. This is the optimum state of adaptation of what is understood or known and is maintained by the processes of accommodation and assimilation.	Challenged the dualism of the external world and the internal world of the child. He understood these to be mutually 'interpenetrating' (Askew et al., 1997: 461). In other words, the child and the world in which he existed could not be separated.
Believed that social factors only influenced, positively or negatively, the child's natural development.	Believed that external social and cultural phenomena were not just sources of information, feedback and disequilibrium, but were 'concrete external media'.
Understood the child as the primary analytical 'unit'.	Understood that function was undertaken by the child and other people.
Understood the child expecting differences in understanding and knowledge from an adult but finding most disequilibrium and therefore assimilation and accommodation experiences to come from peers.	Understood that as the child is gradually socialised into the culture, adults assist and encourage new learning in a way that peers cannot do.
Bruner (1997) Piaget's theory of psychological constructivism	**Bruner (1997) Vygotsky's theory of social constructivism**
Theorised that the fundamental role of mental activity is in logical operations.	Theorised that mental activity has the capacity to appropriate culture, social norms and history as 'tools of mind'. That it had the function of 'making meaning' of language in the social and cultural context in which the language was found.

(Continued)

Figure 5.2   (Continued)

Commented on the importance of disequilibrium in order to promote mental growth by the dual processes of assimilation and accommodation.	Acknowledged the significant importance of language and culture itself on the development of knowledge and meaning.
Proposed a global developmental sequence. Did not attend to the question of cross-cultural norms. Believed that human cognitive characteristics were universal in that they were normal human development. Piaget understood cognition to be an independent process that was exclusive to the individual and abstract.	Understood development to be in response to practical activity and to the learning that occurred across different types of activities. Believed that 'leading' or most dominant activities at different stages of development within the society to which the child belonged depended on the: • timing of the onset of the activity • the duration of the activities • what form the activities took • the content of the activities. In this manner, placed significance on the specific social, cultural and historical circumstances in which that child was developing
Primarily concerned with the human capacity for interpretation and understanding	Understood knowledge as localized; that content was bound to specific contexts. Indicated that he understood meaning as situated in the specific context. Vygotsky was primarily concerned with situated 'meaning making'; situated cognition.

Figure 5.2   Fundamental Differences in Piaget's Theory of Psychological Constructivism and Vygotsky's Theory of Social Constructivism (adapted from Duncan, 1995, and Bruner, 1997)

this has been criticised by others, citing the differences as being too great to combine to provide a constructivist learning theory and corresponding pedagogy (Bruner, 1997; Cole and Wertch; Duncan, 1995). These differences, as identified by Duncan (1995) and Bruner (1997), are summarised in Figure 5.2. It is important to consider these in the context of the philosophical traditions and social circumstances in which each of these theorists lived and worked.

There are similarities in the two theorists' work, however. Both pursued a developmental approach to understanding the learning process. They both also emphasised that qualitative, transformative developmental change was important for human development. They both framed the major theories in terms of the relationship between the mind and the outside world and acknowledged social influences, although they theorised their impact very differently (Duncan, 1995). However, one of the most important points made by Bruner (1997) is the lack of 'intersubjectivity' in Piaget's work. Intersubjectivity can be understood as the capacity for someone outside of the individual to sense what is needed for the learner to be challenged and engage with new learning if the learner cannot do this independently. This is because:

There remains a good deal of truth, objectivity and rationality within communities that share conceptual schemes and paradigms because such communities inherently incorporate standards that serve as the basis for their identities and for intersubjectivity judgements among their members. (Howe and Berv, 2000: 27)

If the child is the sole constructor of knowledge, as in Piagetian theory, how then can others systematically have common ideas about the thinking of the individual in order to support and encourage new learning, albeit, perhaps, by creating a state of disequilibrium, where prior knowledge is challenged by that which is currently presented? Vygotsky provides pedagogical opportunities for this intersubjectivity in his view of constructivism. The introduction of the notion of the Zone of Proximal Development (ZPD), a situation in which the learner cannot proceed unaided in the learning process, and the discussion of how an adult can offer learning support by using a number of pedagogical strategies, illustrates Vygotsky's understanding of the importance of the social context of shared understanding. In this model the tutor can sense what a learner needs and help to develop it. Primary among these pedagogical strategies that are strongly associated with Vygotsky's work are scaffolding (sequencing the steps incrementally to support understanding), identifying critical features of a problem, negotiating the understanding (conferencing) and shielding the learner from distraction (Bruner, 1997). The latter strategy may be one that you might find particularly challenging, depending on your capacity to know your students and what interests them. This brings you back to the notion that all constructivist pedagogies necessitate not only building on prior knowledge but working with the interests of the students (Howe and Berv, 2000). This is also a prerequisite for learning as presented by cognitive scientists (Reese, 1998; Seligman, et al., 2009). Without their interest, it can be very difficult to motivate students to engage in their learning tasks (Sellars, 2003).

Questions for Reflection

- Q1. Are there any new ideas in this discussion of constructivist pedagogy for you?
- Q2. Are there any pedagogical ideas discussed that you have seen in practice or that you have used yourself in your professional experience?
- Q3. Is it difficult to employ and/or identify a pure model of any of the pedagogical models discussed in actual practice in classrooms? Validate your answer.
- Q4. Which pedagogical model would you think that you would be most comfortable working out of in your own classroom? Why?
- Q5. Is there one characteristic of any of the models that you believe is essential in any teaching context if you wish students to learn successfully? What do you think it might be?

(Continued)

(Continued)

- Q6. With reference to the Holy Trinity for Teachers, which pedagogical model might be the most demanding for teachers to implement in their classrooms? Validate your answer by indicating which teacher competency or competencies are required for your choice of pedagogical model.
- Q7. Which of the pedagogical models matches most closely with the ways in which learners actually learn, as proposed by the findings of neuroscience? Validate your choice.
- Q8. Think back to your school days. Are the demands of teachers and students the same now as they were then? What is different in twenty-first century demands?
- Q9. Which pedagogical model do you think is the best for today's students?

Engagement and Motivation

When students are engaged in their learning tasks and are managing successfully to ignore the many other stimuli and distractions in order to pursue their tasks, they are perceived as being motivated. Psychologists differ in their understandings of what exactly causes individuals to be motivated but it is generally recognised that there are two types of motivation: intrinsic motivation is not stimulated by external factors, rewards or grades, while external motivation is the result of any one of a variety of influences, pressures and responsibilities that are external to, or unrelated to, the task itself. Reeve (in Woolfolk and Margetts, 2007), astutely draws attention to what may be an obvious, but a critical, point for educators: namely, that it is not possible to determine what type of motivation students are engaged in by observation alone. This is because the essential difference in the two types of motivation is centred around the 'locus of causality' or the reason that the student has engaged in the task initially or is currently engaging in the task (Woolfolk and Margetts, 2007: 376). In order to establish the nature of the motivation that has produced the observable behaviours of on-task engagement, it is important to know why individuals engage in tasks. Establishing this is not always simple.

Woolfolk and Margetts (2007) indicate that the notion of intrinsic and extrinsic motivation as the extreme ends of one continuum (Woolfolk, 2004) has been challenged. The most recent understanding of motivation is that intrinsic motivation and extrinsic motivation are discrete constructs and that individuals can be motivated by a degree of each at any one time. The extrinsic motivators that served as the initial prompts for individuals to engage in a task may still be present, but at some point during the task the task itself becomes the primary reason for continued absorption and engagement. The traditional research approaches to motivation include those from four main perspectives. Firstly, behavioural approaches focus on the stimulus–response relationship. If individuals are rewarded for specific behaviours and discouraged or punished for indulging in others, then the continual reinforcement of the approved behaviours encourages these individuals to habitually exhibit the behaviours that are rewarded. Incentives or rewards are fundamental components of this approach, which results in individuals adopting an exclusively extrinsic motivational approach to tasks (Pintrich and Schunk, 1996; Woolfolk, 2004; Woolfolk and Margetts, 2007). Secondly, an equally exclusive, but conflicting view is presented by the humanist approach. Among these models, which focus on human dignity and fulfilment of the Hierarchy of Needs model developed by Maslow (1943), is the mostly commonly utilised in school contexts. The model comprises five levels of need. The first four levels consider the needs common to all humans and without which individuals' personal development would be impaired. Maslow theorised that once these basic human needs were met, then another level of needs became important: the need for self fulfilment, creativity and productivity. This fifth level of need in turn provided an explanation for motivation: the human need for self actualisation (Maslow, 1943). This theory proposes that the final level of psychological development that can be achieved is when all basic and mental needs are already fulfilled and the 'actualisation' of the full personal potential takes place. However, while this perspective presents a rather simplistic argument that discusses motivation as an exclusively intrinsic characteristic, which is unable to be activated until all more basic needs are first satisfied, Maslow (1943) does invest in a holistic view of individual development. This not only contrasts with behaviourist views, but highlights the complex and highly individual nature of how and why individuals choose their behaviours and tasks.

Thirdly, cognitive theorists attribute motivation to the processes that individuals engage in when thinking about their behaviours and those of others in order to establish explanations and causes for successes and failures. Weiner (in Elliott and Dweck, 2005) relates attribution theory to educational contexts but it is unclear where exactly this version of attribution theory is placed in terms of a range of theoretical perspectives. Weiner (2000, in Elliott and Dweck, 2005) offers what he terms the 'intrapersonal theory of motivation' and the 'interpersonal theory of motivation'. Intrapersonal theory, as expected, is concerned with the individual endeavouring to make sense of their own thoughts and feelings regarding a particular event or result. Interpersonal theory is concerned with the impact of the comments, judgements or reaction of others to the same event or result on the individual. He suggests that, although explained as separate theories, these two perspectives – the intrapersonal and the interpersonal – are closely intertwined. He believes that the emotional reactions to the result or the event, both the individual's and those of others, are heavily influenced by the reasons students give for the result itself.

Fourthly, expectancy and value theorists (for example Bandura, 1994) combine the importance of the impact of individual thinking and the consequences of behaviour to explain motivation. The importance of Bandura's (1994) work on self efficacy may easily be determined by the impact of self efficacy beliefs on motivation. Unfortunately, the two foundational tenets of this theory are both problematic in terms of the multiple intelligences perspective of executive function (Gardner, 1983, 1993, 1999a, 1999b; Moran and Gardner, 2007).

- Firstly, the learning tasks must have defined characteristics and individuals must be able to assess their competencies against the skills required to complete a task successfully.
- Secondly, the learning task must be valued by the individual.

The difficulty is that this approach does not explain how individuals become motivated to accept challenges where problems may not become apparent until a degree of progress has been made. Although Bandura and his colleagues (Bandura, 1994; Pajeres, 2000; 2001; Pajeres and Valiante, 1996; Pintrich and Schunk, 1996) and Weiner (2000, in Elliott and Dweck, 2005) offer theories that are all about self knowledge components, which are an important aspect of motivation, they do not appear to be concerned with the accuracy of individuals' self knowledge. They seem to assume that students' self perceptions are consistently precise and correct. They also do not appear to take into consideration the impact of social and cultural expectations, which are a major influence on student motivation. This is one of the reasons that quality teachers have high expectations of their students and support them appropriately in quality social environments (Alison and Patrick, 2001). Among the discouraging influences are their anxiety, their fears, their family's stresses and their negativity. Among the encouraging influences are supportive parents and teachers, personal involvement and identification with the learning community and their positive feelings about themselves. These positive feelings have been shown to have strong links to motivation (Munns, 2004). Also with strong links to motivation is the notion of metacognition (Kuhn, 2000a), which is the individual student's capacity:

- to know and understand how they learn best
- to identify which strategies they find the most useful to use in their learning tasks and
- to acknowledge how they feel when they are learning successfully.

The positive feelings that may be part of a student's metacognitive understanding of themselves as learners are also those that can motivate them to engage with, and persevere with, their learning tasks.

What Does This Mean for You?

In reality, it is possible that students are motivated to learn at different stages and in different contexts for any combination of reasons that are explored in the four perspectives discussed. One important notion for you to understand is that the type of motivation and the reasons that individual students are engaged or motivated are rarely the same all of the time or in every context. Some thoughts on engaging students that may be useful for you to remember include:

- While it is important to have high expectations for all students, they must be realistic and achievable. They must be within what students can reasonably achieve as individuals.
- It is important to allow students to be motivated to engage in tasks for their own sake. It is not always useful to give students rewards in the form of points, pencils, computer time and so on. Competition is not always good or beneficial in learning contexts.
- Consider the societal expectations that students are subjected to and ensure as far as possible that these are matched by compensatory social support systems. If students are expected to do well in a task that requires work to be completed outside of the classroom, then the degree of support offered by parents, caregivers and others should match the degree of expectation that is centred on the student. However, the appropriateness of the task must still be within reasonable reach of the student's current competencies as Vygotsky describes by his notion of Zone of Proximal Development. As a teacher you can also have a powerful influence on student motivation that can be directly related to your professional relationships with them as individuals.
- Feedback is important. It is suggested that encouragement is more beneficial than praise and that the assessment of the product should be mediated by the amount of effort the students had expended. Students may expend a great deal of personal energy being engaged in a task and are highly motivated to complete it but may not produce a wonderful piece of work. Select feedback comments carefully in order to ensure that they are encouraged to attempt similar tasks enthusiastically in the future.
- Remember that students need to have accurate knowledge of their capacities. They need to know how they learn best. They need to know how to select and evaluate their strategies. Students may need to be taught how to do this and how to use this knowledge to engage effectively in tasks.
- You may need to be creative to engage students in areas of work that are less interesting for them. You need to adapt your pedagogy to the students' attitudes and interests and make otherwise onerous tasks interesting for them.

Metacognition

Metacognition is a term introduced in 1976 by Flavell, an academic in the Piagetian tradition (Flavell, 1996). Loosely understood to be thinking about your own thinking (Day, 2003), Flavell (1977: 232) defined his concept in this way:

> Metacognition refers to one's knowledge concerning one's own cognitive processes or anything related to them, e.g., the learning-relevant properties of information or data. For example, I am engaging in metacognition if I notice that I am having more trouble learning A than B; if it strikes me that I should double check C before accepting it as fact.

Metacognition is generally understood to be expressly linked to improved cognition and motivation (Walker and Debus, 2002). It is generally discussed in terms of three components (Flavell, 1977; Livingston, 1997). These are:

- strategic knowledge (knowledge about strategies)
- task knowledge (knowledge about tasks and their content)
- self knowledge (knowledge about yourself and how you know and use the other types of metacognition).

However, Kuhn (2000b) goes further, and details the meta-levels of metacognition and then describes how these impact positively on learners and learning in a cyclical manner. Additionally, Schneider (2008), in a longitudinal study, found that the development of declarative metacognitive knowledge, knowing 'about' things or knowing 'that' (Zohar, 1999), was developed differently and more readily than procedural metacognitive knowledge; that is, knowing about strategies. Hartman (2001) confirms the view that metacognition can be learnt and is not a fixed construct, but one that is capable of gradually evolving, a view that is shared by other writers (Kuhn and Dean, 2004; Kuiper, 2002). Hartman (2001) links metacognition primarily with reflection, but also with other skills relating to successful learning, skills that can be improved with practice such as:

- questioning
- self checking learning behaviours
- making decisions about how to attempt tasks using the strategies that are personally most accessible and successful.

She states 'reflective thinking is the essence of metacognition' (2001: xi). So, in addition to reflection being an important aspect of your professional life and ongoing development (Leat, 2003), reflection is also important for the cognitive and metacognitive development of the students that you teach in your classes (Hine, 2000). This may be especially so when metacognitive development is specifically designed to promote 'deep approaches' to learning (Case and Gunstone, 2002) and is discussed as a complex set of cognitive strategies and knowledge, rather than just as 'thinking about one's thinking' (Hacker and Dunlosky, 2003; Livingston, 1997). The increasing popularity, in education, of the theory of metacognition, resulted in Gardner coining it a 'buzzword' (Gardner, 1999b: 62).

Gaskins and Pressley (2007: 27) note that 'metacognition involves knowing about thinking and knowing how to employ executive function processes to regulate thinking'. They also include the students' own knowledge of their personal attributes and beliefs in their interpretation of metacognition. They do not, however, explicitly discuss the impact of emotion on the cognitive processes or on the students' awareness of their emotions in their own thinking and learning. The 'awareness of one's mental processes', or self knowledge associated with metacognition appears to be purely knowledge about an individual's capacity to evaluate, monitor and regulate their relative strengths and limitations in terms of the strategies they have to complete a specific task. Despite this, the development of metacognitive strategies and knowledge has been identified as important to students' improved learning outcomes at all stages of development and in various educational contexts; including teaching and learning in mathematics (Desoete et al., 2001), improving reading outcomes (Hall and Myers, 1998), science teaching and learning (Hennessey, 1999; Wu and Tsai, 2005), developing skills in music composition (Jeanneret and Cantwell, 2002) and in drama for young learners (Johnson, 2002).

Questions for Reflection

- Q1. Have you observed any classroom strategies that could be identified as helping students to know about their thinking and what they find easier or harder to learn? You could list these.
- Q2. Why do you think that motivation and metacognition can be easily linked theoretically?
- Q3. Do you think that you could incorporate explicit strategies into your teaching in order to give your students opportunities to know themselves as learners? Would this fit into your notion of the type of teacher you are hoping to develop into? Give your reasons.
- Q4. What sort of difficulties might teachers have in trying to encourage their students to become increasingly metacognitive with regard to their learning in classrooms?
- Q5. Do you think that by a certain age, or with a certain degree of experience in formal learning contexts, students should have ideas about how they learn best without specifically being taught strategies to enhance metacognition?

Scenario Five

Miss White was talking to her class of 7- and 8-year-old learners. She was discussing how they might construct a paragraph correctly. They did not come up with any really useful ideas and did not seem to be particularly interested in the idea at all. Sensing this, she thought about the recent Olympic Games and decided to use this topic as the focus for the joint construction she had planned. The children had all been really interested in this event and had talked a lot about it when they came back to school. Handing out the strips of paper she had prepared, she asked them to each write one sentence about anything to do with the Olympics. They could even partner up with a classmate and make a sentence to begin with. When the sentences were written, she asked the students let her know if their sentence was about the Olympic Games themselves, about the events, about a particular event or about a particular Olympian. Having sorted these themselves and grouped against the different walls of the classroom, the children were asked to peg their sentences to the clothes line she had prepared in the room in a specific group order. When this was done, they all sat and listened to what had been written. Suggestions from the learners regarding the order of the sentences in the paragraph followed. Many of them could say that the general statements about the Olympics should come first and then the more specific sentences. They then discussed why it might be done in that order and Miss White sensed that they were getting quite involved in this idea. After they had shuffled and rearranged the sentences to their satisfaction, the learners were asked to write two sentences each, if they could, on their paper strips. They could work in groups and could choose from topics that Miss White knew interested learners in the class. When these were written, the group would then organise their sentences and make a short paragraph. These were then read and the class discussed if they had made paragraphs or not, what might help to bring the sentences together as a short paragraph for each topic and group, and who would like to make another sentence to fill out the paragraph a little more. Miss White supported the learners who were having difficulty by constantly referring to the joint construction as an example. Learners could then undertake to write a short paragraph on anything they wished, either individually or in pairs or triangular groups. Miss White had to smile when she read through these after school in preparation for the next lesson. One of the class members had written as the opening sentence: 'Today we are learning about paragraphs.' She had ended it with the conclusion: 'It was not as boring as I thought it would be.'

Questions for Reflection

- Q1. What do you think of Miss White's strategies to get her students interested in a mandatory part of the curriculum?
- Q2. What sort of pedagogical model was Miss White working from?
- Q3. Are there ethical and professional issues here? List any you can identify.
- Q4. What sorts of strategies do you think Miss White's students learned in this lesson about paragraphs?
- Q5. Do you think it would have been better to just explicitly teach paragraph construction? Validate your answer.
- Q6. What comment could you make about the practices described in this scenario?
- Q7. Can you identify any scaffolding that was implemented in this lesson?
- Q8. Why do you think the activities were so short during the lesson?
- Q9. List the explicit steps that Miss White took to motivate and engage her students.

Conclusion

The discussions in this chapter focused on the major learning theories that are currently being implemented in many classrooms, most of which can be identified as basically constructivist in origins. Some attempts to link the content discussed in the previous chapter, regarding the findings of neuroscientists, were able to be made, however tenuous. The importance of student interest and initial engagement was a common theme in learning theories. In the behavioural model detailed (Gagne in Anderson and Dron, 2011), 'getting the student's attention' was the initial trigger for engagement, without any reference to student interest or making links explicitly with prior knowledge, although the latter does come later in the teaching sequence. The two most dominant constructivist pedagogical models have been examined in detail and their differences identified, in addition to the implications these may have for you in your classroom. As student engagement is a considered a prerequisite for learning, several perspectives of motivation have also been discussed. The notion and importance of students actively being engaged as active participants in their own learning is enhanced by the concept of metacognition, which is discussed as being important, both for improved learning outcomes and for motivation.

What remains for you to determine is how you might use this information in the context of your own teaching. The information presented incorporates many challenges for the beginning teacher, but also allows you to understand more fully the impact of your choice of your implementation strategies and learning tasks for your students. You are also able, at this point, to use your understanding of 'self' and your reflective activities to guide your thinking about the type of teacher you want to be. However, there is one more construct to be discussed that will have a major influence on how you relate to your students: the ways in which you support their learning and the manner in which you perceive your professional role. That construct is what you believe to be the nature of intelligence. This will be the focus of the discussions in the next chapter.

References

Abbott, J. and Ryan, T. (1999) Constructing knowledge, reconstructing schooling. *Educational Leadership*, 57 (3): 66–8.

Alison, R. and Patrick, H. (2001) The classroom social environment and changes in adolescents' motivation and engagement during middle school. *American Educational Research Journal*, 38 (2): 437–60.

Anderson, L. and Krathwohl, D. (2000) *Taxonomy of Teaching and Learning: A Revision of Bloom's Taxonomy of Educational Objectives*. New York: Longman.

Anderson, T., and Dron, J. (2011) Three generations of distance pedagogy. *International Review of Research in Open and Distance Learning*, 12 (3): 1–19. Retrieved from www.irrodl.org/index.php/irrodl/article/view/890 (accessed 30th August 2013).

Askew, M., Brown, M., Rhodes, V., William, D. and Johnson, S. (1997) *Effective Teachers of Numeracy: Report of a Study Carried out for the Teacher Training Agency*. King's College, University of London.

Bandura, A. (1994) 'Self efficacy.' In V.S. Ramachaudran (ed.), *Encyclopedia of Human Behaviour*, Vol. 4. New York: Academic Press. pp. 71–81.

Boyles, D. (2006) Dewey's epistemology: an argument for warranted assertions, knowing, and meaningful classroom practice. *Educational Theory*, 56 (1): 57–68.

Bruner, J. (1997) Celebrating divergence: Piaget and Vygotsky. *Human Development,* 40 (2), 63–73.

Case, J. and Gunstone, R. (2002) Metacognitive development as a shift in approach to learning: an in-depth study. *Studies in Higher Education*, 27 (4): 459–470.

Cole, M. and Wertsch, J. (1996) Beyond the individual-social antimony in discussions of Piaget and Vygotsky. *Human Development*, 39: 250–256.

Darling-Kuria, N. (2010) *Brain Based Early Leraning Activities: Connecting Theory and Practice*. St Paul MN: Redleaf Press.

Day, L. (2003) Thinking about thinking. *Educare News*, 1 (140): 20–3.

Desoete, A., Roeyers, H. and Buysse, A. (2001) Metacognition and mathematical problem solving in grade 3. *Journal of Learning Disabilities*, 34 (5): 435–49.

Dewey, J. (1903) Democracy in education. *The Elementary School Teacher*, 4 (4): 193–204.

Dewey, J. (1910) *How We Think*. Boston, MA: D.C. Heath.

Dewey, J. (1933) *How We Think: A Restatement of the Relation of Reflective Thinking to the Educative Process*. Boston, MA: D.C. Heath.

Dewey, J. (1958) *Experience and Nature*. New York: Dover Publications.

Dewey, J. (1966a) *Democracy and Education*. New York: The Free Press.

Dewey, J. (1966b) *Philosophy of Education (Problems of Men)*. Littlefield, NJ: Adams and Co.

Dixon-Krauss, L. (1996) *Vygotsky in the Classroom: Mediated Literacy Instruction and Assessment*. White Plains, NY: Longman USA.

Duncan, M. (1995) Piaget and Vygotsky revisited: Dialogue or assimilitation? *Developmental review*, 15 (4): 458–472.

Elliott, A. and Dweck, C. (eds) (2005) *Handbook of Competence and Motivation*. New York: The Guilford Press.

Flavell, J. (1976) 'Metacognitive aspects of problem solving.' In L. Resnick (ed.), *The Nature of Intelligence*. Hillsdale, NJ: Erlbaum.

Flavell, J. (1977) *Cognitive Development*. Oxford: Prentice–Hall.

Flavell, J. (1996) Piaget's legacy. *Psychological Science*, 7 (4): 200–3.

Gardner, H. (1983) *Frames of Mind: The Theory of Multiple Intelligences*. New York: Basic Books.

Gardner, H. (1993) *Multiple Intelligences: The Theory in Practice*. New York: Basic Books.

Gardner, H. (1999a) *The Disciplined Mind: What All Students Should Understand*. New York: Simon & Shuster.

Gardner, H. (1999b) *Intelligence Reframed: Multiple Intelligences for the 21st Century*. New York: Basic Books.

Gaskins, I.W. and Pressley, M. (2007) 'Teaching metacognitive strategies that address executive function processes within a schoolwide curriculum.' In L. Meltzer (ed.), *Executive Function in Education: From Theory to Practice*. New York: Guilford Press. pp. 261–86.

Gordon, S. (1995) A theoretical approach to understanding learners of statistics. *Journal of Statistics Education*, 3 (3). Available from www.amstat.org/publications/jse/v3n3/gordon.html (accessed 24th September 2013).

Gruber, H. and Voneche, J. (1977) *The Essential Piaget*. London: Basic Books.

Hacker, D. and Dunlosky, J. (2003) Not all metacognition is created equal. *New Direction for Teaching and Learning*, 95: 93–97.

Hacker, D., Dunlosky, J. and Graesser, A. (1998) *Metacognition in Education Theory and Practice*. Mahwah, NJ: Lawrence Erlbaum Assocaites.

Hall, K. and Myers, J. (1998) 'That's just the way I am': metacognition, personal intelligence and reading. *Reading*, 38 (2): 8–13.

Hartman, H. (2001) *Metacognition in Learning and Instruction*, Vol. 19. Norwell, MA: Kluwer Academic Publishers.

Hein, G. (1991) Constructivist learning theory. Paper presented at the International Committee of Museum Educators Conference, Jerusalem, Israel.

Hennessey, M. (1999) Probing the dimensions of metacognition: implications for conceptual changes in teaching and learning. Paper presented at the Annual Meeting of the National Association for Research in Science Teaching (NARST).

Hine, A. (2000) Mirroring effective education through mentoring, metacognition and self-reflection. Paper presented at the Australian Association for Research in Education Conference.

Howe, K. and Berv, J. (2000) 'Constructing constructivism: epistemological and pedagogical.' In D. Phillips (ed.), *Constructivism in Education: Opinions and Second Opinions on Controversial Issues*. Chicago, IL: The University of Chicago Press. pp. 19–40.

Jeanneret, N. and Cantwell, R. (2002) Self efficacy issues in learning to teach composition: a case study of instruction. *Australian Journal of Educational and Developmental Psychology*, 2: 33–41.

Johnson, C. (2002) Drama and metacognition. *Early Child Development and Care*, 172: 595–602.

Kuhn, D. (2000a) Metacognitive development. *New Direction for Teaching and Learning*, 9 (5): 178–181.

Kuhn, D. (2000b) Metacognitive development. *Current Directions in Psychological Science*, 9 (5): 178–81.

Kuhn, D. and Dean, D. (2004) Metacognition: a bridge between cognitive psychology and educational practice. *Theory into Practice*, 43 (4): 268–74.

Kuiper, R. (2002) Enhancing metacognition through the reflective use of self-regulated learning strategies. *The Journal of Continuing Education in Nursing*, 33 (2): 78–87.

Leat, D.L. (2003) Developing a pedagogy of metacognition and transfer: some signposts for the generation and use of knowledge and the creation of research partnerships. *British Educational Research Journal*, 29 (3): 383–415.

Livingston, J. (1997). *Metacognition: An Overview*. Unpublished manuscript. State University of New York Buffalo.

Maslow, A. (1943) A theory of human motivation. *Psychological Review*, 50 (4): 370–96.

McCarty, L. and Schwandt, T. (2000) 'Seductive illusions: Von Glaserfeld and Gergen on epistemology and education.' In D. Phillips (ed.), *Constructivism in Education*. Chicago, IL: University of Chicago Press. pp. 41–90.

Moran, S. and Gardner, H. (2007) '"Hill, skill and will": Executive function from a multiple-intelligences perspective.' In L. Meltzer (ed.), *Executive Function in Education: From Theory to Practice*. New York: Guilford Press. pp. 19–38.

Munns, G. (2004) You say motivation, I say engagement: can we work this whole thing out. Paper presented at the 3rd International Biennial SELF Research Conference, Berlin, 4th-7th July.

Pajeres, F. (2000) *Seeking a culturally attentive educational psychology*. Available from www.des.emory.edu/mgp/AERA2000Discussant.html (accessed 5th August 2005).

Pajeres, F. (2001) 'Self beliefs and schools success: self efficacy, self concept and school achievement.' In R. Riding and S. Raynor (eds), *Perception*. London: Ablex Publishing. pp. 239–66.

Pajeres, F. and Valiante, G. (1996) Predictive utility and causal influence of the writing self efficacy beliefs of elementary students. Paper presented at the Annual Meeting of the American Educational Research Association, New York.

Parr, G. (2004) Professional learning, professional knowledge and professional identity: a bleak view, but oh the possibilities. *English Teaching: Practice and Critique*, 3 (2): 21–47.

Piaget, J. (1964) Part I: Cognitive development in children: Piaget development and learning. *Journal of Research in Science Teaching*, 2 (3): 176–86.

Pintrich, P. and Schunk, D. (1996) *Motivation in Education: Theory, Research and Applications*. Englewood Cliffs, NJ: Prentice–Hall.

Posner, G. (2005) *Field Experience: A Guide to Reflective Teaching*. Sydney: Pearson.

Prawat, R. (1999) Social constructivism and the process/content distinction as viewed by Vygotsky and the Pragmatists. *Mind, Culture, and Activity*, 6 (4): 255–73.

Reese, A. (1998) Implications of results from cognitive science research for medical education. *Medical Education Online*, 3 (1). Retrieved from www.utmb.edu/meo/ (accessed 30th August 2013).

Richardson, V. (2003) Constructivist pedagogy. *Teachers College Record*, 105 (9): 1623–40.

Robertson, M. and Gerber, R. (eds) (2000) *The Child's World: Triggers for Learning*. Melbourne: ACER Press.

Rowe, K. and Berv, J. (2000) 'Constructing constructivism, epistemological and pedagogical.' In D. Phillips (ed.), *Constructivism in Education*. Chicago: University of Chicago Press. pp. 19–41.

Schneider, W. (2008) The development of metacognitive knowledge in children and adolescents: major trends and implications for education. *Mind, Brain, and Education*, 2 (3): 114–21.

Seligman, M., Ernst, R., Gillham, J., Reivich, K. and Linkins, M. (2009) Positive education: Positive psychology and classroom interventions. *Oxford Review of Education*, 35 (3): 293–311.

Sellars, M. (2003) *The affective component of effective education*. Master of Education Research. Sydney: Australian Catholic University.

Splitter, L. (2009) Authenticity and constructivism in education. *Studies in Philosophy and Education*, 28 (2): 135–51.

Stevens, D. (2010) A Freirean critique of the competence model of teacher education, focusing on the standards for qualified teacher status in England. *Journal of Education for Teaching*, 36 (2): 187–96.

van der Heijden, M.K. (n.d.) A holistic Vygotskian operational definition of approach behaviour for the study of personality and learning. Retrieved from http://psych.hanover.edu/vygotsky/heijden.html (accessed 23 August 2005).

Vygotsky, L.S. (1968) The problem of consciousness. *Collected Works of L.S. Vygotsky* Retrieved from www.markists.org/archive/vygotsky/works/1934/problem-consciousness.htm (accessed 23 August 2005).

Waite, T. (2003) Activity theory. Retrieved from www.slis.indiana.edu/faculty/yrogers/act_theory2/ (accessed 23 August 2005).

Walker, R. and Debus, R. (2002) Educational psychology: advances in learning, cognition and motivation. *Change: Transformations in Education*, 5 (1): 1–25.

Woolfolk, A. (2004) *Educational Psychology*. Boston, MA: Pearson Education.

Woolfolk, A. and Margetts, K. (2007) *Educational Psychology*. Frenchs Forest, NSW: Pearson Education.

Wu, Y. and Tsai, C. (2005) Development of elementary school students' cognitive structures and information processing strategies under long term constructivist-orientated science instruction. *Science Education*, 89 (5): 822–846.

Zohar, A. (1999) Teachers' metacognitive knowledge and the instruction of higher order thinking. *Teaching and Teacher Education*, 15 (4): 413–29.

Chapter 6: Theories on the Nature of Intelligence

- Q1. What do think about the nature of intelligence?
- Q2. Do you think intelligence can be changed or improved?
- Q3. Do you think there are different types of intelligence?
- Q4. Do you think that intelligence is easily measured, or able to be measured at all?
- Q5. Are there occasions when you have been challenged by other people's ideas about intelligence? Why?
- Q6. Do you think that what individual teachers think about the nature of intelligence matters?

Introduction

The nature of intelligence has been a contentious issue for some decades, despite the existence of a very large number of definitions for this construct. Generally, intelligence is understood to be the human capacity to learn effectively. Originally the debate focused on the nature versus nurture argument, but currently, additional considerations have brought more complexity to the debate than before. In the previous chapters you have considered the impact of issues directly related to your professional work, the significance of the way the brain works in the learning process and the understandings that educational psychologist have brought to pedagogical models. All of these topics are important to you as an aspiring or beginning teacher. However, much of your discussion and reasoning may easily have been influenced by your notions of the nature of intelligence. Many of the mandatory teaching standards implicitly suggest that all students have the potential to learn. This is frequently indicated in the statements that relate to you providing for all learners by the ways in which you plan teaching and learning activities. What you think about the nature of intelligence itself underpins everything you do in your classroom. It determines what and how you prepare your teaching activities to support students' learning, how you perceive and design students' assessment tasks and how you actually interpret student progress and evidence of learning. The tensions created by systems and funding bodies do little to support you and other beginning teachers who are struggling to combine the conservatism of the financial supports for learners and the implicit demands of the teaching standards. On one hand the funding for learners who may require additional support in regular classrooms is often inextricably linked to IQ testing, but on the other hand, there appear to be expectations that these students have their learning supported by you and other teachers who employ more recent, inclusive understandings of the nature of intelligence and its potential to be enhanced and strengthened.

What Does the Literature Say about Theories of Intelligence?

Binet has been credited with being the first psychologist to make a serious contribution to the understanding and measurement of intelligence (Anderson, 1999: xv). He was commissioned by the French authorities at the end of the nineteenth century to devise some way of identifying children who would need extra educational support. Anderson (1999) concludes that Binet's contribution to understanding intelligence is threefold: his understanding of intelligence as higher-order properties of the mind which has provided a challenge to Spearman's theory of general intelligence; his formulation of the notion of 'mental age'; and the fact that he later gave Piaget a job, which entailed him developing the Binet IQ tests. The notion that there is a single, biologically predetermined potential for intelligence that is unaffected by other, environmental factors is largely unacceptable in today's educational contexts. This perception of intelligence has largely served the conservative, male, middle class white population (Kincheloe et al., 1999: 1). Anderson (1999: 9) discusses Eysenck's belief that many of the important aspects of intelligence will have to wait for the findings of neuroscience. However, Anderson himself contends that finding a precise neurological explanation for intelligence will not wholly explain or settle the current debates regarding the nature of intelligence. This is simply because of the other important environmental factors that are always variables. What is agreed, however, is that, for many theorists, intelligence is only what the intelligence tests are testing. Styles (1999: 23) discusses three 'fundamental doctrines of human ability' taken from Spearman and Jones. She describes these as:

- Monarchic: the notion that intelligence is a single entity as espoused by Spearman's notion of general intelligence or Cattell's fluid intelligence.
- Oligarchic: the idea that intelligence comprises several broad features such as those described by Thurstone and by Gardner in his Multiple Intelligences (MI) theory.
- Anarchic: the theory that intelligence consists of many specific abilities as described by Guilford's structure of intellect model of intelligence.

Styles (1999) concurs with Spearman and Jones that there may be value in each of these perspectives. She also advocates that scale and a hierarchical model of the development of intellectual growth are important to the measurement of intelligence in varying contexts. However, in the conclusion of her detailed discussion of measurement and factor analysis, Styles (1999) is optimistic about the current possibility of integrating theoretical models of intelligence and measurement with the inclusion of the affective factors that influence human cognition. It also appears that while the discussion of genetic determination in intelligence has received very little research attention, the questions that geneticists are asking in this area reflect a more dynamic view of intelligence, its development and its structure (Hay, 1999).

Cattell's original thinking about intelligence was that it was of the nature of fluid intelligence. This concept was then developed further by Cattell and his colleague. The Horn–Cattell (1967) notion of fluid intelligence was developed as part of their theory of fluid and crystallised intelligences. They speculated that intelligence is made of many abilities that work together to make up a single entity that produces intelligent behaviour. They proposed that fluid intelligence was one type of two varieties of intelligence that humans possess. This fluid intelligence was viewed as a type of natural capacity for problem solving and abstract thinking. It was considered natural in the sense that it was not learned, nor was it influenced by environmental factors; it was an inherent human capacity that began to decline during adolescence and continued to decline as people aged. Crystallised intelligence, on the other hand, was developed as the result of education and experiences and was constantly being strengthened and informed by new learning that was based on prior learning. This type of intelligence was thought to be based on facts and did not deteriorate with age. Spearman (1904) developed the notion of general intelligence or *general factor* which became simply known as *g*. As in Cattell's theory, this mental activity was identified as a single, biological capacity that produced intelligent behaviour. Spearman reached his conclusions about the nature of intelligence by using a statistical approach that analysed the correlations among the variables. This statistical technique is called factor analysis and Spearman showed that the results on mental tests could be positively correlated by using this method, leading him to believe that intelligence was a single entity.

These theories that espouse the notion of intelligence as a fixed, inherited trait that is unaffected by the social and cultural environment in which all individuals live, have attracted some severe criticism from a sociological perspective. Leistyna (1999: 51) comments that:

> From this perspective, it is as if the cognitive and psychological makeup of each person were somehow formulated outside of history and politics and thus unaffected by ideology, power relations and such socially constructed categories as capitalism, race, class, gender and sexual orientation.

The impact of adopting this perspective in educational, or indeed other contexts, is that 'thinking, speaking and knowing' (Leistyna, 1999: 63) are socially and culturally orientated. Tests that are structured to measure intelligence are taking the values and understandings of a specific social and cultural group and applying them to individuals in the name of 'measuring' intelligence. Leistyna recommends that critical educators need to acknowledge that the mind is socially constructed and, in contrast to Piagetian thinking, the ways in which individuals speak, know and understand the world and construct their individual sources of knowledge are the result of their experiences in a social and cultural environment. Kincheloe (1999: 9) also includes Piagetian constructivism in his critique of mainstream educational psychology, which he sees as dominated by the understanding of intelligence as 'fixed and innate – a mysterious quality found only in the privileged few'. His discussion of postmodernism, like Connella's (1999) challenge to conservative teacher educators, confronts educationalists. He specifically challenges those who prepare new teachers to make more sense of their students' social contexts and to revise their notions of intelligence and the construction of knowledge, By doing this he proposes that there will be a democratisation of intelligence and the development of a 'transformative educational psychology' (Kincheloe et al., 1999: 10).

The next category of intelligence as identified by Styles (1999) includes those theories that have several broad features identified as intelligence. Decades ago Thurstone (1938) proposed the first multifactor approach to intelligence. He named seven 'primary mental abilities' that constituted intelligence, in opposition to theories such as the one developed by Spearman (1904) which, as you have read, had placed much significance on *g* – general ability – which was determined by testing. These primary mental abilities were identified by Thurstone (1938) as independent components. They were:

- word fluency
- verbal comprehension
- spatial visualisation
- number facility
- associative memory
- reasoning
- perceptual speed.

Also in contrast to Spearman (1904), Thurstone (1938) found that individuals showed different capabilities in each of these seven mental abilities, but not that the seven were totally separate from each other. Perhaps the most well known theory of multifactor intelligence is proposed by Gardner (1983) in his theory of Multiple Intelligences. Gardner (1983a-c, 1993a, 1993b, 1999a, 1999b, 2000) developed his ideas about intelligence as a result of 'a comprehensive, thorough and systematic review of empirical data from studies in biology, neuropsychology, developmental psychology and cultural anthropology' (Chen, 2004: 5). His view of intelligence can be succinctly described as 'a biopsychological potential with an emergent, responsive and pluralistic nature' (Chen, 2004: 5) Gardner strongly opposes standardised means of measuring intelligence, not only because of the interactive nature of the multiple intelligences, but because some intelligence domains are impossible to measure by traditional pen and paper tests. His theories are opposed by those who are concerned by the lack of empirical evidence. However, as postmodernist endeavours across the disciplines are reactions against theoretical efforts to explain reality in terms of science or objectivity, Kincheloe (1999: 22) writes, from a postmodernist perspective of the nature of intelligence as socially situated, that:

> In Gardner's expansion of the concept of intelligence, we find his relevance not only to post formal democratic effort but also to the attempt to educate intelligence. If we know better what intelligence involves and the variety of forms it takes, we have a much better chance of cultivating it.

Gardner's Multiple Intelligences theory is based on two major assumptions. Firstly, it is a cognitive theory (Bereiter, 2000; Gardner, 2000a-c, 2003; Shephard, 2001; Stuss and Levine, 2002) based on the most modern research into the functions of the brain, specifically frontal lobe functions. As we have seen in an earlier chapter, Reese (1998: 1–3) has explained that the brain is comprised of 'semi-independent' modules for different functions. The modules are all interconnected and influence one another and other functional areas of the brain reciprocally. Additionally, they are influenced by hormones

and 'neuropeptides, many of which are central to emotional states'. He identifies these functional centres as being the physical basis for Gardner's (1983,
1993a, 1999a, 1999b) Multiple Intelligences theory. Secondly, in refuting the
theory that intelligence is a single, fixed, uniform phenomenon, Gardner
(1983, 1993a) proposes a much wider and more encompassing view of
intelligence in eight intellectual domains. Initially, Gardner (1983, 1993a)
identified seven intelligence domains. These then grew to eight intelligence
domains with inclusion of naturalist intelligence. It appears Gardner is still
open to the possibility of adding others, namely existential intelligence, and
very recently there has been some informal discussion of pedagogical intelligence (Hutchins n.d.; Khalsa, 2013). Gardner comments that 'there is not,
and can never be a single, irrefutable and universally accepted list of human
intelligences' (1993a: 59). The eight domains are linguistic intelligence, logical–mathematical intelligence, visual–spatial intelligence, bodily–kinaesthetic
intelligence, musical intelligence, interpersonal intelligence, intrapersonal
intelligence and naturalist intelligence. Gardner's (1983, 1993a, 1999a, 1999b)
eight 'signs' that determine the inclusion of an intelligence are multidisciplinary. However, he sums up his notion of intelligence as 'a set of skills of
problem-solving – enabling the individual to resolve genuine problems or
difficulties' (1993a: 60), adding that these skills must also be culturally
valued.

Gardner (1993a, 1993b, 1999b) proposes that everyone possesses all eight
intelligences as part of their genetic inheritance. What is significant is that
no two people are exactly alike. An intelligence profile developed using
Multiple Intelligences theory is as unique as a fingerprint each individual
profile comprises a set of relative strengths and relative limitations. To add
further complexity to the profile, cultural influences and personal experiences constantly impact on the intelligences (Gardner, 1993a, 1993b, 1999b),
changing the profile of the individual and the relationship of the intelligences, one to another. Kincheloe (1999: 22) notes that Gardner's theory is
a social construction 'reflecting the values of individuals from particular
cultural locations at specific times in history', which implies strongly that in
the current educational climate in the Westernised world, it is important for
every individual to have some area in which they are 'smart'. This notion is
also reflected in Gardner's concept of the intrapersonal domain, which will
be discussed in detail in later chapters. He asserts that 'knowing yourself' in
terms of your relative strengths and limitations is a critical part of this intelligence domain.

The 'anarchic' category uses Guilford's model, which he named the 'Structure
of the Intellect' (Barlow, 2000). It is indeed a very tightly structured model of
the nature of intelligence. It was, however, one of the first models of intelligence
to acknowledge the importance of creativity, which previously had been rather
taken for granted. The model comprised three dimensions – content, product

and process – and from these 150 independent thinking skills are able to be developed. Two of these three dimensions are described in Figure 6.1.

Content Guilford observed that different individuals demonstrated a preference for one or more of the following ways to receive information	• Symbolic, which referred to words and symbolic meanings conveyed • Visual, which was actually information gleaned by the senses, including pictorial and images • Auditory, which was also information from the senses and visuals • Semantic, which was generally associated with words but not always • Behavioral, this was about information received by individuals who were sensitive to the mental states and behaviours of others. Barlow (2000) notes that this type of intelligence has been made popular in recent times by Goleman (1995) under the title of emotional intelligence. This is the topic of Chapter 7.
Products The different types of information that could be processed from the content sources	• Units, which means the individual can understand single units such as words, symbols or facial expressions from the information received • Classes, which meant that the individual was able to organize the units of information into groups effectively according to their commonality • Relationships, which allows the individual to see the connections between two units • Systems, which is the capacity to see the relationships and connections between more than two units • Transformations, which is the ability to understand and gain information from the units when they are changed or altered in subtle ways: for example, when a figure is rotated or when there is a play on words or a pun • Implications, is to do with the expectancy that if one set of information is true or correct then other information may also be true or correct, the capacity to predict from one set of information, various facts about another

Figure 6.1   Guilford's Model of the Structure of the Intellect

Content and product are the two dimensions that detail what people are able to think about. Individuals receive information in various ways that reflected their personal preferences about how information was most easily obtained. It is then processed into the various products, or types of information, that were meaningful for the thinker.

• Process describes the various ways that the brain interacts with the information it receives:

   o Cognition is the capacity to perceive the information and to make meaning from it.
   o Memory is an individual's capacity to store information. It also refers to the differences in the types of information that individual people choose to remember and to the capacity of individuals to retrieve what they have stored in their individual memory.

- o Divergent production is the capacity to find large numbers of items in the memory that fit certain criteria.
- o Convergent production is the capacity to find a specific piece of information in the memory, for example a correct answer to a problem. It is thought that convergent production may be initially the process of divergent memory findings which are then evaluated for correctness. This is the type of thinking that is most often required to respond to IQ tests.
- o Evaluation is the process by which identical characteristics of items are established, the differences in items are identified and value judgements related to which information is better for the context or circumstances are made.

The motivation for Guilford (1967) to become involved in research was his initial interest in creativity. This interest is found in his notion of divergent production. Most tests of creativity are designed as divergent production tests.

In addition to the cognitive psychologists that are identified by Styles (1999), there is another who has made a considerable contribution to the understanding of the nature of intelligence. The work of Sternberg (Sternberg, 2004; Sternberg et al., 2000; Sternberg and Kaufman, 2006; Sternberg and Williams, 1998) has also contributed greatly to our understanding of intelligence in educational contexts. Sternberg hypothesises that intelligence can be demonstrated in three different ways. His theory of intelligence comprises three distinct types of intelligence:

- Analytical: to do with academic problem solving, the type of intelligence traditionally measured by testing that comprises academic puzzles and tasks.
- Creative: to do with creativity, having insight and finding new and innovative ways to react to situations that are novel or previously encountered.
- Practical: the intelligence needed to deal with practical problem solving in everyday life. It can entail adapting or changing strategies or procedures or contexts so that everyday tasks are completed.

All of these are amenable to improvement in response to learning experiences and materials. Sternberg et al. (2000: xi) additionally defines practical intelligence as 'common sense' and indicates that it is the truly necessary intelligence for everyday life. He has expressed particular interest in one vital component of this practical intelligence: an aspect he calls 'tacit knowledge'. Tacit knowledge as understood by Sternberg et al. (2000) is the procedural knowledge that is part of life in every culture and in all walks of life for all ages of individuals. It is also considered to be distinct from academic intelligence, which he identifies as the analytical intelligence of his Triarchic

Theory of Intelligence (Sternberg and Williams, 1998). The reason these are separate and distinct from each other is discussed in terms of the types of problems that necessitate engagement with each of these types of intelligence. Like Gardner, Sternberg also discusses the potential of intelligence to be strengthened and emphasises the important of individuals identifying their relative strengths and limitations in order to succeed more easily.

What Does This Mean for You?

One of the most important constructs that you can reflect on is what exactly you think about the nature of intelligence. This is because it impacts on everything you do as a teacher. It influences your expectations of your students, your planning for learning and your classroom decisions and interactions. There may indeed be value in each of the perspectives discussed here. However, if you believe the monarchic perspective alone, then you are investing in several specific notions, including the following, which will impact in these ways on your professional work.

- You will have to accept that the IQ scores of your students reflect what they are able to achieve in life.
- Nothing you do as their teacher makes any difference to their learning potential.
- Nothing in the learning environment will have an impact on the students' achievements.

As a result of this perspective, there is no need for you to employ strategies that may increase students academic success as these would have no effect on the capacity of the students to learn more readily.

You cannot easily plan for the students' learning potentials as this perspective identifies intelligence as fixed. As a result, your efforts would not have any influence on the learners' innate, regulated capacity for learning.

You are ignoring a very important finding from neuroscience: the impact of emotion on mental capacities.

You are also proposing that the mind and intelligence are not social constructs.

If, however, you believe in any of the theories that propose that intelligence is not fixed, not measurable and has the potential to be enhanced, then your professional practice will look very different. You would be committed to a range of different pedagogical strategies, including the following:

- Supporting students' understanding of how exactly they each are smart and not defining intelligence narrowly in terms of literacy and logic but realising the students' potentials to have other strengths that can be used to facilitate more successful academic learning.

- Offering multiple representations of concepts and strategies so that each student has an opportunity to think about the learning in their own ways, i.e. differentiating tasks to support different learning preferences.
- Using students' strengths to help them learn more effectively in other content areas.
- Providing a quality environment in which students can learn effectively. Supporting students' efforts, being sensitive to individual differences relating to readiness to learn in some areas, having high expectations for all students.
- Endorsing the notion that every child has the potential to become an effective, successful learner.
- Valuing the potential of all students to develop their learning possibilities through appropriate engagement with suitable tasks, resources, environments and interactions with others.
- Understanding that a relative limitation in any area of learning does not indicate an inability to learn successfully in others.

Questions for Reflection

- Q1. Have you seen any pedagogical practice in classrooms that you can identify as being influenced by one of these theories of intelligence?
- Q2. What were the characteristics of this pedagogical practice?
- Q3. Have you seen texts with lessons developed using any of these notions of intelligence as a framework? Identify these.
- Q4. Which of these theories of intelligence would you be most comfortable using as a framework for your practice?
- Q5. Do you think it matters which theory of intelligence you use to underpin your professional practice? Validate your response.

Intelligence Matters

What students think of as intelligence and how they apply their notions to their own sense of competency has important ramifications according to research. Dweck (2000) describes and explains two diametrically opposed views of the nature of intelligence and their impact on motivation, achievement, development and personality. The 'traditional' understanding of intelligence portrays this construct as a fixed, inherited trait that cannot be changed, rather like a genetic inheritance, such as the colour of an individual's eyes. This is termed 'entity theory'. Dweck (2000) and her colleagues found in their research that there were many negative repercussions for students holding this view. Firstly, they may worry about how intelligent they actually are and what sort of IQ score they might attain if tested. More importantly, they felt considerably challenged by any tasks that presented some difficulties as these tasks threatened their self esteem. When faced with difficult tasks for which students did not have immediate answers, students who embraced the 'entity view' of intelligence were observed to use strategies that undermined their potential to succeed, engaging in 'self handicapping' (Dweck, 2000: 4) to protect their sense of self worth. They associated effort with low intelligence, feeling that 'smart' people always found tasks easy. They self handicapped by not attempting to solve difficult problems, excused poor results by claiming they didn't bother to study and claiming they were not taught properly in the first place, thus shifting the responsibility to the teacher. All of this impacted negatively on their motivation for future learning, their actual academic achievement in learning contexts and their capacity to develop traits such as perseverance, persistence and resilience in their learning.

In contrast, students who understood intelligence as a 'trait' that could be strengthened and cultivated through meaningful activities and experiences were more proactive in the learning process, especially when challenged by difficult tasks that required a great deal of effort and perseverance. Naming this notion of intelligence 'the incremental theory of intelligence', Dweck (2000), and her various collaborators in a number of studies, found that repercussions of subscribing to this belief were singularly positive for students' learning and academic achievements. The students valued effort and persistence. One research result (Henderson and Dweck in Dweck, 2000: 28–32) that is of particular interest focused on the coping capabilities of learners moving from primary school settings to junior secondary or to middle school contexts. Traditionally, these transitions have proven difficult for some students and their academic progress has been less consistent than it was previously. This is considered to be because the work gets harder, often the teachers differentiate less for individual learning preferences, grades become more important and the workload increases as the students undergo physical, cognitive and emotional changes (Blakemore and Choudhury, 2006). The researchers found, among other things, that students who were undergoing the transition with high confidence and who held the entity theory of intelligence were among those who managed only low academic success. In contrast, the students who subscribed to the incremental theory of intelligence were found to be more successful. Several individuals from the latter group were students who had expressed low confidence in their intellectual ability. However, the latter group were able to rise to the challenges presented in the transition itself and in the secondary classroom and were working towards improving their competencies. They had achieved the most impressive academic gains. The students from the two groups also differed in the explanations they would give if they did not achieve highly at school. Those whose beliefs were based on incremental theory were more likely to say that they needed to make more effort or to revise their learning strategies. The students whose beliefs were based on entity theory were more likely to say that they were not smart enough.

What Does This Mean for You?

Dweck's research challenges you to encourage your students to think of themselves as potentially successful learners, irrespective of their current levels of academic success. As you have read, there is an interesting question relating to the issue of effort and persistence. As you know from the previous chapter, student attitudes and motivation are critical components in the learning process. As a result, the manner in which you evaluate students' work becomes an important influence on their willingness to persevere with their learning tasks. If you wish to encourage your students to work hard, increase their levels of competencies and value an incremental theory of intelligence, you need to adopt specific pedagogical strategies. These may include:

- Developing tasks so that all students have an appropriate degree of difficulty in their learning. Do you think it would be considered ethical to have some students complete tasks with little or no effort and have others who have to struggle constantly to achieve the smallest academic success? Differentiation is important.
- Do not set tasks for the entire class that some students can do quickly and competently and then have 'extension' tasks. This has the capacity to create an elitist group in the class who may become over-confident or believe that they are the only ones who have any intelligence or who may be viewed by their peers as 'clever'.
- Plan for students' needs and avoid praising fast finishers. For some students finishing first means they are very clever when in fact they are capable of a better learning outcome. Being first is not always appropriate or beneficial when learners understand that education is a process, not a race.
- Complete individual assessments of the formative (ongoing) and summative types to establish progress instead of grading students in ranks according to their performance on a test. Avoid competition. Instead encourage students to respect difference and diversity.
- Consider the implications of praising students who are 'the best' or who produce the 'best' work. Consider the effort that students expend as the first criterion in order to firmly establish with your students that effort and persistence is valued in your classroom.

(Continued)

(Continued)

- Be positive and affirming in your feedback to students. Find and acknowledge students' relative strengths and provide opportunities for each of them to learn in their preferred ways.
- Model your own 'growth mindset' (see below) with your students by identifying your own relative strengths and limitations as accurate self knowledge where professionally appropriate.

It is difficult to understand how exactly the students who held the incremental theory of intelligence were able to independently develop the strategies and *modus operandi* required to succeed in a more complex and demanding learning context, while the other group of students were not. Perhaps Dweck provides a clue in a later publication, where she states:

> Howard Gardner, in his book *Extraordinary Minds*, concluded that exceptional individuals have 'a special talent for identifying their own strengths and weaknesses'. It is interesting that those with the growth mindset seem to have this talent. (2006: 11)

The growth mindset to which she refers is the perspective of those who believe the incremental theory of intelligence. While Dweck's (2006) theory on growth mindset and achieving success appears to have a sound theoretical background, there is a lack of detail on how exactly individuals can acquire the skills, knowledge and attitudes that can facilitate success. It appears that subscribing to one specific conceptualisation of the nature of the construct understood generally as 'intelligence' would be an important start, but how exactly do students, in particular young students, turn this perspective into academic success? Obviously, the understanding of intelligence potential may motivate students to try harder, but there are occasions when trying harder alone would not be enough to make a substantial difference (Dweck, 2006; Ng, 1998, 2000, 2002). Similarly, accepting that poor grades do not necessarily mean that individuals are not intelligent is a useful and positive perspective, but how do students revise strategies and find other ways to make personal meaning of their learning? These practical considerations are part of the essence of the teaching and learning dynamic engaged in daily in educational contexts and are important questions that are left unanswered by Dweck's (2006) theory of 'mindsets' based on individuals' perceptions of the nature of intelligence. It could be, however, that the emphasis placed by both Gardner and Sternberg on the importance of students' self knowledge in respect of acknowledging their individual, relative strengths and limitations could be major component of the students' strategies. This suggestion is made with the knowledge that both Gardner's and Sternberg's theories of intelligence are clearly formulated in what Dweck (2000, 2006) terms the 'incremental model' of intelligence.

Questions for Reflection

- Q1. Have you encountered students who self handicap? Why do you think they do this?
- Q2. What is your perspective on intelligence: entity or incremental?
- Q3. Why do you believe that you have this view? Give your reasons.
- Q4. Are you surprised that the students who transitioned with a high degree of confidence going into secondary school were not the most successful academically? Validate your answer.
- Q5. How do you think the students themselves developed their opinions about the nature of intelligence?
- Q6. Do you think that teachers can be influential in developing students' understanding of what it is to be intelligent? How or why?

Implications for Teaching

What you believe to be the nature of intelligence impacts on every aspect of your professional life. The implications for teachers are profound at every level of practice. In the big picture, how you understand the nature of intelligence impacts on your understanding of the nature and purpose of schooling and education. On another level, it influences the sort of teacher you wish to develop into and the ways in which you interpret teachers' work and your role in the school and community. It impacts on your everyday pedagogies. Your perspectives influence the ways in which you:

- organise your classroom
- select the materials you provide for your students
- debate and determine ethical solutions to professional problems
- make decisions that impact on the lives of your students.

At the beginning of the chapter there was a mention of the tension often created in schools and educational systems by specific funding procedures and the ways in which you may understand the nature of intelligence and its potential to be enhanced. If you understand that intelligence is a single, fixed entity that students have in measures that are not able to be changed by interaction with artefacts, environments, interactions with others or in

community experiences, then you may simply have to present the mandatory curriculum in way in which you understand it best. You may decide to
differentiate tasks and learning for those displaying different levels of understanding and development in your classes, but you may have to assess each
individual on 'one size fits all' tests, especially in the areas of logic and
language, irrespective of their ability to complete the test or assessment task
successfully. You may encourage all your students and try to have high
expectations for them, but implicitly acknowledge that some students will
never have the intellectual capacity to effectively learn what matters most in
terms of academic attainment.

If, however, the perspective of intelligence that you hold is that, by its
nature, it is not fixed, is able to be enhanced by a variety of activities and
interactions and is, in many respects, developed and understood in socially
constructed language and norms, then you have a much more complex
situation within which to practise your profession. You will be constantly
adapting the classroom materials and learning tasks for students in order to
provide an optimal environment in which learners at all levels of cognitive
development can be challenged. All learners will have different needs and
different relative strengths and limitations. You will be busy knowing each
of your students and how they learn most effectively. The challenge for you
then will be to develop learning tasks that use their relative strengths as a
point of departure from which to work with new areas of understanding.
Fortunately, there are many research findings that will support your work
and numerous examples of how best to structure learning for all your students, irrespective of their differences and diversity. The view of the nature
of intelligence that you hold mandates you to ensure that all students learn
effectively and are confident about their capacity to be successful learners.
Whist greater detail on differentiation, scaffolding learning and understanding the implications of cultural diversity are discussed in detail in later
chapters, the impact of one theory of intelligence is discussed below.

Gardner's Multiple Intelligences (MI) theory (Gardner, 1983, 1993a)
appears to have received the most attention from educators in classrooms.
Evidence of the degree and scope of the attention educationalists have paid
to Gardner's (1983, 1993a) cognitive theory include positive comment from
the following authors regarding the impact that activities designed around
MI theory have had on the learning of students in their classrooms: Berman
(1995), Davidson (2005), Ellison (1992, 2001), Hine (2002) – all of whom
consider the implementation of multiple intelligences in primary educational
contexts. Additionally, Morris and Le Blanc, (1996), Glasgow (1999) and
Wahl (2002) discuss the benefits of the application of Gardner's MI theory
in various secondary school subject domains. Armstrong (1994, 2003), Noble
(2002; Noble and Grant, 1997) and Diaz-Lefebre (2004) also recommend that
teachers examine the possibilities of utilising MI theory (Gardner, 1983,

1993a) to improve teaching and learning outcomes. Hoerr (2004) provides some insight into why these teachers and educators would be enthusiastic about using theory in regular classrooms, irrespective of the age of the students. Thomas Hoerr, principal of the New City School in St Louis, Missouri, since 1981, suggests why this would be so. He describes MI as having 'two powerful lures' (Hoerr, 2004: 1). Firstly, he asserts more children find success at school when students are offered different pathways to learning. Secondly, he stresses that 'using MI transforms the role of the teacher'.

Questions for Reflection

- Q1. What do you think of as the nature of intelligence?
- Q2. What implications do you see this perspective having for your teaching?
- Q3. Would you agree that the way in which you understand the nature of intelligence impacts on every aspect of your professional life? Give your reasons
- Q4. Do your mandatory standards imply that a particular notion of the nature of intelligence underpins them? How can you tell? Does this perspective make you comfortable as an aspiring teacher?
- Q5. Why do you think that Gardner's theory has been so popular in educational contexts in ways in which other theorists who espouse the 'incremental' nature of intelligence have not?
- Q6. What do you think Hoerr means when he suggests that using MI 'transforms the role of the teacher'? Would agree with this? Validate your answer.

Scenario Six

Mr Tan's students were working well in their classroom. They had the freedom to get the resources they needed from the cupboards, access the computers and generally organise themselves. They were working with others or independently, according to their personal preferences for this particular task. They were able to do this because they were working towards the goals that they had set for themselves in history. Mr Tan had written the multiple intelligences domains on the whiteboard on the previous Friday and had invited students to select where they would like to concentrate their efforts in relation to the jigsaw activity that was to consolidate the learning in this topic. He had planned to look at as many aspects of the topic as possible so when the students came together with

(Continued)

(Continued)

their efforts, the 'jigsaw' or the 'entire picture' of that time in history could be appreciated by everyone in the class without everyone being required to learn a little about all the different social, cultural and practical aspects of the period. On Monday morning, a significant number of students had placed their names in the linguistic intelligence domain and the remainder were scattered among the other intelligence domains. In order to create a framework within which the students could work effectively, Mr Tan asked the students complete a form for his records so that he could more readily support the learning. The form required the students to complete the following information. He told them they could wait until after the break as they might find that others would like to work with them once the list of who was working in which intelligence domain was completed.

The forms comprised these questions:

Name:
Intelligence domain selected:
Working independently or with:
Would like to investigate:
My goal (or our goal) is to:
I will need:

Mr Tan was pleased to see some collaborative work was planned in addition to individual projects. He was even happier to see the variety of tasks that students had undertaken as their goals. On the presentation day he was looking forward to the students sharing their products. There was some dance, a song created to reflect life at the time being studied, some PowerPoint presentations on different perspectives, a short play depicting some of the customs and social etiquette of the day, including a conversation about a current political topic, a traveller's diary with contemporary comments about how he felt as he travelled the country each day and what he saw that was important to him or made him angry or concerned, there were a number of local recipes and one student was cooking a dish of the period and had already arranged for her mother to come into school and assist her! There was even a spreadsheet with data from the period about a wide variety of habits and ideas that included the percentage of each gender who smoked, salaries for each gender, jobs available and anything else they could find, including acreage under local crops and the statistical probability of growing other crops successfully in the particular weather conditions of specific geographical areas.

As he looked around the room, Mr Tan reflected on the journey these students and he had made together. It had been very challenging for students at first and rather frustrating for him personally, but he felt it had all been worthwhile.

They had been a difficult group to get to know but when he decided to share his love for singing with them, they had gradually joined in and accepted that he had some rather unusual ideas. Now, when the music was played and he started singing to signal a break in the work, most of the students just sang along as they were getting organised! They appeared to favour loud songs from musical theatre. *Oklahoma!* was very popular, even though they had no idea about the show itself! They also responded to quieter music, but in a very different way. The trick was knowing the students and being able to tell when they were totally engrossed, needed a break or just needed to reflect on their own work. They each had so much to offer and were learning to respect each other's talents and work. As a beginning teacher, Mr Tan understood that he was a learner, as were his students. He was getting increasingly competent at supporting his students' learning efficiently and the improved academic outcomes were evidence that the students were making progress and learning in the ways that they each found best.

Questions for Reflection

- Q1. What do you think is happening here?
- Q2. Do you think that student capabilities can be measured on an IQ test? Give your reasons.
- Q3. Why do you think Mr Tan shared his singing?
- Q4. Do you think you could organise learning in this manner? Validate your answer.
- Q5. Do you like the way that Mr Tan facilitated learning? Why?
- Q6. What is Mr Tan's perspective on the nature of intelligence?
- Q7. What might be the difficulties Mr Tan and his students experienced before they got to this stage of organisation in the classroom?
- Q8. What pedagogies would underpin this practice?
- Q9. Do you think this is an acceptable way to teach the curriculum? Validate your answer.

Conclusion

Discussions on the nature of intelligence are usually challenging, not least for individuals who, like you, have most likely enjoyed sufficient success in the current educational systems to enable you to study at a tertiary educational institution. The irony is, as always, that the individuals who are preparing to teach the next generations of learners are not the individuals that the educational system has failed. This makes it more difficult for some individuals to become agents of change in educational contexts. The discussions here not only presented current theories of education for reflection, but also critiqued these theories from the sociological view of postmodernists who believe that the education system itself could be instrumental in creating a more democratic society by working from a more inclusive, more culturally sensitive understanding of intelligence. In order to do that, the current measures of intelligence, which are culturally and socially biased, would need to be disregarded in favour of an understanding that better fits the current neurological research and the global community – a perspective of intelligence that honours and respects different, socially constructed understandings of what it means to be smart in today's multicultural, technological world.

No discussion of intelligence can be complete without a consideration of the social, cultural and historical context in which the various theories were developed. In this chapter the sociological views of Kincheloe and his colleagues (1999) provide a considerable ethical challenge for you to reflect upon within the context of the nature of intelligence. The chapter also challenges you to reflect on the ways in which the strictures and structures of educational systems are used to maintain current educational practices that may easily discriminate against those who are not from white, middle class, English-speaking backgrounds. It is considered an ethical challenge, not only because your understanding of the nature of intelligence is foundational to your personal pedagogies, but also because if, ethically, you are committed to developing and practising pedagogies that promote fairness, equity, honesty and justice then you need to consider the role of education and schooling in endorsing these principles in their demonstrable policies and practices. You may easily disagree with some of the theories that are presented here as theories of intelligence, preferring to understand some of them as theories of talents, mental abilities, personal competencies or other constructs. However, as we will see, the use of the word 'intelligence' itself is no longer conservative and has been applied to other mental capacities, the most popular, and possibly the most controversial, of which is the notion of emotional intelligence, which will be the major focus of the next chapter.

References

Anderson, M. (ed.) (1999) *The Development of Intelligence*. Hove: Psychology Press.

Armstrong, T. (1994) *Multiple Intelligences in the Classroom*. Alexandria, VA: Association for Supervision and Curriculum Development.

Armstrong, T. (2003) *The Multiple Intelligences of Reading and Writing: Making Words Come Alive*. Alexandria, VA: Association for Supervision and Curriculum Development.

Barlow, C. (2000). Guildford' Structure of the Intellect. Retrieved from www.cocreativity.com/handouts/guilford.pdf (accessed 1 September 2012).

Bereiter, C. (2000) Keeping the brain in mind. *Australian Journal of Education*, 44 (3): 226.

Berman, S. (1995) *A Multiple Intelligences Road to a Quality Classroom*. Cheltenham, VIC: Hawker Brownlow Education.:

Blakemore, S. and Choudhury, S. (2006) Development of the adolescent brain: implications for executive function and social cognition. *Journal of Child Psychology and Psychiatry*, 47 (3/4): 296–342.

Burgh, G., Field, T. and Freakley, M. (2005) *Ethics and the Community of Enquiry: An Approach to Ethics Education*. Melbourne: Thomson Social Science Press.

Chen, J.-Q. (2004) Theory of Multiple Intelligences: is it a scientific theory? *Teachers College Record*, 106 (1): 17–23. Retrieved from www.tcrecord.org/PrintContent.asp?ContentID=11505 (accessed 3 August 2005).

Connella, G. (1999) 'Postformal thought as critique: Reconceptualization and possibility for teacher education reform.' In J. Kincheloe, S. Steinberg and L. Villaverde (eds.), *Rethinking Intelligence*. New York: Routledge. pp. 145–64.

Davidson, J. (2005) Multiple intelligences. Retrieved from www.childdevelopmentinfo.com/learning/multiple_intelligences.htm (accessed 29 April 2005).

Diaz-Lefebre, R. (2004) Multiple intelligences, learning for understanding, and creative assessment: some pieces to the puzzle of learning. *Teachers College Record*, 106 (1): 49–57.

Dweck, C. (2000) *Self Theories: Their Role in Motivation, Personality and Development*. Lillington, NC: Taylor and Francis.

Dweck, C. (2006) *Mindset*. New York: Random House.

Eliot, L. (2000) *What Is Going On in There? How the Brain and Mind Develop in the First Five Years of Life*. New York: Bantam Books.

Ellison, L. (1992) Using multiple intelligences to set goals. *Educational Leadership*, 50 (2): 69–72.

Ellison, L. (2001) *The Personal Intelligences: Promoting Social and Emotional Learning*. New York: Corwin Press.

Gardner, H. (1983) *Frames of Mind: The Theory of Multiple Intelligences*. New York: Basic Books.

Gardner, H. (1993a) *Frames of Mind. Tenth Anniversary Edition*. New York: Basic Books.

Gardner, H. (1993b) *Multiple Intelligences: The Theory in Practice*. New York: Basic Books.

Gardner, H. (1999a) *The Disciplined Mind. What All Students Should Understand*. New York: Simon & Shuster.

Gardner, H. (1999b) *Intelligence Reframed: Multiple Intelligences for the 21st Century*. New York: Basic Books.

Gardner, H. (2000a) *The Disciplined Mind*. Ringwood, VIC: Penguin Books Australia.

Gardner, H. (2000b) Howard Gardner on making the most of young minds. *The Education Digest*, 65 (2): 4–6.

Gardner, H. (2000c) *The Disciplined Mind: Beyond Facts and Standardized Tests: the K-12 Education Every Child Deserves*. New York: Penguin Books.

Gardner, H. (2003) Audiences for the Theory of Multiple Intelligences. *Teachers College Record*, 106 (1): 212–20.

Given, B. (2002) *Teaching to the Brain's Natural Learning Systems*. Alexandria, VA: Association for Supervision and Curriculum Development.

Glasgow, J.N. (1999) Recognising students multiple intelligences in cross age buddy journals. *English Journal*, 23 (1): 88–96.

Goleman, D. (1995) *Emotional Intelligence: Why It Can Matter More than IQ*. New York: Bantam Books.

Guilford, J. (1967) *The Nature of Human Intelligence*. New York: McGraw-Hill.

Hay, D. (1999) 'The developmental genetics of intelligence.' In M. Anderson (ed.), *The Development of Intelligence*. Hove: Psychology Press. pp. 75–104.

Hine, C. (2002) Developing multiple intelligences in young learners. Retrieved from www.earlychildhood.com/articles (accessed 10 November 2002).

Hoerr, T. (2004) How MI informs teaching at a New City school. *Teachers College Record*, 106 (1): 40–8.

Horn, J. and Cattell, R. (1967) Age differences in fluid and crystallized intelligence. *Acta Psychologica*, 26: 107–29.

Hutchins, P. (n.d.) Building pedagogical intelligence. *Carnegie Perspectives*. Retrieved from www.carnegiefoundation.org/perspectives/building-pedagogical-intelligence (accessed 16 January 2013).

Khalsa, S. (2013) Pedagogical intelligence. Retrieved from http://plsclasses.com/wp-content/uploads/2013/01/plsclasses_successful_teaching_for_acceptance_of_responsibility_online_syllabus_may_13.pdf (accessed 29th June 2013).

Kincheloe, J. (1999) 'The foundations of a democratic educational psychology.' In J. Kincheloe, S. Steinberg & L. Villaverde (eds.), *Rethinking Intelligence*. New York: Routledge. pp. 1–26.

Kincheloe, J., Steinberg, S. and Villaverde, L. (1999) *Rethinking Intelligence*. London: Routledge.

Leistyna, P. (1999) 'The personality vaccuum: Abstracting the social from the psychological.' In J. Kincheloe, S. Steinberg and E. Vialleton (eds.), *Rethinking Intelligence*. New York: Routledge. pp. 51–68.

Morris, C. and Le Blanc, R. (1996) Multiple intelligences: profiling dominant intelligences of grade eight students. *McGill Journal of Education*, 31 (2): 119–41.

New South Wales Institute of Teachers (2005) *Professional Teaching Standards*. Retrieved from www.nswteachers.nsw.edu.au/Main-Professional-Teaching-Standards/ (accessed 29 June 2013).

Ng, C.-H. (1998) I'm motivated because of who I am: the effects of domain specific self-schemas in students' learning engagement patterns. Paper presented at the Annual Conference of Australian Association for Reearch in Education, Adelaide. Australia.

Ng, C.-H. (2000) A cross cultural comparison of the effects of self schema on learning engagement. Paper presented at the Annual Conference of Australian Association for Research in Education.

Ng, C.-H. (2002) Relations between motivational goals, beliefs, strategy use and learning outcomes among university students in a distance learning mode: a longitudinal study. Paper presented at the AARE, Brisbane, Australia.

Noble, T. (2002) Blooming with multiple intelligences. A planning tool for curriculum differentiation. *Learning Matters*, 7 (3): 27–33.

Noble, T. and Grant, M. (1997) An interview with Howard Gardner. *EQ Australia*, 5 (1): 24–6.

Reese, A. (1998) Implications of results from cognitive science research for medical education. *Medical Education Online*, 3 (1). Retrieved 30th August 2013 from www.utmb.edu/meo/.

Shephard, P. (2001) *Brainworks: Whole Brain Thinking and Learning*. Malaysia: Brain Dominance Technologies Sdn Bhd.

Spearman, C. (1904) General intelligence: objectively determined and measured. *American Journal of Psychology*, 15 (2): 201–92.

Sternberg, R. (2004) Culture and intelligence. *American Psychologist*, 59 (5): 325–38.

Sternberg, R. and Kaufman, A.S. (2006) Human abilities. *Educational Theory*, 56 (1): 325–38.

Sternberg, R. and Williams, W. (1998) *Intelligence, Instruction and Assessment*. Mahwah, NJ: Lawrence Erlbaum Associates.

Sternberg, R., Forsythe, G., Hedlund, J., Horvath, J., Wagner, R., Williams, W., Snook, S. L. and Grigorenko, E. (2000) *Practical Intelligence in Everyday Life*. Cambridge: Cambridge University Press.

Stuss, D. and Levine, B. (2002) Adult clinical neuropsychology: lessons from studies of the frontal lobes. *Annual Review of Psychology*, 53: 401–33.

Styles, I. (1999) 'The study of intelligence – the interplay between theory and measurement.' In M. Anderson (ed.), *The Development of Intelligence*. Hove: Psychology Press. pp. 19–42.

Thurstone, L. (1938) *Primary Mental Abilities*. Chicago, IL: University of Chicago Press.

Wahl, M. (2002) Multiple intelligences power up math teaching Retrieved from www.reourcefulhomeschooler.com/files/MarkWahlMathArticle.html (accessed 29 April 2005).

Chapter 7: Emotional Intelligence

- Q1. What do you know about emotional intelligence?
- Q2. Does it sound like an important part of mental activity to you?
- Q3. Have you found any programmes used in schools to enhance emotional intelligence?
- Q4. Make a list of what you think emotional intelligence may be about.

Introduction

As you read in the previous chapter, the word 'intelligence' is currently used in the context of any mental activity that involves thinking and learning. You read that Guilford's understanding of intelligence (Barlow, 2000: 60; Guilford, 1967) included the capacity to receive information from the body language and expressions of others. This was considered to be an early understanding of emotional intelligence and the inclusion of this aspect of receiving information indicates how important the awareness of the emotional life of oneself and of others was considered to be in Guilford's theory of intelligence. Earlier chapters have also found that emotion and cognition are inextricably linked. The findings of neuroscientists confirmed that the brain and emotions were interdependent and the various pedagogical models based on constructivist theories of cognition emphasised the role of interest in the students' motivation to engage with learning tasks. The cognitive science perspective of cognition stresses that among all the stimuli that students encounter, it is the one that catches their interest that provides the trigger for learning. As a result, the emotional life of the students has a considerable impact on their learning and is an aspect of human cognition that you will need to consider when planning for learning with your students. The ways in which you interact with learners and the social culture that you develop in your classroom will depend on your personal capacity to be emotionally intelligent. Your capacity to maintain classroom harmony will also depend on your capacity to support your students in becoming emotionally intelligent, to encourage them to be socially appropriate in their interactions with you and with their peers and to be sensitive to the feelings and emotional lives of the individuals in your classroom community. An overview of the major theorists contributing to the body of work on emotional intelligence is provided below as there is substantial evidence that theories of emotional intelligence have impacted significantly in educational contexts (Fernandez and Extremera, 2006). What is important about all of these theories is that they all stem, in various degrees, from Gardner's (1993) understandings of knowledge of self and knowledge of others.

What Does the Literature Say about Emotional Intelligence?

It may be that the first name that comes to your mind when emotional intelligence is mentioned is that of Daniel Goleman (1995), who did much to popularise the idea of emotional intelligence almost two decades ago although not everyone was totally convinced of the value of the construct (Daus and Ashkanasy, 2003). However, as you will read, Goleman is not the only theorist who has an interest in emotional intelligence. He is joined by others whose work differs slightly in conceptual terms and who have developed widely different measures to assess their constructs (Conte, 2005). However, as Gardner's (1983b) Multiple Intelligences theory has had at least an initial impact on the development of the entire concept of emotional intelligence, most specifically his intrapersonal and interpersonal intelligence domains, it is important to preface the theories of emotional intelligence with some information about the constructs from which they were inspired.

Intrapersonal and interpersonal intelligences are known as Gardner's (1983a) 'personal intelligences'. Intrapersonal development, as expressed in the original edition of the 1983 text (pp. 239–40), is the capacity to know yourself in terms of your own emotions. It is accessed by looking inward to acknowledge and identify your personal feelings. It is the capability to distinguish between these feelings, name them and use them effectively to guide and inform personal behaviour. At its most sophisticated, it is described as the capacity to 'detect and to symbolise complex and highly differentiated sets of feelings' (Gardner, 1983a: 240). The other intelligence domain, inter-personal intelligence, requires you to look outwards and to 'notice and distin-guish between other individuals' (Gardner, 1983a: 240) and to most specifically attend to their feelings, their intentions, their moods and their motivations. In its most sophisticated form, this intelligence domain allows you to read and understand the temperaments, motivations and needs of others, even when these are not explicitly stated or made obvious in other ways. Interpersonal intelligence also allows you to act on this knowledge in order to plan or to determine your actions. Gardner (1983a) comments that these personal intel-ligences have much more varied capacities than any of the other intelligence domains. This is because they are socially constructed and understood. Each culture has its own symbol systems and codes of enculturation which are readily identifiable to the cultural participants of the society of origin but that may not be easily comprehended by members of other cultures or societal groups. Gardner (1983a) also identifies another difference between these intelligences and the others. He places the two personal intelligences together, although each has its own characteristics and 'neurological repre-sentations'. He does these explicitly to acknowledge the normal course of human development. It is unlikely that any human survives totally without human contact, irrespective of the degree of human interaction or the cultural climate and norms. Knowledge of self is therefore mediated and impacted upon by others in the context in which children are nurtured and socialised. It is the inclusion of these personal intelligences in a theory of cognition that caused other modern theorists to review their work on aspects of human nature and develop models of emotional intelligence.

Although influenced by Gardner's thinking about intelligence, Salovey and Mayer's (1990) original writing on emotional intelligence was indicative of the resurgence of interest in social intelligence by psychologists in the West-ernised countries. Historically, this concept was investigated by theorists such as Thorndike and Cronbach (Cronbach, 1960; Thorndike, 1920; Thorndike and Stein, 1937). Salovey and Mayer (1990) established a com-prehensive definition for emotions, describing them as interdisciplinary 'organised responses' that arise in response to events that are meaningful for the individual. The interdisciplinary nature of these responses as described by Salovey and Mayer (1990) was, at the time, understood as breaching the boundaries of seemingly separate psychological subsystems, including those that regulate cognition and motivation. This definition was important in reflecting the authors' interest in the relationship between cognition and emotion (Bryan, 2007; Mayer, 2004, 2005, n.d.; Mayer et al., n.d.; Mayer & Salovey, 1997). Integrating this notion of emotions with Wechsler's (1958) definition of intelligence, Salovey and Mayer (1990) labelled the set of skills that they hypothesised contributed to the appraisal, regulation and expression of the emotions of self and others as 'emotional intelligence'. This description was later clarified (Mayer and Salovey, 1997) and the emotional intelligence model developed by these theorists was then defined as:

> The capacity to reason about emotions, and of emotions to enhance thinking. It includes the abilities to accurately perceive emotions, to access and generate emotions so as to assist thought, to understand emotions and emotional knowledge, and to reflectively regulate emotions so as to promote emotional and intellectual growth. (Barlow, 2000: 60)

However, it was in their original writing that Salovey and Mayer (1990) provided a definitive explanation of the relationship between the work of Salovey and Mayer and that of Gardner (1983b), describing emotional intelligence as a 'part' or 'subset' of Gardner's personal intelligences (1983a). They portray emotional intelligence as 'quite close' to one aspect of Gardner's personal intelligences: that of the intrapersonal intelligence, as it was defined in the original edition of *Frames of Mind* (1983a: 239). In that edition, Gardner had written about intrapersonal intelligence in this way:

> The core capacity at work here is access to one's own feeling life – one's range of affects or emotions: the capacity instantly to effect discriminations among these feelings and, eventually, to label them, to enmesh them in symbolic codes, to draw upon them as a means of understanding and guiding one's behaviour. (Guilford, 1967: 5)

Coupled with interpersonal intelligence, this aspect of intrapersonal intelligence is a particularly important component of emotional intelligence. Salovey and Mayer (1990) acknowledge, however, that further aspects of intrapersonal intelligence that are identified by Gardner (1983a) in this first edition of his work on multiple intelligences are not included in their conceptual model of emotional intelligence. They had consciously excluded the aspects of intrapersonal intelligence that refer to an awareness of self in other dimensions and the capacity to use the knowledge that is the result of that awareness effectively in life to achieve personal goals. In this manner the emotional intelligence model they developed was influenced by Gardner's (1983a) theory of intrapersonal intelligence, but is neither synonymous with intrapersonal intelligence nor identical to Gardner's personal intelligence domains. In their later works on emotional intelligence Mayer and Salovey (Mayer & Salovey, 1997; Mayer et al., 2004) consistently acknowledge that their thinking on emotional intelligence was influenced by the psychologists seeking to broaden thinking about intelligence, especially those who developed theories of specific multiple intelligences, including Gardner (1983a, 1993, 1999a, 1999b).

The development of their four branch taxonomy of emotional intelligence skills and competencies continues to focus exclusively on emotions (Mayer and Salovey, 1997; Mayer, et al., 2004). The simplest is perceiving and the most complex, managing emotions.

- Perceiving emotions. This branch of the model indicates the need for individuals to understand emotions correctly in order to perceive them accurately. It includes the understanding of non-verbal emotional indicators such as facial expressions and body language.
- Reasoning with emotions. This branch of the model requires individuals to acknowledge the role of emotions in cognition and to have an understanding of the role of interest in triggering attention and engagement.
- Understanding emotions. This branch of the model explains that emotionally intelligent people, while the may perceive emotions expressed by others accurately, need to have an awareness of the wide range of possible meanings that these expressed emotions can have.
- Managing emotions. This branch of the model presents the most complex and sophisticated aspect of emotional intelligence. Emotionally intelligent people regulate their emotions appropriately in a variety of social contexts, in pursuit of their goals and in their interactions with others.

Salovey and Mayer (1990) have developed their own criteria that qualify emotional intelligence as a both a general intelligence theory and a development theory. However, unlike some other theorists, Mayer and Salovey (1997) do not explicitly place emphasis on skill development within social and cultural contexts. Admittedly, it would be rare for any individual to live without human contact or interaction with society, but to conclude, as they do, that the maturation process of emotional intelligence is determined by chronological age and not the quality of interaction and self reflection that the individual is engaged in is rather unusual, unless they are taking the social nature of humankind as understood, in which case it would be useful for them to have noted this premise.

What Does This Mean for You?

The important aspect of the various theories of emotional intelligence is the ways in which the authors connect emotion to cognition. This relates back to the findings of neuroscience discussed in a previous chapter. One of the major impacts of emotional intelligence education in schools is to facilitate improved learning outcomes for students. As you will read in this chapter, some theorists do not explicitly link their theory with cognition at all. If you select, or are required to work with a programme that supports emotional intelligence in the learning context, there are some questions that may need to be asked. Among these may be:

- Which theory of intelligence is this programme based on? This will allow you to understand how closely the principles of the programme parallel your

(Continued)

(Continued)

understanding of the brain and how it works. Identifying the foundational tenets of any programme will allow you to reference the original theory and assess how closely it relates to developing knowledge of self and of others.

- Whose standards, behaviours, attitudes and values are being reflected in these programmes? This is a topic for critical reflection and for you to examine your perspective on the purpose of schooling. As Gardner indicates, the intrapersonal and interpersonal intelligence domains are complex because they are socially and culturally mediated. As a result there are a number of inevitable variables.

As you read further, consider the issues in these questions and return to reflect on them.

- How might any programme relating to educating for emotional intelligence be implemented effectively in a class of culturally and socially diverse students?
- What may be the effect of implementing a programme designed to support emotional intelligence on your understanding of the student as an individual?
- Which would you envisage being more beneficial for students in all areas of their development: accurate self knowledge and the capacity to use this to achieve their goals coupled with an understanding of the attitudes, needs and perspectives of others, both spoken and unspoken, or the theory of emotional intelligence as developed by your selected theorist?
- Do you believe that all the above options have the same capacity to impact positively on your students' academic progress?
- Do you think that school culture (explicit and implicit), classroom culture and students' own social background have the potential to impact on what emotionally intelligent behaviour looks like?

Salovey and his colleagues are not alone, however, in their interests in emotional intelligence. Other well-known theorists include Bar-On (Bar-On et al., 2003; Bar-On and Parker, 2000) and, of course, Goleman (Boyatzis et al., 2000; Goleman, 1995), who have both developed theories of emotional intelligence. Goleman (1995) in particular did much to bring the notion of emotional intelligence to the notice of the general public. The initial chapters of Goleman's (1995) text were devoted to the current research findings of neuroscience and provided a great deal of information about how the brain works in a work designed for a wide-ranging audience. The subtitle of the text indicated that emotional intelligence ratings were more important for success than the intelligence (IQ) scores that were measured on psychometric tests such as those already discussed in the previous chapters. He also suggests that the more senior individuals become in their organisations, the more emotional intelligence competencies matter (Salopek and Goleman, 1998). A similar suggestion has been made in terms of school leadership, as it has been proposed that principals who have the task of reviving low-performing schools should have emotional intelligence criteria added to the list of required competencies (Cai, 2011). Goleman's theory is identified as the EI model and he has also developed an Emotional Intelligence Inventory. This inventory is detailed in Figure 7.1.

It has been suggested that the major notion contained in Goleman's (1995) theory was that emotional intelligence was demonstrated as the development of attitudes, values, behaviours and beliefs that reflected a specific type of society and culture. This could be summarised as the capacity to identify,

The self awareness cluster	Emotional awareness Accurate self assessment Self confidence
The self regulation cluster	Self control Trustworthiness Innovation Conscientiousness Adaptability
The motivation cluster	Achievement drive Commitment Optimism initiative
The empathy cluster	Understanding others Developing others Service orientation Leveraging diversity Political awareness
The social skills cluster	Influence Communication Conflict management Leadership Change catalyst Building bonds Collaboration and cooperation Team capabilities)

Figure 7.1   Goleman's Emotional Intelligence Inventory (adapted from Boyatzis et al., 2000: 4)

accept and conform to the status quo that was maintained by particular groups of individuals within which you hoped to be successful. However, the success of Goleman's text (1995) was, according to Mayer et al. (2000), not necessarily a result of the calibre of intellectual content, but the result of societal tensions at that time. The social climate to which they refer was caused by an issue that was dividing American society. Educationalists in North America at this time had reintroduced widespread national testing for students of specific ages and the results were subsequently being used to determine a wide range of evaluative statements about schools and school districts. Many perceived this initiative as a backward step. Freedman (n.d.) argued that the promotion of an intelligence, that anyone could have, that gave individuals the potential to overcome difficulties and promote greater success in a variety of learning and workplace contexts, came at a time when societal tensions rendered the public most susceptible to this notion, having undergone the revival of standardised testing during the late 1980s and 1990s.

Despite its wide public appeal, Goleman's initial work on emotional intelligence (1995) appears to have attracted a significant degree of academic criticism. Mayer, et al. (2000: 102) comment that 'at first it was presented as a journalistic account of our own theory', despite the resultant publication by Goleman containing significant differences to their work; most notably the absence of any attempt to develop or explore any relationship between emotion or cognition, which is a critical focus of the work of Salovey et al. (2004). Another issue centres around Goleman's (1995) reluctance to decide on a definition for emotional intelligence. While Gardner may have developed and refined the definition of intrapersonal intelligence (Gardner, 1983a, 1993, 1999a, 1999b; Moran and Gardner, 2007) over a period of many years and as the result of reflection, Goleman's definition 'snowballed' within the text until the traits included in his final definition were described by Mayer et al. as encompassing 'the entire model of how one operates in the world' (Mayer et al., 2000: 101–2). Gardner (Noble and Grant, 1997) also appears to have some problems with Goleman's model of emotional intelligence, while acknowledging that the theory had its source in his own work on multiple intelligences (1983a):

> Interpersonal and intrapersonal intelligences add up to Dan Goleman's emotional intelligence. But I think he goes on to talk about other things like having a certain stance on life ... My major quibble with his book is that he kind of collapses description and prescription ... I think that Dan wants people to be a certain way ... (Gardner quoted in Noble and Grant, 1997: 24–6)

This comment illustrates that Gardner himself has some problems with Goleman's (1995) model of emotional intelligence, and the most significant of these is that this model goes beyond the boundaries of Gardner's own understanding of the personal intelligences, which are part of a theory of cognition. It is possible that the prescriptive nature of Goleman's work actually places boundaries on the potential of individuals to develop these intelligences and that it may even promote a type of homogeneity that is contrary to Gardner's emphasis on the need to find personal meaning and understanding in life. While Gardner's (1983a, 1993, 1999a, 1999b) intrapersonal intelligence domain requires individuals to express their intrapersonal capacities as the skills of executive function, which will be discussed in detail in a later chapter, the most critical objection of Goleman's (1995) theory of emotional intelligence appears to be the need for individuals to conform to a particular perspective of life that is the most socially acceptable. This is at the heart of Gardner's comment. The author of the third most prominent theory of emotional intelligence has not explicitly referred to his work as a derivative or development of Gardner's multiple intelligences theory, but there appear to be several indications that Bar-On (1997) was at least cognisant with Gardner's theory.

Bar-On's (1997) emotional intelligence theory is also problematic for several reasons. These include the use of the terms that are normally associated with Gardner's (1983a, 1993, 1999a, 1999b) intrapersonal intelligence and the total exclusion of any cognitive traits. Bar-On's definition (1997: 14) of emotional intelligence is similar to Goleman's in that it is an extensively inclusive collection of non-cognitive traits. Bar-On defines emotional intelligence as 'an array of non-cognitive capabilities, competencies and skills that influence one's ability to succeed in coping with environmental demands and pressures'. The Bar-On model (1997) can be divided into two main parts. The first part is his theory of emotional–social intelligence and the second part is the psychometric scale which is his measure of emotional–social intelligence, which was based on his theory and designed to assess his specific model. These two aspects of the model have also been referred to as (a) the Bar-On conceptual model of emotional–social intelligence and (b) the Bar-On psychometric model of emotional–social intelligence, while (c) the Bar-On model of emotional–social intelligence refers to both the conceptual and the psychometric aspects of this model combined into one entity. Using an analysis of his own self reporting scale, the value of which is disputed by others in the field (Mayer et al., n.d.) but affirmed by the evaluative study conducted by Dawda and Hart (2000) and others (Fletcher et al., 2009), Bar-On has developed five categories of competencies, each containing a number of facets that characterise that particular aspect of his (1997) theory of emotional intelligence. These are detailed in Figure 7.2.

Intrapersonal component (capacity for self awareness and self expression)	Self Regard (being aware of, understanding and accepting ourselves as individuals) Emotional Self Awareness (being aware of and understanding our emotions) Assertiveness (expressing our feelings and ourselves in a non-destructive manner) Independence (being self reliant and free of excessive emotional dependency on others) Self Actualization (the capacity for setting and achieving goals to realise our potential)
Interpersonal component (capacity to socialize with and understand others)	Empathy (being aware of and understanding how others feel) Social Responsibility (identifying with and feeling a sense of belonging with larger groups of people) Interpersonal Relationship (establishing and maintaining mutually satisfying relationships)
Stress management	Stress Tolerance (effectively and constructively managing our emotions with regard to stressful situations or contexts) Impulse Control (effectively and constructively controlling and monitoring our emotions)
Change management	Reality Testing (validating our feelings and thinking objectively about reality) Flexibility (coping with and adapting to minor and significant life changes) Problem Solving (generating effective solutions to problems of a personal nature or in relationships with others)
General mood	Optimism (having a positive outlook and looking at the brighter side of life) Happiness (feeling content with ourselves, others and life in general)

Figure 7.2   Bar-On's Emotional Intelligence Theory (adapted from Bar-On, 1997)

This represents a very different view of intrapersonal intelligence from that defined and redefined by Gardner (1983a, 1993, 1999a, 1999b; Moran and Gardner, 2007). While the intrapersonal and interpersonal components of Bar-On's emotional intelligence have similar titles to Gardner's 'personal intelligences', they are very different in nature and, once again, do not form part of a theory of cognition, despite the neurological relationship of emotion and cognition and some attempts to highlight the relationship (Bryan, 2007) and use the terms interchangeably (Ellison, 1992, 2001).

Like Goleman's work, Bar-On's model of emotional intelligence has been understood to be simply a renaming of personality theories and research (Mayer et al., 2000). Mayer et al. (2000: 103) 'take issue' with theories that are relabelling all the parts of personality as emotional intelligence and comment that these theories have moved significantly away from their base – which was Gardner' s intrapersonal and interpersonal intelligence domains.

In doing so, they have widened the gap between intrapersonal intelligence (Gardner, 1983a, 1993, 1999a, 1999b; Moran and Gardner, 2007), and theories of emotional intelligence that have no relationship to cognition. This is despite the fact that the capacities to understand one's emotions and generate them to support more effective thinking are integral to sound intrapersonal intelligence (Gardner, 1983a, 1993, 1999a, 1999b; Moran and Gardner, 2007), especially in the component of executive function identified by Moran and Gardner (2007) as the 'will' or motivational aspects of cognitive capacities. Emotional intelligence theories, therefore, although remaining conceptually linked to intrapersonal intelligence (Gardner, 1983a, 1993, 1999a, 1999b; Moran and Gardner, 2007), have developed and evolved in a direction that is significantly different to that taken by Gardner.

Questions for Reflection

- Q1. What do think of the usefulness of these theories of emotional intelligence?
- Q2. Why do you think they are so popular in industry and in education?
- Q3. Do you think that strong emotional intelligence can promote or facilitate academic success, directly or indirectly?
- Q4. Are there any aspects of any one of the theories that you feel would be beneficial for you to promote in your classroom to develop a community of successful learners?
- Q5. Are there any aspects of the theories that were described in detail that you feel are embedded in prescribed curricula for your class?
- Q6. Are there any aspects of the theories that were described in detail that you feel you would like to find embedded in prescribed curricula for your class?
- Q7. Does anything in the emotional intelligence theories presented cause you to be concerned as an educator?
- Q8. What do you think of Goleman's statement that EQ (emotional quotient) can actually matter more than IQ (intelligence quotient)? Validate your perspective.

Implications for Teaching

There has been considerable interest in emotional intelligence since its initial appearance in the 1990s (Elias and Arnold, 2006). Studies continue to be conducted and measures of emotional intelligence developed and tested for validity. Many of these are conducted in organisational contexts where emotional intelligence has gained great popularity (Ashkanasy and Daus, 2005). So, while not all of these described briefly here are implemented in educational settings, the findings of these studies may be of interest to educators. Brackett et al. (2006) found in one of their studies that there are gender differences in the perceptions of emotional intelligence, with self reporting males more accurately assessing their degrees of emotional intelligence competencies than their female counterparts. Cherniss (2000) discusses why emotional intelligence matters in the workplace in the current climate of rapid, substantial change. His reasoning could also be applied to educational contexts where teachers are facing substantial changes to the identity and professional work. In a study of the emotional intelligence capacities of adolescents entering a private boarding school, it was found that the male students who lacked emotional intelligence exhibited the most disturbing behaviours (Erasmus, 2007). These included depression and sleeplessness, which not only impacted on the students' dispositions, but also on their academic progress. Another school-based study of the relationships between emotion-based perceptions of self efficacy and academic achievement of 565 students in their first six years of schooling offers interesting findings (Mavroveli and Sánchez-Ruiz, 2011). The researchers concluded that although the correlations between the emotion-based perceptions of students' self efficacy in 8-year-olds and their academic achievement was 'modest', emotion-based self efficacy was an important construct with many possible advantages for the socialisation of students in primary schools. They also found that emotion-based self efficacy scores were significantly lower for students with special educational needs. This may be interesting for educationalists, especially when combined with the findings of another study (Ciarrochi et al., 2000), this time conducted with Australian undergraduate participants, which found that although no correlation between IQ and emotional intelligence could be established, a certain degree of general intelligence was needed to correctly interpret and understand the emotional intelligence process. Others studies did find a firm relationship between academic achievement and emotional intelligence in year eleven students in the US (AbiSamra, 2000).

Qualter et al. (2007) investigated students who were transitioning from primary school to secondary school. They found that students with high levels of emotional intelligence coped better and fewer concerns were displayed regarding their home study and their classroom achievements and behaviours. They also found that an intervention programme designed to support higher levels of emotional intelligence for the students who initially attained low scores on the measures of emotional intelligence achieved some success. Similar results were found in a another study implemented in comparable circumstances (Parker et al., 2004), which focused on the academic achievement of students transitioning from primary schools to secondary school. Saklofske et al. (2007) studied the possible relationship between student's wellbeing and coping strategies in a Canadian secondary school. They found that emotional intelligence both facilitated and provided successful coping strategies, along with the students' tendencies towards the consumption of healthy foods and regular exercise.

A strong case for including emotional and social learning in school can be based on a number of compelling arguments that incorporate diverse perspectives related to the importance of inclusion of emotional learning in school curricula (Zins et al., 2004). Among the major arguments is the acknowledgement of schools as social places and of the learning process as social interaction that is a consequence of compulsory schooling. As a result of this, there are subsequent disadvantages suffered by students who are not able to interact successfully (Zins et al., 2004). McCombs (2004: 23) comments on the 'unacceptably high' rates of school violence, bullying, school dropout, youth suicide and other negative behaviours and the resultant negative impacts on the entire school communities. She suggests that schools need to build appropriate frameworks of supporting social and emotional learning that can be openly embraced by all students and not just the less academic students with whom programmes of this nature are commonly associated. Christenson and Havsy (2004: 60) also comment on the high percentage of school dropout in American schools, citing the disparities between students' lives in their 'multiple worlds' and their limited capacities to cope with these. They suggest that students who dropout:

> demonstrate the most extreme form of disengagement. They are more likely to have exhibited behaviour and disciplinary problems, poor attendance, low motivation to succeed, low aspirations for academic achievement, poor self concept, an external locus of control and alienation from school.

Weare (2004) suggests that traditionally many Western cultures are afraid of emotion, to the detriment of student learning and inclusion in the social nature of learning itself and of the school community in general. She outlines strategies for using students' emotional lives to enhance and enrich their academic understandings and growth, their self regulatory skills, autonomy and sense of belonging. Johnson and Johnson (2004), in discussing the lifelong importance of developing sensitivity to one's own and others' emotional lives, suggest that all programmes for supporting social and emotional learning should incorporate three major themes. They identify these as students developing competencies in (i) engaging in and sustaining cooperative experiences, (ii) utilising non-aggressive strategies for conflict resolution, and (iii) attending to and internalising civic values.

What Does This Mean for You?

If you look at Johnson and Johnson's suggestion and work to develop your classroom culture around these themes, your classroom environment and planned implementation would have several distinctive features in addition to the types of interaction that took place. These may include:

- Plans for substantial discussion time.
- Details of teams or groups who regularly work together productively.
- Resources. These can include narratives, songs and film. Commonly found are posters, reminders, cartoons of what students can do if ... These would include strategies for managing strong negative emotions such as the thermometer that indicates if you are annoyed, and a specific coping strategy. The pattern then continues towards the more intense emotions, each with a strategy to help students cope. Many of these suggestions might come from the students themselves as the result of your planning in the next activity.
- Planned role play on a regular basis. Students can act out a variety of experiences and aggressive responses in small groups or pairs. Everyone joins in to provide strategies for better, fairer or less aggressive solutions. These then become the strategies that are explicitly discussed in relation to the behaviours and taught as alternative ways of coping with these emotions in the students themselves or in others. There are several resources available that can be used to support these activities, depending on the age of your students. There are pictures expressly designed to help younger students develop the language they need to identify and discuss their emotions.
- Explicit strategies and resources to develop an awareness and common understanding of the nature of civic values. Depending on the age of the students, this may include visits from service organisation personnel who help others as their occupation, visits to hospitals, nursing homes to engage in specific activities and so on. Agreed definitions of respect, care and other selected civic values join the other resources on the walls along with examples of how these may be demonstrated in the classroom community.
- Positive sayings, mottos and other resources that indicate or illustrate the positive impact of getting along, working collaboratively, learning from each other and helping each other.
- Understanding the potential for emotional learning from real characters in history and in literature and even from fictional or fantasy characters. Given (2002) comments on some strategies used in various schools to support the development of strong emotional learning. These included implementation of curricula rich in personal relevance which allow students to explore the

feelings of others without having to relate a personal story. She indicates that activities such as these help heal hurt and facilitate a healthy understanding of feelings and emotions while focusing on a story character. This maintains a safe emotional distance for the students while helping them understand their own and others' feelings in various circumstances.

- Responding to the different emotional pressures of diverse environments, Given (2002) also describes how teachers in some schools develop their students' emotional learning by examining the environments they frequently find troublesome. She describes how one teacher asked her students to draw a plan of the school, indicate on it where they most often got into trouble or were upset, and then supported the students' investigations of the particular characteristics of the context or the specific type of interactions that the students engaged in when at these particular places.

Lopes et al. (2003) focus on the benefits of social and emotional learning to enhance the capacity of young people to emotionally adapt to the increasingly rapid rate of change in the society in which they will become adults. They assert that changes in curriculum and pedagogy can support students and impact positively on their social and emotional capacities. It is for this purpose also that Fleming and Bay (2004) argue that teaching standards need to incorporate social and emotional learning for aspiring teachers in each of the following areas:

- How they interpret and teach content knowledge.
- How they understand human development and the stages of learning.
- How to understand and cope effectively with diversity.
- What they consider in their planning for teaching.
- How they develop the inclusive learning environments they provide for their students.
- How to monitor their pedagogical practices in order to allow for students to take responsibility for their learning.
- How they communicate effectively with their students to facilitate student self awareness and executive function skills.
- How they assess authentically using a variety of techniques and involving student input.
- How they communicate with and develop positive, collaborative relationships with students, parents and caregivers and the wider community. This includes strategies designed to develop, manage and model collaborative relations with colleagues, parents and community to promote effective learning climates and school ethos.

- At what levels aspiring teachers engage in reflective practice to determine, individually and with colleagues, the impact their decisions and choices have on students and communities.
- Maintaining standards of professional conduct, taking initiative and demonstrating leadership skills.

What Does This Mean for You?

If research indicates that studies in emotional intelligence help students cope with change and adapt more readily to new demands and contexts, then it is likely that you will have an opportunity to work with this construct in some way with your students. The suggested changes recommended by Fleming and Bay may or may not become a part of newly developed standards in an explicit manner but they are already implicit in your professional and ethical work. Because of this it may be useful to expand their ideas and the implications for you. These include:

- Developing a high degree of sensitivity towards how you understand present curriculum content requires you to be particularly insightful about any opinions, prejudices or bias you may have around the subject matter itself. This can mean having a controversial view on a topic, avoiding teaching anything that is not clear to you or with which you do not agree or simply not teaching enthusiastically because you may not feel accomplished in that particular area. It is not anticipated that you are 'objective' but it would be expected that you reflect on and assess your personal approach to implementing the curriculum with regard to the emotional and academic needs of your students.
- Understanding stages of development and how these impact on students' capacities to learn various concepts and respond in specific ways is integral to your success as a teacher. If you look back to your reading on the findings of neuroscience, you will find useful information about listeners, visual representations and kinaesthetic activity. In the chapter on learning developmental stages many types of thinking are discussed. At different stages of development students are able to listen differently and for longer or shorter periods of time and this may not always be age-related. Some students are genuinely able to understand someone else's perspective at a younger age than others. Much of the social understanding that is expected at school is impacted upon quite substantially by a number of variables not related to chronological age.
- Understanding and planning for diversity is the sole topic of Chapter 10 and requires much self reflection. For example, with good intentions you may feel that the sooner students settle into the dominant culture the better they will be, but in reality is this an ethically sound opinion?

- What you consider in your planning for teaching is directly related to the first criterion and is clearly significant as the decisions you make as a teacher regarding your pedagogical strategies, attitudes and implementation of planning have a huge impact on your students.
- Your interactions with your students mirror your emotional intelligence in many ways. How you structure your class rules and enforce them, how you view the triadic ethics components and prioritise the aspect of consistency, care and consequences for each individual case is important to your class culture. The language, intonation and non-verbal communications you use with your students also serve as a model for how they might treat each other and is a professional issue for reflection. The degree of attention you pay in your planning to giving your students choices, listening to their perspectives in a non-judgemental manner and using strategies that facilitate student ownership of their work and opportunities to self regulate indicates to them your understanding of teachers' work and the degree to which you personally need to be authoritarian.
- Your assessment tasks need to be designed to allow students to show what they can do and what is important to them, not just give the correct answers to what you think is important about the topic. This demonstrates your sensitivity to the frustration of students who have different opinions, knowledge and interests and how you might honour this in a professional manner.
- Communicating respectfully is often the key to developing sound relationships with parents and communities, irrespective of the purpose of the communication. It may be difficult to understand or even value the opinion that others have of your work, your school or your colleagues but it is important to recognise these and deal with them in appropriate ways, even when you cannot professionally defer to them.
- Needing the skills to think purposefully about the professional decisions you make and how these impact on your students, their parents and the wider community.
- Retaining your professional integrity in your actions, responses and engaging authentically with all of the other criteria. You would also have to demonstrate the innovation, negotiation skills, empathy and initiative that characterises good leadership either as a classroom leader or as a school or department leader.

This interest in emotional intelligence by diverse sections of the educational community has led to the development of a wide range of resources for use with students or simply by students in schools to help develop their emotional intelligence competencies. These resources are often marketed as social–emotional teaching and learning resources and cover a wide range of topics that can be associated with the diverse models of emotional intelligence. Some suggest ways in which technology can be utilised to enhance emotional intelligence, either directly or indirectly by differentiating the curriculum appropriately in order to promote students' improved academic success and, indirectly, their emotional intelligence (Furger, 2001). It appears that emotional intelligence is even considered to be an appropriate area for inclusion in school curricula (Six Seconds, 2007) and there are even suggestions that if emotional intelligence learning is not able to be taught in the classroom then it can be facilitated in school 'spaces' by making suitable mentors available to students during their breaks from class. New models of emotional intelligence are being developed for use with students in schools (Low et al., 2004) and there are many websites that discuss emotional intelligence in terms of student well-being and scholarly success and recommend programmes suitable for pre-school and nursery-aged children in addition to those developed for use with primary and secondary students (for example Vinando, 2012). Other websites discuss the programmes that have been customised and implemented in specific schools as after-school programmes and give details of the impact of their instruction (for example Wings Team, n.d.) or as part of their curriculum studies (Low and Nelson, n.d.). Many other resources discuss strategies for developing specific attributes that are aspects of or associated with emotional intelligence, such as activities for discussion and strategies to promote support the development of student resilience (for example McGrath and Noble, 2003) and texts that contain material that can support teachers and learners to develop positive relationships and engage with empathetic pedagogy (Arnold, 2005).

Questions for Reflection

- Q1. Do you think that social and emotional learning can impact positively on academic achievement? Validate your answer.
- Q2. What do you think about the research findings that focused on emotional intelligence?
- Q3. Why might it be really difficult to conduct authentic research on a construct such as this?
- Q4. What do you think of the three themes that Johnson and Johnson have identifies as essentials of any social and emotional learning programme for students? Do these bring to mind any ethical concerns or criticism of Goleman's theory of emotional intelligence?

- Q5. Can you find, in your professional standards, the aspects of professional work that Fleming and Bay identify as elements within which social and emotional learning should be incorporated?
- Q6. What do you think of their suggestion? Would social and emotional learning help you as a pre-service teacher to undertake your work and improve your performance in these professional elements more effectively? Validate your answer
- Q7. Would you like to have social and emotional aspects of the standards included in your teacher preparation courses? Validate your answer.
- Q8. Emotional and social learning is all about being nice to everyone, not causing any trouble or controversy and accepting the school or workplace customs, values or ways of operating. Critically discuss and reflect. Validate your answer.

Scenario Seven

Bradley was a charming student. He had only one year of high school to complete and was a close contender for election as school captain. He was much admired by the younger students as a competent sportsman and by the staff as a polite, dutiful and conscientious student. He had represented his prestigious school on several occasions as captain of the debating team and as a member of several sports teams. He was always cheerful and cooperative. He impressed others as an atypical teenage boy as he appeared mature and wise beyond his years. He frequently helped his form master with his computer problems and that is how he gained access to the end of year exam results, even though he should not have had access to his form master's password. Realising that his marks were not as good as he had hoped and may exclude him from the school captaincy, Bradley changed his scores to reflect the marks he felt he would have got if he had studied harder. He reasoned that he was hurting no one and doing no actual damage. The exam results were processed on to the end of year reports without any incident, printed and sent home to parents. The staff met, as usual, to discuss the appointment of the school captains and the principal distributed profiles of the candidates. Glancing over the profiles, the form master was surprised to see Bradley's profile in front of him. He was even more surprised to see the exam results that had been recorded for him, simply because as the marks came in, he distinctly recalled that Bradley's marks were disappointing and that he would almost certainly not be

(Continued)

(Continued)

considered for the school captaincy as a result. He realised that Bradley must have taken the opportunity, when he helped with his new software, to gain access to the results files and alter his marks. No one else had access to his computer. What was he to do now? The reports had gone out to parents; if he argued against Bradley's appointment it would be very suspicious as he was the one who had suggested him in the first place. He was thinking what he could possibly do when he realised that Bradley's profile was up for discussion next ...

Questions for Reflection

- Q1. What is the problem for Bradley's form master – after all, he was the person who nominated Bradley for consideration for the captaincy?
- Q2. What are his options for action?
- Q3. What would you do? Why?
- Q4. Do you think that Bradley has a high degree of social and emotional intelligence? Why?
- Q5. Do you think that Bradley would make a good school captain and represent the school well?
- Q6. Do you think that Bradley should be considered for the captaincy? Why? Or why not?
- Q7. Do you think your social and emotional intelligence impacts on your reflection in this case study?
- Q8. What do you think about Bradley's degree of self knowledge?
- Q9. Given Bradley's character in general, is this something he may typically do?
- Q10. Do you think that Bradley's form master was jumping to conclusions? Validate your answer.

Conclusion

In this chapter you have had the opportunity to become familiar with the major theories related to the construct of emotional intelligence. You have read how persuasively some theorists have presented strong emotional intelligence as a vital criterion for becoming successful in any context, not just in education. The impact of the research and study of emotional intelligence and its potential to improve some aspects of schooling for a diverse cohort have also been presented. Bearing in mind the importance that neuroscientific research has had on your understanding of the ways in which the brain works – the impact of emotion on cognition – you are now challenged to consider these models in terms of the ethical considerations that were presented in an earlier chapter, the understanding of how learning actually occurs, the social constructive theory of teaching and learning, and the notions that you have personally regarding the nature of intelligence. You are also challenged to evaluate these emotional intelligence models in terms of how you might usefully employ some of these ideas to support your students' academic and social outcomes and to improve your understanding of various aspects of your professional practice, including how you might interpret and implement the requirements of mandatory standards and other professional documents. You may also wish to assess any aspects of emotional intelligence that are explicit or implicit in the suggestions and discussions presented in the following chapters.

References

AbiSamra, N. (2000) The relationship between emotional intelligence and academic achievement in eleventh graders Retrieved from http://meltingpot.fortunecity.com/zaire/131/research-intell2.html (accessed 9 June 2002).

Arnold, R. (2005) *Empathic intelligence: Teaching, learning and relating.* Sydney: University of New South Wales Press Ltd.

Ashkanasy, N. and Daus, C. (2005) Rumours of the death of emotional intelligence in organizational behaviour are vastly exaggerated. *Journal of Organizational Behaviour*, 26 (4): 441–52.

Bar-On, R. (1997) *Bar-On Emotional Quotient Inventory: Technical Manual.* Toronto: Multi-Health Systems.

Bar-On, R. and Parker, J. (eds.) (2000) *The Handbook of Emotional Intelligence.* San Francisco: Jossey-Bass.

Bar-On, R., Tranel, D., Denburg, N. and Bechara, A. (2003) Exploring the neurological substrate of emotional and social intelligence. *Brain*, 126 (8): 1790–1800.

Barlow, C. (2000) *Guildford' structure of the intellect.* Retrieved from http://www.cocreativity.com/handouts/guilford.pdf (accessed 1st September 2013).

Boyatzis, R., Goleman, D., and Rhee, K. (2000) 'Clustering competence in emotional intelligence: Insights from the emotional competence inventory (ECI).' In R. Bar-On and J.D.A. Parker (eds), *Handbook of Emotional Intelligence.* San Francisco: Jossey Bass. pp. 343–462.

Brackett, M., Rivers, S., Shiffman, S., Lerner, N. and Salovey, P. (2006) Relating emotional abilities to social functioning: a comparison of self-report and performance measures of emotional intelligence. *Journal of Personality and Social Psychology*, 91 (4): 780–95.

Bryan, S. (2007) Emotional intelligence and intrapersonal conversations. Paper presented at the 3rd European Conference on Management Leadership and Governance, University of Winchester UK, 19–20 April.

Cai, Q. (2011) Can principals' emotional intelligence matter to school turnarounds? *International Journal of Leadership in Education*, 14 (2): 151–79.

Cherniss, C. (2000) Emotional intelligence: What it is and why it matters. Paper presented at the Annual Meeting of the Society for Industrial and Organizational Psychology, New Orleans, USA.

Christenson, S., & Havsy, L. (2004) 'Family -school- peer relationships: significance for social, emotional and academic learning.' In J. Zins, R. Weissberg, M. Wang & H. Walberg (eds), *Building Academic Success on Social and Emotional Learning*. New York: Teachers College Press.

Ciarrochi, J., Chan, A. and Caputi, P. (2000) A critical evaluation of the emotional intelligence construct. *Personality and Individual Differences*, 28 (3): 539–61.

Conte, J. (2005) A review and critique of emotional intelligence measures. *Journal of Organizational Behavior*, 26 (4): 433–40.

Cronbach, L. (1960) *Essentials of Psychological Testing*, 2nd edn. New York: Harper and Row.

Daus, C. and Ashkanasy, N. (2003) Will the real emotional intelligence please stand up? On deconstructing the emotional intelligence. 'Debate' retrieved from http://eqi.org/real_ei.htm (accessed 15 December 2005).

Dawda, D. and Hart, S. (2000) Assessing emotional intelligence: reliability and validity of the Bar-On Emotional Quotient Inventory (EQ-i) in university students. *Personality and Individual Differences*, 28 (4): 797–812.

Elias, M.J. and Arnold, H. (eds) (2006) *The Educator's Guide to Emotional Intelligence and Academic Achievement*. Thousand Oaks, CA: Corwin Press.

Ellison, L. (1992) Using multiple intelligences to set goals. *Educational Leadership*, 50 (2): 69–72.

Ellison, L. (2001) *The Personal Intelligences: Promoting Social and Eemotional Learning*. New York: Corwin Press.

Erasmus, C. (2007) The role of emotional intelligence in the adaptation of adolescent boys in a private school. Unpublished Thesis for Master of Education with specialisation in guidance and counselling, University of South Africa.

Fernandez, B. and Extremera, N. (2006) Special issue on emotional intelligence: an overview. *Psicothema*, 18 (Suplemento): 1–6.

Fleming, J., and Bay, M. (2004) Social and emotional learning in teacher preparation standards. In J. Zins, R. Weissberg, M. Wang & H. Walberg (eds), *Building Academic Success on Social and Emotional Learning*. New York: Teachers College Press. pp. 94–111.

Fletcher, I., Leadbetter, P., Curran, A. and O'Sullivan, H. (2009) A pilot study assessing emotional intelligence training and communication skills with 3rd year medical students. *Patient Education and Counseling*, 76 (3): 376–9.

Freedman, J. (undated) Have the originators of EI missed the point of their own research? Part 1: The problem. Retrieved 15th December 2005 from www.unh.edu/emotional_intelligence/ei%20Controversies/eicontroversy%20missed

Furger, R. (2001) Digital technology: tools to enhance emotional intelligence. Retrieved from www.edutopia.org/digital-technology-tools-help-enhance-emotional-intelligence (accessed 19 October 2012).

Gardner, H. (1983a) *Frames of Mind*, 1st edn. London: William Heinemann Ltd.

Gardner, H. (1983b) *Frames of Mind: The Theory of Multiple Intelligences*. New York: Basic Books.

Gardner, H. (1993) *Frames of Mind. Tenth Anniversary Edition*. New York: Basic Books.

Gardner, H. (1999a) *The Disciplined Mind. What All Students Should Understand*. New York: Simon & Shuster.

Gardner, H. (1999b) *Intelligence Reframed: Multiple Intelligences for the 21st Century*. New York: Basic Books.

Given, B. (2002) *Teaching to the Brain's Natural Learning Systems*. Alexandria, VA: Association for Supervision and Curriculum Development.

Goleman, D. (1995) *Emotional Intelligence*. New York: Bantam Books.

Guilford, J. (1967) *The Nature of Human Intelligence*. New York: McGraw-Hill.

Johnson, D., and Johnson, R. (2004) 'The three Cs of promoting social and emotional learning.' In J. Zins, R. Weissberg, M. Wang & H. Walberg (eds), *Building Academic Success on Social and Emotional Learning*. New York: Teachers College Press. pp. 76–102.

The Jossey Bass Reader on the Brain and Learning (2008) San Francisco: Jossey Bass.

Lopes, P.N., Salovey, P. and Straus, R. (2003) Emotional intelligence, personality, and the perceived quality of social relationships. *Personality and Individual Differences*, 35 (3): 641–58. doi:10.1016/s0191-8869(02)00242-8

Low, G. and Nelson, D. (n.d.) Emotional intelligence: effectively bridging the gap between high school and college. Retrieved from www.prenhall.com/success/FacultyRes/emotional. html (accessed 5 July 2013).

Low, G., Lomax, A., Jackson, M. and Nelson, D. (2004) Emotional intelligence: a new student development model. Paper presented at the National Conference of the American College Personnel Association, Philadelphia, PA.

Mavroveli, S. and Sánchez-Ruiz, M. (2011) Trait emotional intelligence influences on academic achievement and school behaviour. *British Journal of Educational Psychology*, 81 (1): 112–34.

Mayer, J. (2004) A classification system for the data of personality psychology and adjoining fields. *Review of General Psychology*, 8 (3): 208–19.

Mayer, J. (2005) A tale of two visions. Can a new view of personality help integrate psychology? *American Psychologist*, 60 (4): 294–307.

Mayer, J. (n.d.) How does this model compare to other approaches to emotional intelligence? Retrieved from www.unh.edu/emotional_intelligence/ei%20Waht%20is%20EI/ei%20 model%20co (accessed 10 January 2006).

Mayer, J. and Salovey, P. (1997) 'What is emotional intelligence?' In P. Salovey and D. Sluyter (eds), *Emotional Development and Emotional Intelligence*. New York: Basic Books. pp. 3–37.

Mayer, J., Carrochi, J. and Michela, J. (n.d.) Can self report measures contribute to the measurement of emotional intelligence? Retrieved from www.unh.edu/emotional_intelligence/ ei%20Controversies/eicontrovery%20why% (accessed 15 December 2005).

Mayer, J., Salovey, P. and Caruso, D. (2000) Emotional intelligence, as zeitgeist, as personality, and as a mental ability. In R. Bar-On and J. Parker (eds.), *The Handbook of Emotional Intelligence*. San Francisco: Jossey-Bass. pp. 92–117.

Mayer, J., Salovey, P. and Caruso, D. (2004) Emotional intelligence: theory, findings and implications. *Psychological Inquiry*, 15 (3): 197–215.

McCombs, B. (2004) 'The learner-centered psychological principles: a framework for balancing academic achievement and social-emotional learning outcomes.' In J. Zins, R. Weissberg, M. Wang & H. Walberg (eds), *Building Academic Success on Social and Emotional Learning*. New York: Teachers College Record Press. pp. 23–39.

McGrath, H. and Noble, T. (2003) *Bounce Back! Classroom Resiliency Program*. Sydney: Pearson Education.

Moran, S. and Gardner, H. (2007) '"Hill, skill and will": Executive function from a multiple-intelligences perspective.' In L. Meltzer (ed.), *Executive Function in Education: From Theory to Practice*. New York: Guilford Press. pp. 19–38.

Noble, T. and Grant, M. (1997) An interview with Howard Gardner. *EQ Australia*, 5 (1): 24–26.

Parker, J.D.A., Summerfeldt, L.J., Hogan, M.J. and Majeski, S.A. (2004) Emotional intelligence and academic success: examining the transition from high school to university. *Personality and Individual Differences*, 36 (1): 163–72.

Qualter, P., Whiteley, H., Hutchinson, J. and Pope, D. (2007) Supporting the development of emotional intelligence competencies to ease the transition from primary to high school. *Education Psychology in Practice*, 23 (1): 79–95.

Saklofske, D., Austin, E., Galloway, J. and Davidson, K. (2007) Individual difference correlates of health-related behaviours: preliminary evidence for links between emotional intelligence and coping. *Personality and Individual Differences*, 42 (3): 491–502.

Salopek, J. and Goleman, D. (1998) Train your brain. *Training and Development*, 52 (10): 26–35.

Salovey, P. and Mayer, J. (1990) *Emotional Intelligence*. Amityville, NY: Baywood Publishing.

Salovey, P., Caruso, D. and Mayer, J. (2004) 'Emotional intelligence in practice.' In P. Lindsay & S. Joseph (eds.), *Positive Psychology in Practice*. Hoboken, NJ: John Wiley and Sons. pp. 447–63.

Six Seconds. (2007) *A Case for Emotional Intelligence in Our Schools*. Retrieved from www.6seconds.com.au/pdf/Case-for-EQ-in-Our-Schools-au.pdf (accessed 5 July 2013). Bloomington IN: Solution Tree Press.

Thorndike, E. (1920) Intelligence and its uses. *Harpers Magazine*, 140, 227–35.

Thorndike, E. and Stein, S. (1937) An evaluation of the attempts to measure social intelligence. *Psychological Bulletin*, 34: 275–84.

Vinando, Y. (2012) Social and emotional learning programs for schools. Retrieved from www.happychild.com.au/articles/social-and-emotional-learning-programs-for-schools (accessed 19 October 2012).

Weare, K. (2004) *Developing the Emotionally Literate School*. London: Paul Chapman Publishing.

Wechsler, D. (1958) *The Measurement and Appraisal of Adult Intelligence*, 4th edn. Baltimore, MD: Williams and Wilkins.

Wings Team (n .d.) Wings: helping kids soar. Retrieved from www.wingsforkids.org/about-us/what-is-wings/our-programs (accessed 5 July 2013).

Zins, J., Bloodworth, M., Weissberg, R. and Walberg, H. (2004) 'The foundations of social and emotional learning.' In J. Zins, R. Weissberg, J. Wang & H. Walberg (eds.), *Building Academic Success on Social and Academic Learning*. New York: Teachers College Press. pp. 3–22.

Chapter 8: The Importance of Positive Thinking

- Q1. What do think is so important about positive thinking?
- Q2. Have you read anything that links to this idea?
- Q3. Is positive thinking in education about letting the students have fun instead of learning?
- Q4. Do you think it is important that students learn that they have to work at school even if they do not want to or are not interested? Validate your answer.
- Q5. Do you think positive thinking is for students or teachers?

Introduction

As teachers today, you face many stresses and anxieties associated with your professional work in classrooms. There are numerous decisions to be made every day that affect the welfare and the schooling of your students. Students themselves are frequently unhappy or disinterested in the classroom, indicating that not all students are able to remain positive about their learning, their peers or their learning environment. While it is not possible to alleviate all of the stresses that exist within schools and communities, there is an amount of research that indicates the potential of developing positive perspectives and positive thinking. As you saw in the previous chapter, many of these studies have a focus on emotional intelligence.

However, there are a number of other notions about positive perspectives which support the work of neuroscientists who have identified the importance of emotion in the learning process – most especially in effective cognition. This chapter presents some of those that have had a major impact on educationalists and their work, including details on the notions of the 'flow' experience (Csikszentmihalyi, 1988, 1991b), positive psychology (Fredrickson, 2000; Seligman, 2002, 2004), self efficacy (Bandura, 1986; Pajeres, 2002; Pintrich and Schunk, 1996; Zimmerman et al., 1996) and how the use of technology can engage students positively and enhance their learning outcomes.

What Does the Literature Say about Theories on Positive Thinking and Related Ideas?

For many years there was a specific focus on negativity and the impact that it had on students and teachers alike. This was because it was problematic. Everyone who has had experiences with negative students, parents or other community members is aware of the tendency of negative comments and attitudes to subdue other perspectives and even to be contagious. Negativity was also found to limit and restrict student engagement in exploration, to rebuff curiosity and to disallow feelings of hope that things could work out well or that improvement was possible. Negativity has the effect of making students more cautious and to hold back. Because of this negativity students had less diverse experiences from which to learn and to grow. There existed few studies into the opposite of this emotional outlook in educational and in other contexts until the work of Csikszentmihalyi (1991a, 1991b, 2000) on 'flow' or optimal experience. This theory of flow (Csikszentmihalyi, 1988, 1991b) considers the development of personal potential from a holistic perspective and identifies the characteristics of tasks that may facilitate optimal experience.

Csikszentmihalyi's (1988) investigations into the state of consciousness known as 'flow' appear to have developed as a reaction to the trends of twentieth-century behaviourist scholars to espouse reductionist theories of human action, in their attempts to explain behaviour in increasingly scientific terms. Reductionist theory tends to ignore many of the factors that can explain the 'how' or the 'why' of human behaviour (Dupré and O'Neill, 1998). Many reductionist theories ignore concepts such as the construct of 'soul' and explain all human behaviour in terms of very simple rules or principles. These principles can be biological, such as the way in which the brain is biologically structured to function, or psychological, in which case explaining behaviour is couched in terms of cognitive functioning and conditioning. These theories do not make provision for the understanding of individuals and their personal notions of 'self' which may also contribute to their behaviours.

Csikszentmihalyi tracks the development of the notion of 'self' and maintains that once the self is established in one's consciousness, its main purpose is its own survival. To this end, the self represents its interests as goals. Most goals are genetically determined, such as the need for shelter, food and the basic necessities of survival; or culturally determined, although individual choice does exist within these frameworks. New information is received in terms of supporting the goals of self, or not. Csikszentmihalyi's (1988, 1991b) work is important because, while as you have read, there appears to be a significant amount of information available on the negative response of self, much of which neglects the dimensions of affect and motivation, a great deal less has been known about the extreme positive response: 'a condition of consciousness known as physic negentropy, optimal experience, or flow … [this] is obtained when all the contents of consciousness are in harmony with each other, and with the goals that define the person's self' (Csikszentmihalyi, 1988: 24). Once experienced, the total compatibility of the self and its own goal-directed structure becomes a personal priority and the 'self' seeks these optimal experiences as an ongoing process. This is what Csikszentmihalyi (1988: 24) terms the 'teleonomy of self, the goal seeking tendency that shapes the choices we make among alternatives'. In addition to the biological and cultural teleonomies, a principle that proposes that the body systems function to ensure survival of the body in various aspects, this is the third of the three teleonomies that individuals use to safeguard the consciousness of self. Little is known about this third teleonomy, although the other two have been extensively investigated. It is suggested that pleasure (biological teleonomy), power (cultural teleonomy) and participation (teleonomy of self) are all used to shape consciousness. However, Csikszentmihalyi (1988) asserts that consciousness evolves. He maintains that pleasure, power and participation are not sufficient motivation to account for the new goals that people pursue. He believes that when individuals have new, unprecedented experiences that are as positive in nature as to be exhilarating, the activity that created these experiences will be sought out again and again. When individuals expend psychic energy on goals that exhilarate, they begin to build a sense of self based on these emergent goals. Csikszentmihalyi (1988: 28) terms this 'autotelic motivation'; in other words, the task is done for its own sake because the goal is actually the experience itself; the goal is not any resultant product.

The flow experience appears to create similar responses irrespective of the content domain or specific contexts. What is interesting is that in order to sustain the flow experience Csikszentmihalyi (1988) noted that the complexity of the challenge must increase with the frequency of the experience. The flow experience forces individuals to develop new competencies and skills. A key component of experiencing flow is that individuals have suffi-cient, accurate self knowledge in order to recognise activities for which they have skills and to evaluate the level of challenge embedded in the tasks. It appears that accurate intrapersonal intelligence (Gardner, 1993, 1999b) is a prerequisite for flow. Csikszentmihalyi (1988) observed that if the challenge level in a task is too high then anxiety, frustration and other negative responses will replace the flow experience. If the challenge level is low or non-existent, or the task is intrinsically simple, then boredom or apathy may easily replace the flow experience. Flow experiences can only occur when the individual's skills and challenge level are balanced.

Flow experiences can occur in everyday situations when the complexity or challenge of a routine task is raised. It can also occur whether individuals anticipated enjoying the task or not; or even when they originally do not want to do the task! Among the common characteristics of flow are, as men-tioned, the correct balance of skills and challenge, clear goals and immediate feedback. However, it appears that other characteristics are commonly expe-rienced. These include a total focus to the exclusion of everything else going on around which is the state of totally focused consciousness also described by Moran and Gardner (2007), as when individuals have graduated to the 'master stage' of executive functioning. This occurs when individuals have integrated their goals so extensively into their perceptions of self and future that they are generally not conscious of the efforts they expend in pursuit of their goals. Other characteristics of the flow experience include the feel-ings of complete control, the distortion of one's sense of time, a disregard for problems and the total lack of self consciousness. Csikszentmihalyi (1988: 35) conceptually links the flow experience with the development of intrapersonal intelligence (Gardner, 1983, 1993, 1999b; Moran and Gardner, 2007) and the cognitive processes as expressed as the skills of executive function when he states that 'the flow experience is important because it provides a key for understanding the strivings of self' (Csikszentmihalyi, 1988: 35). The pursuit of flow experiences that have the capacity to enrich and develop 'self' are inspired by autotelic motivation, otherwise known as intrinsic motivation; but it has been demonstrated that this type of motiva-tion is not always what initially prompts individuals to engage in tasks, irrespective of the experiences that are provided by the processes of engag-ing in the task itself. One of the very real indicators that students are posi-tively engaged when in 'flow' experiences is the responses they gave to random 'in task' questions for reflection.

The very real benefits of being open to and embracing 'flow' experiences have been documented by Csikszentmihalyi (1988) in his research findings. His research participants were disillusioned, disenfranchised youths who had dropped out of school without any formal academic qualifications. As participation in these studies was not mandatory but of a voluntary nature, then it can be assumed that the teenagers who participated had retained enough curiosity about life experiences to volunteer for the study, even if they were not anticipating any pleasure in the self selected tasks or did not particularly wish to engage with them.

What Does This Mean for You?

The notion of engaging students in 'flow' may seem an idealistic suggestion that is well outside of regular classrooms. However, if you recall the discussion on Vygotsky's notion of Zone of Proximal Development, the challenges that surround the notions of intelligence and being 'clever' and the theories related to engagement and motivation, demonstrate a role for encouraging 'flow' in teaching. Planning for 'flow' experiences for your students may be complex but it can be achieved by reflecting conscientiously on a number of aspects of your professional life and the lives of your students in classroom environments. Focal points for reflection and then action (lesson or task planning) would necessarily include the following:

- **Do my students** have sufficiently accurate knowledge of their own relative strengths and relative limitations to be able to nominate or negotiate a learning task that challenges and raises the levels of competencies and skills? If not, do I have the strategies and resources to help them develop an increasingly deep understanding of these aspects of self? Do I have the professional capacity to remain positive and motivated and to motivate my students to engage positively?
- **Am I positive myself** about my profession and is my belief that all my students can learn effectively truly authentic and foundational to my professional pedagogies and practices?
- **How well do I know my students?** Am I aware of the tasks they appear to enjoy more than others? Are they naturally positive in school or do they bring negative attitudes about their capacities to learn, their abilities to understand and the mandatory nature of schooling? Do any students think that the curriculum is boring, irrelevant or that they are not part of this learning community because of variable differences that they perceive between themselves and the dominant culture? What do I know about how my students like to learn? Do I know what would interest them and provide an appropriate challenge, even if they are reluctant to initially engage with the task
- **Can I** gather and use all this information to plan suitable learning tasks? How effective are my skills in modifying tasks and finding different ways of

(Continued)

(Continued)

presenting the curriculum material? Do I know the curriculum content well enough to modify it and find the alternative pathways? (If the answer is no, stay positive. This is discussed extensively in Chapter 11 and lots of strategies are provided to start you thinking.) Am I prepared to negotiate these learning task designs with my students individually?

- **Do I have the capacity** to develop learning tasks that have the components to sustain the optimal functioning of students who have experienced 'flow' and have the desire or autotelic motivation to engage in other tasks that will require similar engagement and further challenge to their new level of competencies?

- **Am I organised** enough to ensure I can manage these negotiated learning goals when implemented in my classroom? Do I have the resources? Do I have the disposition, given that students typically lose track of time and become totally absorbed in learning, that elicits the 'flow' experience?

The power of positivity has been investigated by a group of researchers who identify their work as 'positive psychology'. This work is designed to explore the potential of positive emotion on wellbeing and happiness without seeking to replace what is already known and established regarding human suffering and disorders (Seligman et al., 2005). The work of Seligman and his colleagues (Dupré and O'Neill, 1998; Seligman, 2002, 2004; Seligman et al., 2009) has contributed considerably to the work of educational professionals. Using his PERMA model, he has led school staff and their pupils to understand and employ ways in which they may engage with their work more positively and implement classroom strategies to maximise what he now terms 'wellbeing' in their everyday interactions (Seligman, et al., 2009). Seligman now offers the PERMA model, which comprises five measurable areas of wellbeing which each have three characteristics in common. They are measured independently from each other, are each pursued for their own sake and each contribute to wellbeing. They are described here:

Positive emotions – happiness and life satisfaction, the pleasant life. This was originally the goal and first element of the Authentic Happiness theory but is now one of the elements of the wellbeing theory.

Engagement – Seligman discusses this in terms of flow, the concentrated engagement that utilises all your cognitive and emotional energies so you are 'lost in the moment'. Also originally one of the elements of the Authentic Happiness theory.

Relationships – positive relationships are built on the premise that very little that is positive is solitary; it is about other people and nothing that is accomplished, identified around positive relationship, is a solitary activity.

Meaning – belonging to and serving something that is 'bigger' than self. The third element of the Authentic Happiness theory is now presented as not solely subjective but as meaningful in a wider sense and to a wider audience.

Accomplishment or achievement – pursuing, achieving or mastering something for its own sake, not for reward, positive emotion or positive relationships. (Seligman, 2011)

The work of another of Seligman's colleagues has also been valuable for educationalists. The evidence that Fredrickson (2000, 2001) brings to her 'broaden and build' model of positive emotions provides a clear link to cognition, interest, attention and intrinsic motivation. Her hypothesis focuses on the potential of positive emotions – namely joy, interest, pride, contentment and love – to 'broaden people's momentary thought-action repertoires, widening the array of the thought and actions that come to mind' (2001: 220). In one example of the impact of positive emotions, she explains how interest creates the urge to explore and take in new information and experiences. In much the same way as Csikszentmihalyi's (1988, 1991a, 1991b) flow experiences facilitate personal growth, Fredrickson (2000, 2001) details how this process of exploration allows for an 'expansion of self' (2001: 220). While these findings are important for the promotion of emotional, cognitive and, perhaps, physical wellbeing, they are also an important consideration in any attempt to understand the complexity of factors that influence motivation. In this context, it could be that positive emotions both encourage initial engagement and perseverance and facilitate more successful outcomes. If this is so, then individuals may become encouraged to continually extend their efforts to develop an increasingly intrinsic motivational focus. Evidence supporting Fredrickson's 'broaden and build model' (Fredrickson, 2001: 220) also highlights another important benefit of positive emotions; the development of psychological resilience. The link is clear: resilient individuals are able to recover from adversity and disappointment more rapidly than their less resilient peers.

The impact of positive emotions may also make some contribution to understanding the importance of self efficacy beliefs in education. Pride, a positive emotion that is the result of personal achievement, not only influences current feelings of competence, but encourages individuals to strive for greater achievements and successes. A feeling of contentment may form part of the self efficacy beliefs of individuals and form the foundation that facilitates the reconceptualisation of self beliefs that is observed as improved self efficacy. The impact of positive emotion may even inform Dweck's theories (2000, 2006) of psychology for success. Individuals who hold an incremental view of intelligence have hope. By embracing theories of intelligence that allow them to exert some control over their potential to improve their performances, they are able to anticipate changes for the better. If they believe that there are strategies they can implement that may impact positively on the probability of improved outcomes, then this must influence motivation. It is not difficult to envision the potential of love itself on motivation: love of an area of learning, love of school life and community, can have a positive impact on motivation as the contexts of safe, enjoyable relationships are acknowledged as powerful indicators of student success (Arthur-Kelly et al., 2007; Cope, 2005; Foreman, 2005; Groundwater-Smith et al., 2003; Latham et al., 2006; Woolfolk and Margetts, 2007). What is remarkable about the benefits of positive emotions is that they are not lost after the experiences that engendered the feelings have passed. They remain in the memory as a support mechanism for times of adversity and difficulty.

What Does This Mean for You?

After the discussion of the impact of emotion on the cognitive functions of the brain, it is probably not a surprise for you to read that research findings in educational psychology have confirmed this. These findings provide you with a further opportunity to maximise your students' opportunities to deepen their self knowledge, to develop the capacities to acknowledge and benefit from positive relationships and to become increasing resilient as their optimism allows them to think more clearly, explore more options and retain their positive notions of self when faced with difficulties. These difficulties may be present in any of their 'multiple lives' without diminishing their capacity to think positively and remain optimistic regarding finding a suitable solution or exploring different options. There are many ways in which you can professionally support the development of wellbeing and promote student optimism. These could include:

- Demonstrate genuine optimism yourself.
- Work towards developing the characteristics of an emotionally intelligent class community.
- Negotiate learning tasks that engage students in the 'flow' experience.
- Implement plans for teaching and learning with the other stakeholders, namely the students. Model collaboration and cooperative strategies in your relationships with your students. Develop appropriate, professional positive relationships with your students as individuals.
- Develop a culture of helping and supporting others in your classroom and the wider school community. Sometimes this requires that the students help you or support your efforts to achieve something for its own sake. Share and celebrate success as a community in the same ways that you work together to solve problems and overcome difficulties.

While not expressly a theory of positive thinking, the importance of Bandura's (1986) work on self efficacy may easily be determined by the impact of high and low self efficacy beliefs on motivation. There are two foundational tenets of this theory in relation to educational contexts. Firstly, the learning tasks must have defined characteristics so that individuals are able to assess their competencies against the skills required to complete a task successfully. Secondly, the learning task must be valued by the individual. There are a significant number of research studies that explore the impact of self efficacy beliefs on students' learning potential, many concluding that self efficacy beliefs have a positive impact on student academic progress. The underpinnings of the theory are more widely developed. In his theory, Bandura (1986, 1994) stresses the importance of self efficacy beliefs for all individuals in everyday life. He proposes that self efficacy is the belief individuals have regarding their personal capacities to perform at predetermined levels of competence. He specifically identifies the self efficacy beliefs that individuals have concerning events or tasks that are important or may significantly impact on their lives. He proposes that these beliefs impact on the way individual think, feel, motivate themselves, make decisions and behave in their everyday lives. This process has its foundations in four major processes: affective, cognitive, motivational and selection processes. The affective processes are related to the emotions that are aroused or experienced in relation to the event being assessed and the possible regulation of these feelings. Cognitive processes relate to the manner in which the information regarding the task is accessed, understood, organised and implemented. The motivational considerations are those that determine how a task is approached, what methods are utilised, the degree of persistence the individual may demonstrate in the undertaking of the task and the intensity of concentration that is applied to the completion of the specific assignment. The final process is the combination of factors that are foundational to an individual's degree of self efficacy and that subsequently determine the choices that are made in relation to selecting events and tasks with which an individual may engage.

The most interesting aspect of this theory for you, as aspiring teachers, are the means by which Bandura (1986, 1994) proposes self efficacy beliefs are developed and strengthened or are weakened. Certainly, failure in completing the satisfactory level of task competencies undermines students' self efficacy beliefs, which is an important point to consider. However, it is equally important to take into account the expectations of those who routinely experience success easily. While it would be reasonable to expect that these students have a high degree of self efficacy beliefs, the ease with which they are able to complete tasks to the required level or standard can actually be a disadvantage in that it does not support the development of persistence or resilience in students who find things easy to achieve. As a consequence, when these students are faced with task they cannot easily accomplish, their self efficacy is easily undermined and they have a tendency to give up very easily. This has important implications for teaching practice and the provision of tasks suitable for students' learning needs. However, it is not only the experiences of the students themselves that Bandura views as influential for the development of personal self efficacy beliefs. Bandura also recognises that students can become confident and develop self efficacy beliefs vicariously by witnessing the success of others with whom students can identify and relate to as individuals who have similar strengths and limitations as themselves. The success of others who are regarded by students as being dissimilar to themselves, however, does not have the same influence or impact, and the failure to achieve of others who are identified by students as similar to themselves has a negative impact on students' self efficacy beliefs, causing them to have weaker self efficacy beliefs regarding their capacities to complete the tasks in question successfully.

Bandura identifies this influence of others on students and people in general as the influence of social models. He expresses the belief that modelling is a highly effective means by which to raise self efficacy beliefs in those who seek out appropriate social models because not only can individuals identify with their models, the models themselves can 'transmit' (Bandura, 1994: 72) knowledge by demonstrating their thinking and strategies for problem solving. This, in turn, can provide increased self efficacy levels by presenting the observers with additional means by which problems can be solved and tasks completed effectively at the standard of competency required. In addition to mastery of experiences and social modelling, Bandura describes two other methods of developing or promoting self efficacy beliefs. He identifies this as social persuasion, a context in which the individual is verbally encouraged to believe that they can successfully complete the task or solve the problems presented. The final condition concerns an attention to the students' emotional states and their actual physical reactions to the prospect of undertaking a task. The points of caution Bandura offers for you as a teacher trying to raise student self efficacy are as follows:

- Social persuasion alone is the least effective manner of changing self efficacy beliefs as the individuals who have their efficacy beliefs raised unrealistically may suffer greater disappointment with a poor result than others and this impacts negatively on their levels of self efficacy and their potential to be improved.
- Teachers and others are not only relied upon to demonstrate effective means of problem solving or task completion but also need to be sensitive to the importance of:

o finding the positive aspects in their appraisal comments of student's efforts

o matching the student's capabilities to the appropriate tasks and learning conditions

o ensuring that students are not placed in learning situations for which they are unprepared or do not have the skills, knowledge or concepts to complete with a degree of success. Situations in which students feel stressed or anxious are interpreted as being indicative of their vulnerability to failure if they do not already have the degree of self efficacy beliefs required in that context.

Bandura indicates that levels of self efficacy impact on student and individual performance in the four major ways already mentioned briefly. These are now investigated in some detail in order for you to further understand and recognise what Bandura understands as the impact of self efficacy beliefs on human functioning.

• Cognitive processes: These are demonstrated in several ways. For example, it is proposed that students with higher levels of self efficacy are able to set higher-reaching personal goals as they assess their own capabilities in a positive manner and are optimistic about their chances of succeeding.

• In order to achieve their goals they visualise their efforts as successful and use this mental visual imagery as a way to relate to the goal, to engage positively and to anticipate success.

• In engaging positively and anticipating success, these students are enabled to persevere more persistently in the face of difficulties, interruptions and other non-productive events and phases in the work that comprise their goal.

• In each of these cognitive process factors, if the individual's sense of self efficacy is low, then self doubt and negative thinking impact on the goals that are set and the chances of successful completion.

• Motivational processes: Bandura believes that self efficacy beliefs are the key to self regulation and therefore to motivation. He explains that self efficacy beliefs are implicit in the three major theories of motivation.

• Self efficacy beliefs impact on causal attributions (attribution theory) in that highly self efficacious students attribute a poor result to not working hard enough, while students with low self efficacy attribute their poor performance to lack of ability to complete the tasks successfully.

• In expectancy-value (outcome expectancies) theory, students are motivated by the expectancy that specific behaviours produce specific results and the value of these results. Bandura proposes that people are motivated by what they believe they can do in addition to the expected results and its values.

- Goal theory (theory of cognised goals) requires students to make self satisfaction a condition of the motivational and goal setting process. Self efficacy beliefs are foundational to the types of goals individuals set, how they assess their progress, how they respond in times of difficulty, how they reassess and reset their goals, how positively and to what degree they expend their energies and to what extent they are able to persist and persevere in their attainment.
- Affective processes: the capacity to recognise, understand and then control anxiety and other negative thoughts and visual thought patterns affecting the development and exercise of self efficacy beliefs. Conversely, the inability to control negativity undermines self efficacy and causes individuals to dwell on their perceived shortcomings which further diminishes self efficacy beliefs.
- As mastery experiences are the principal factor in the promotion and maintenance of self efficacy, even the most self depreciating and anxious student must be provided with learning experiences in which they can become successful, almost despite themselves. Supports such as 'mastery aids' can be provided until they are no longer needed, at which stage the student's self efficacy beliefs are sufficient to motivate engagement with appropriately designed tasks.
- Selection processes: when provided with choice, students with high self efficacy beliefs are able to make sound choices regarding their tasks, the level of difficulty embedded in them and the amount of sustained effort they need to expend to complete them successfully. As with the other factors, this capacity is diminished if low self efficacy beliefs are held regarding the student's competencies in relation to the task.

Bandura (1994) discusses the notion of self efficacy in the context of personal ownership and personal agency in that self efficacy beliefs are part of what comprises an individual notion of 'self'. Although Bandura and a number of other writers whose work will be discussed in the following section offer theories that encompass self knowledge components, which are an important aspect of motivation, the accuracy of individuals' perceptions of self do not appear to be of importance in these hypotheses. It appears to be assumed that students' self perceptions are consistently precise and correct, which may be a concern for you as reflective practitioners. Additionally, these writers neglect other factors that may contribute to motivation. One of these factors concerns the individual's perceptions of other important aspects of self; another concerns the impact of social and cultural expectations (Sellars, 2009), both of which will be discussed more thoroughly in the chapters to come.

Questions for Reflection

- Q1. What do you think of these theories about positive thinking?
- Q2. From your experience, do you think they may be useful to engage within school contexts? Why or why not?
- Q3. Can you think of any specific advantages of thinking positively as a teacher?
- Q4. Do you think it would be useful to encourage your students to think positively?
- Q5. What benefits could you anticipate positive thinking may bring to classroom environments and interactions?
- Q6. Do you think that stress and negative emotions cause the degree of student disadvantage and cognitive limitation that is discussed by some of these theorists? Validate your answer.
- Q7. Do you anticipate any disadvantages with stressing the potential of positive thinking in the classroom? What might these be if you think there are disadvantages?
- Q8. Have you any reservations or would you be cautious about using any of these positive psychology theories or self efficacy theory in your classroom? Validate your answer.
- Q9. Are there any issues or content in this section of writing that relate to content you have read in other chapters? Identify and discuss these.
- Q10. Do you think the criticisms and comments regarding Bandura's theory of self efficacy have any merit? Validate your answer.

Implications for Education: The Positive Education Framework

Issues of student disinterest and lack of motivation in school have been the topic of discussion in many staffrooms and professional debates for a number of years. In some cases, as you will read Chapter 10, which focuses on diversity, these conditions are the result of very complex social, cultural and personal issues. Frequently, however, even in very complex circumstances, research studies have provided a body of evidence that firmly links positive emotion and high self efficacy beliefs to improved classroom interactions and increased academic performance. There are some quite explicit guidelines available for you as prospective teachers who may be anxious to engage positively with your students in the work of Noble and McGrath (2008). They have brought the practical implications of positive thinking together in their framework for positive educational practices and detailed how the framework may be implemented to improve teacher and student wellbeing and success. The framework comprises of five foundations: social and emotional competency, positive emotions, positive relationships, engagement through strengths and a sense of meaning and purpose. What these entail, and strategies that are suggested by Noble and McGrath (2008), are detailed below.

- Social and emotional competencies. These are identified as pro-social values, resilience skills, social skills, emotional literacy skills and personal achievement skills. Pro-social values are identified as being respect, cooperation, acceptance of differences, compassion, honesty and friendliness/inclusion (Noble and McGrath, 2008: 123). It is suggested that deliberate, explicit teaching of these values and then providing opportunities in regular classroom interaction for students to demonstrate their capacities to implement their learning is the most effective way of developing these skills and values in your students (McGrath, 2005).
- Positive emotions. These are feelings of belonging, feelings of safety, feelings of satisfaction, affirmation and pride, feelings of excitement and enjoyment and feelings of optimism about success. The authors suggest that there are many ways in which these positive emotions can be enhanced. Children are more likely to feel that they belong when they are given opportunities to work in small groups, when they are participating in a cooperative learning environment and when they perceive they are cared for in personal ways. Students feel safer when they are in learning environments that have clearly articulated, school-wide behaviour policies, where bullying is minimised and where expectations around these issues are clear. Feelings of pride and affirmation can be supported by the acknowledgement and acceptance of various types of achievement and success, not just those traditionally recognised. Excitement and enjoyment are typically associated with play, both informal interactions and games, which encourage pro-social behaviours and self regulation of emotions such as anger, aggression and feelings associated with winning and losing. Optimism about success is developed when students are aware that their work and the energy that they have expended in the course of their efforts have been recognised in addition to the assessment of the resultant product. Students can also be encouraged to find the positive aspects of their otherwise unsuccessful work attempts, to learn from their mistakes and to challenge their more pessimistic thinking.
- Positive relationships. In this framework, positive relationships are a whole school responsibility. These can be effectively modelled by teachers in their peer relationship in addition to their relationships with the

students. It is suggested that the successful adoption of the school values and goals, displays of altruistic and compassionate behaviour, fair settlement of disputes and inclusive, rather than exclusive attitudes towards others are characteristic of schools that have positive cultures. Noble and McGrath (2008) suggest that group work, circle time and a number of other interactive classroom routines can be effectively utilised as opportunities to promote positive relationships. They suggest that positive teacher–student relationships can be established if teachers get to know their students well and take an interest in them as individuals, manage their classroom discipline situations fairly and unemotionally, and make themselves available to their students outside the regular classroom times for student consultation and support.

- Engagement through strengths. This aspect of the framework relies on students being able to identify what comes naturally and easily to them and can be used to support their learning. There is a body of research that confirms that students are increasingly motivated and engaged in their learning tasks if they are able to use their learning strengths (Sellars, 2008). Strengths are generally recognised as being cognitive or personal. Learning that is accomplished by engaging with personal strengths is more easily understood, more positive in nature, more productive and accomplished and more confidently interacted with than other learning. Using relative strengths does not ignore student relative limitations, but it serves as a means by which new or more complex learning can initially take place with relative ease and success. Teachers need to allow students opportunities to discover their relative learning strengths by providing a variety of strategies, contexts and tasks from which students can develop a deep understanding of their own strengths and limitations (Anderson and Lux, 2005). They suggest that a planning tool such as the Revised Bloom's Taxonomy (Anderson and Krathwohl, 2000) and Gardner's Multiple Intelligences (Gardner, 1993) matrix provides a usable, efficient framework for planning that is designed to meet the learning needs of a diverse group of students, while simultaneously facilitating the opportunities for students to know and understand their preferred ways of learning and how they can use their relative strengths to minimise their relative limitations. Using their strengths also leads the students to the final foundational tenet of the framework.

- Meaning and purpose. It is easy to understand that allowing students to learn 'their way' contributes significantly to the 'personal' aspects of learning. This is considerably enhanced when students have opportunities to use their strength to contribute to the work of others, in a group project or team effort. Purposeful learning is established when students pursue a project or learning goal that is significant for them. In order for this to occur, it is important that students' work has relevance and is connected to their interests and allows some degree of 'ownership'. Community based projects are recommended as suitable learning opportunities as are 'service' type learning experiences where students can participate in learning as part of a wider, more diverse community. Projects that allow students to engage with the community outside the classroom and then outside the school communities have been found to be ideal contexts for learning that has embedded meaning and purpose.

Implications for Education: The Impact of Self Efficacy Beliefs

There are a considerable number of research studies which have been implemented in school contexts in order to establish the importance and relevance of Bandura's (1986, 1994) theory of self efficacy in education. Some of these have focused on teachers' perceptions of their professional self efficacy (Gibbs, 2003), while others have concentrated on establishing what is meant by self efficacy in educational contexts (Pajares, 1996, 2000, 2002; Pintrich and Schunk, 1996). Studies that investigated student performance in relation to their self efficacy beliefs have been conducted in relation to achievement in various content disciplines and at all levels of education. Examples include Jeanneret and Cantwell (2002), who investigated tertiary students' self efficacy beliefs in relation to their competencies in musical composition, Marat (2005), who explored the mathematics self efficacy of secondary school students, Pajeres and Valiante (1996), who considered the self efficacy beliefs of students regarding their competencies and writing, and Zimmerman et al. (1996) who studied the relationship between self regulation and self efficacy beliefs. These studies and others consistently reported that their findings demonstrated strong correlations between self efficacy beliefs and student performance despite the concerns mentioned earlier regarding the appropriateness and accuracy of the students' perceptions of their competencies.

The work of Schunk and Pajeres (2001) on the increasing importance of self evaluation strategies may do much to minimise the impact of the lack of attention that has previously been paid to the accuracy of students' self efficacy beliefs. It may also promote a greater understanding of self efficacy and limit studies that find students' self accuracy beliefs to be inaccurate (Boxall, 2002; Sewell and St George, 2000), and those that find developmental and maturation factors impact negatively on students' self efficacy (Caprara et al., 2011; Harter, 1999; Midgley et al., 1989; Nicolaou and Philippou, 2004). Another concern about self efficacy is that it is not 'future' orientated in the way that it is used by Beare (2003), Burchsted (2003) and other educationalists referring to twenty-first century education (Sellars, 2009).

Self efficacy refers to specifics, namely students' perceptions of their specific competencies in predetermined learning tasks in well-defined subject domains (Bandura, n.d.) in the immediate future. Many of the problems students are faced with in the classroom or in life are not able to be anticipated, have no precedents or are simply too different in their nature or structure to be successfully assessed in terms of self efficacy beliefs. Students are not necessarily sufficiently engaged in reflective, metacognitive processes that promote greater accuracy in perceptions of self and one one's own capabilities.

Questions for Reflection

- Q1. Are there any aspects of the positive education framework that are reflected in other theories and ideas about student learning? Can you identify these and discuss?
- Q2. Are there any ideas in the positive education framework that you feel reflect your understanding of teachers' professional work and responsibilities?
- Q3. Are there any ideas in the positive education framework that you would like to try to implement in your classroom? Can you identify why these would be important to your professional practice?
- Q4. Are there any notions in this chapter that support the Holy Trinity for Teachers (see Chapter 2)? Can you identify them and nominate which of the three teacher competencies each is associated with?
- Q5. Are there any ideas in the positive educational framework that challenge your concept of professional, ethical teacher practice? Can you validate your answer?
- Q6. Why do you think there may be some diversity in the research findings relating to the importance and relationship of self efficacy beliefs to student performance? Give your reasons.
- Q7. Make a note of your thinking that has been (i) challenged by the contents of this chapter and (ii) supported and validated by the contents of this chapter.
- Q8. Can you begin a concept map or other visual display of the ideas that you have read in this text so far? This can be added to as you progress through the text.
- Q9. Are there any circumstances in which you think being positive in a learning context such as a classroom may be inappropriate? Validate your response.
- Q10. Can you identify formal situations when students are required to participate in learning contexts for which they are ill-prepared or have low efficacy beliefs?

Scenario Eight

Miss Scarlett's classroom was as bright as her name! Around the walls were photos of her students working together and underneath each was a written message with the participating students' names and the particular activity in which they were engaged. Included was a short message about the ways in which they were interacting cooperatively. Some indicated the students were actively listening to the child who was explaining an idea to them, others commented on other aspects of pro-social behaviours such as helping, contributing, organising together, sharing resources and collaboratively planning. Even though her students had an average age of 11 years, she knew that they were secretly very proud when a photo of them appeared with affirming comments underneath, even though they said very little about them openly! She had tried to have at least a few new ones every Monday morning as a welcome for the students and made sure she had enough copies of each photo at the end of term to put in their portfolios of work. She was very happy to witness the degree of pride and respect that the students demonstrated in the classroom. Determined to make it their class and not her exclusive domain, she had decided to discuss with the students what they would exhibited on their walls, where and how exactly the work could be arranged most effectively and often allowed the students to actually prepare the wall spaces themselves. She contributed her photos of them at work, which she would pop in small corners or spaces after the students left for the day. She had negotiated the classroom guidelines for behaviour and academic work with the students and these were also on display. She genuinely encouraged her students to think of themselves as successful learners by identifying and planning to use their relative strengths, providing choices and differentiating the curriculum, her pedagogy and the students' possible products as much as possible. She ensured that everyone was included in the photos, managing the classroom displays and making class decisions. She kept checklist just in case someone was so positive and cooperative they ended up being overlooked. Her attitude to disparaging comments from the students about their peers was well known, although not written and the very few boundaries that had been established in negotiation with her students were openly enforced.

Her students selected the work they could take home at the end of term in their portfolios and prior to their parent–teacher meeting. Although there were few students who took this opportunity at first, the numbers had increased dramatically during the year and the portfolios were the topic of discussion and negotiation. She had eventually decided to allow the students to take them any time they wanted on the condition they signed them in and out. Her colleagues had smiled and said she would have none left at the end of the year, but she was pleased she had stuck to her plan. After a few misadventures, all had gone surprisingly well and she still had a portfolio folder for every student which contained their selected works – successful and not so successful – and reflections on their work, including how they had learned from and recovered from their mistakes, and, of course, the photos.

She spent a great deal of her time in class talking to her students about their work and felt they had developed really positive relationships with each other and she could plan for their leaning really effectively. However, she was horrified when she asked them to write their own progress reports halfway through term to accompany the one she had prepared. So many of them had used very negative comments to describe their capabilities that she had to make a lunchtime timetable to discuss her report in relation to the one they had written for themselves. She had always had high expectations of her students and provided suitable academic and social support structures but she had not realised how many of her students felt they should work harder, do better and lacked competencies. Following this experience, she made her expectations about effort and standards very clear but took great care not to be overly demanding in general. This strategy did appear to be effective, she realised, when she met with the students and parents for the teacher–parent meeting. She had discussed the reports with the students individually before they were sent home. The students could sign them and make a comment if they wished. Everyone did. As the students came to the meeting with their parents, she found this a really enjoyable opportunity and the students did most of the talking about their progress with the help of their portfolios and the reports they had each prepared and discussed. She felt she was making good progress too as she listened to the students explain to their parents what they had learned about and what they had learned to do.

Questions for Reflection

- Q1. What is Miss Scarlett's goal for these students?
- Q2. Why would this be important?
- Q3. Do you think that her strategies are useful or appropriate? Validate your answer.
- Q4. What would you do in your classroom to promote positivity?
- Q5. Are there ethical and professional issues to discuss in this situation? Identify them and discuss.
- Q6. Is there anything that you could take away from Miss Scarlett's practice that may help you?
- Q7. Are there any difficulties associated with her practices?
- Q8. Would you use these strategies? Validate your answer.

Conclusion

This chapter discussed the impact of optimistic thinking and positive action and attitude in relation to teaching and learning. Bandura's social cognition theory, which presents the means by which students can be supported and scaffolded in developing their belief in their own capacities to achieve well-defined tasks, has been summarised and the potential of this theory to support student learning has been examined. The findings of the more recently developed group of psychologists who are interested in the potential of positive thinking on both holistic wellbeing and on cognitive capacities have been explored and their possible impact on educational practice and contexts investigated. The importance placed on positivity and optimistic thinking in this chapter may directly oppose and contradict the attitudes and values that you may experience in some educational settings. It is your challenge to reflect on your own self knowledge and explore your potential for positivity and for using this trait to enhance your professional practice and fulfil your ethical and moral responsibilities in your interactions with diverse groups of students and personalities. Noble and McGrath (2008) comment that some of the traditional attitudes and practices found in educational contexts are not necessarily conducive to optimism and productive positivism. A new perspective is needed. In the current educational and economic climates, engaging with students in positive terms may be considered to be more important than ever before. The more difficult or diverse your students are, the more essential thinking and working positively may become for you. One way of working positively with your students and honouring their personal capacities as students and learners is to support them in their efforts to become self directed learners. How and why this strategy may be productive for all involved is explored in the following chapter.

References

Anderson, J. and Lux, W. (2005) Knowing your own strength: accurate self assessment as a requirement for personal autonomy. *Philosophy, Psychiatry, & Psychology*, 11 (4): 279–94.

Anderson, L. and Krathwohl, D. (2000) *Taxonomy of Teaching and Learning: A Revision of Bloom's Taxonomy of Educational Objectives*. New York: Longman.

Arthur-Kelly, M., Lyons, G., Butterfield, N., and Gordon, C. (2007) *Classroom Management: Creating Positive Learning Environments*. South Melbourne, Victoria: Thomson.

Bandura, A. (1986) Self efficacy beliefs in human functioning. Retrieved from www.emory. edu/EDUCATION/mfp/effpassages.html (accessed 15 June 2002).

Bandura, A. (1994) 'Self efficacy.' In V.S. Ramachaudran (ed.), *Encyclopaedia of Human Behaviour*, Vol. 4. New York: Academic Press. pp. 71–81.

Bandura, A. (n.d.) Self-efficacy defined. Retrieved from www.emory.edu/EDUCATION/mfp/ BanEncy.html (accessed 9 July 2002).

Beare, H. (2003) The future school. *Prime Focus*, (32): 2–6.

Boxall, M. (2002) *Nurture Groups in School: Principles and Practice*. London: Paul Chapman Publishing.

Burchsted, S. (2003) Future sudies: peparing learners for success in the 21st century. *New Horizons* (February): 3–6.

Caprara, G., Vecchione, M., Alessandri, G., Gerbino, M. and Barbaranelli, C. (2011) The contribution of personality traits and self-efficacy beliefs to academic achievement: a longitudinal study. *British Journal of Educational Psychology*, 81 (1): 78–96.

Cope, B. (2005) *How to Make a Classrooom Management Plan*. Frenchs Forest: Pearson Education Australia.

Csikszentmihalyi, M. (1988) 'The flow experience and its significance for human psychology.' In M. Csikszentmihalyi and S. Csikszentmihalyi (eds), *Optimal Experience: Psychological Studies of Flow in Consciousness*. Cambridge: Cambridge University Press. pp. 3–37.

Csikszentmihalyi, M. (1991a) Consciousness for the twenty first century. *Zygon*, 26 (1): 7–25.

Csikszentmihalyi, M. (1991b) *Flow: The Psychology of Optimal Experience*. New York: Harper Perennial. pp. 143–63.

Csikszentmihalyi, M. (2000) Happiness, flow and economic equality. *American Psychological Association*, 55 (10): 1163–4.

Dupré, J. and O'Neill, J. (1998) Against reductionist explanations of human behaviour. *Proceedings of the Aristotelian Society, Supplementary Volumes*, 72: 153–71, 73–88.

Dweck, C. (2000) *Self Theories: Their Role in Motivation, Personality and Development*. Lillington, NC: Taylor & Francis.

Dweck, C. (2006) *Mindset*. USA: Random House

Foreman. P. (2005) *Inclusion in Action*. Southbank, Vic.: Thomson Learning Australia.

Fredrickson, B. (2000) Cultivating positive emotions to optimize health and well being. *Prevention and Treatment*, 3. Retrieved from www.unc.edu/peplab/publications/Frednicks on_2000_Prev & Trmt.pdf (accessed 3 September 2013)

Fredrickson, B. (2001) The role of positive emotions in positive psychology. *American Psychologist*, 56 (3): 218–26.

Gardner, H. (1993) *Frames of Mind. Tenth Anniversary Edition*. New York: Basic Books.

Gibbs, C. (2003) Explaining effective teaching: self efficacy and thought control of action. *Journal of Educational Inquiry*, 4 (2): 1–14.

Groundwater-Smith, S., Ewing, R., and Le Cornu, R. (2003) *Teaching Challenges and Dilemmas*, 2nd edn. Southbank: Thomson Learning Australia.

Harter, S. (1999) *The Construction of Self: A Developmental Perspective*. New York, NY: Guilford Press.

Latham, G., Blaise, M., Dole, S., Faulkner, J., Lang, J., and Malone, K. (2006) *Learning to Teach: New Times, New Practices*. South Melbourne: Oxford University Press.

Jeanneret, N. and Cantwell, R. (2002) Self efficacy issues in learning to teach composition: a case study of instruction. *Australian Journal of Educational and Developmental Psychology*, 2: 33–41.

Marat, D. (2005) Assessing mathematics self efficacy of diverse students from secondary schools in Auckland: Implications for academic achievement. *Issues in Educational Research*, 15: 37–68.

McGrath, H. (2005) 'Directions in teaching social skills to students with specific emotional and behavioural difficulties.' In P. Clough, P. Garner, T. Pardeck, F. Yuen and T. Yuen (eds), *Handbook of Emotional and Behavioural Difficulties*. London: Sage. pp. 3–19.

Midgley, C., Feldlaufer, H. and Eccles, J. (1989) Change in teacher efficacy and student self- and task-related beliefs in mathematics during the transition to jumior high school. *Journal of Educational Psychology*, 81 (2): 247–58.

Moran, S. and Gardner, H. (2007) '"Hill, skill and will": Executive function from a multiple-intelligences perspective.' In L. Meltzer (ed.), *Executive Function in Education: From Theory to Practice*. New York: Guilford Press. pp. 19–38.

Nicolaou, A. and Philippou, G. (2004) Efficacy beliefs, ability in problem posing and mathematical achievement. Paper presented at the Third International Biennial SELF Research Conference: Self Concept, Motivation and Identity: Where To From Here? Berlin, 4–7 July.

Noble, T. and McGrath, H. (2008) The positive educational practices framework: a tool for facilitating the work of educational psychologists in promoting pupil wellbeing. *Educational and Child Psychology*, 25 (2): 119–34.

Pajares, F. (1996) Self-efficacy beliefs in academic settings. *Review of Educational Research*, 66 (4): 543–78.

Pajeres, F. (2000) Seeking a culturally attentive educational psychology. Retrieved from www.des.emory.edu/mgp/AERA2000Discussant.html (accessed 5 August 2005).

Pajeres, F. (2002) Overview of social cognitive theory and of self efficacy Retrieved from www.emory.edu/EDUCATION/mfp/eff.html (accessed 5 August 2005).

Pajeres, F. and Valiante, G. (1996) Predictive utility and causal influence of the writing self efficacy beliefs of elementary students. Paper presented at the Annual Meeting of the American Educational Research Association, New York.

Pintrich, P. and Schunk, D. (1996) *Motivation in Education: Theory, Research and Applications*. Englewood Cliffs, NJ: Prentice–Hall.

Schunk, D. and Pajeres, F. (2001) 'Development of academic self efficacy.' In A. Wigfield and J. Eccles (eds), *Development of Achievement Motivation*. San Diego, CA: Academic Press. pp. 15–31.

Seligman, M. (2002) *Authentic Happiness: Using the New Positive Psychology to Realize Your Potential for Lasting Fulfillment*. New York: Free Press.

Seligman, M. (2004) Can happiness be taught? *Daedalus* (Spring): 5–17.

Seligman, M. (2011) *Flourish: A Visionary New Understanding of Happiness and Well-Being*. New York: Free Press.

Seligman, M., Ernst, R., Gillham, J., Reivich, K. and Linkins, M. (2009) Positive education: positive psychology and classroom interventions. *Oxford Review of Education*, 35 (3): 293–311.

Seligman, M., Park, N. and Peterson, C. (2005) Positive psychology progress: empirical validation of interventions. *American Psychologist*, 60 (5): 410–21.

Sellars, M. (2008) *Using Students' Strengths to Support Learning Outcomes: A Study of the Development of Gardner's Intrapersonal Intelligence to Support Increased Academic Achievement for Primary School Students*. Saarbrucken: VDM Verlag. pp. 97.

Sellars, M. (2009) Intrapersonal intelligence, executive function and stage three students. Dissertation, Australian Catholic University, Sydney.

Sewell, A. and St George, A. (2000) Developing efficacy beliefs in the classroom. *Journal of Educational Inquiry*, 1 (2): 58–71.

Woolfolk, A. and Margetts, K. (2007) *Educational Psychology*. Frenchs Forest, NSW: Pearson Education.

Zimmerman, B., Bonner, S. and Kovach, R. (1996) *Developing Self-Regulated Learners: Beyond Achievement to Self-Efficacy*. Washington, DC: American Psychological Association.

Chapter 9: Self Directed Learning

- Q1. What do you think are the characteristics of self directed learners?
- Q2. Are self directed learning tasks suitable for all students or only the really competent academic students?
- Q3. Have you been part of, or witnessed any self directed learning activities in classrooms?
- Q4. Given the current emphasis that is placed on relevant, appropriate tasks for all learners, do you think self directed learning is a useful idea in primary or secondary classrooms or in both?
- Q5. How do you think students develop the cognitive capacities of self directed learners?

Introduction

The notion of asking students what they would like to learn about and then letting them go about organising themselves to complete a self selected task in any manner they would like to may fill some of you with delight and others with dread. Both responses are reasonable and understandable in the current climate of professional standards, standardised testing and increased teacher accountability. However, given what you have already read about the learning process, the demands of education in the twenty-first century and the uncertain future that your students will face in terms of rapid change, it may be time to reconsider your role as a teacher. Encouraging your students to become increasingly self directed and to get to know themselves thoroughly as learners with evolving needs and increasing academic competencies may prove to be a very positive opportunity. In doing so it is important to know what skills and strategies, knowledge and behaviours can support your students' efforts to take responsibility for their own learning. This chapter discusses a range of cognitive capacities collectively known as executive function skills, considers student readiness for independence in aspects of their learning and presents some practical ways that independent learning can be managed for all students. Additionally it draws on the notions from previous chapters and provides opportunities for you to reflect on your own teaching practice in light of this discussion.

What Does the Literature Say about Self Directed Learning?

Although self directed learning (SDL) has been an educational approach for some time (Candy, 1991; Heimstra, 1994; Towle and Cottrell, 1996), some general perceptions exist that are not necessarily accurate. Self directed learning has become synonymous with adult education, whether at the formal tertiary stage or as ongoing lifelong learning. Despite the abundance of literature that discusses self directed learning as a foundational construct in adult learning contexts (e.g. Brookfield, 2009; Merriam, 2001) and the comparative paucity of research related to school learners, especially those in primary schools, there are many opportunities for you to facilitate self directed learning habits and capacities for the students in your classes. Self directed learning is not only for adult learners, nor exclusively for those individuals who are particularly competent in academic matters. It is not necessarily a solitary, isolated pursuit. It is generally agreed that SDL is any learning where the learner determines what is to be investigated, what and how problems may be solved and takes some responsibility for monitoring the progress and quality of their output. Despite being developed in the context of tertiary or adult education, much of the information published in relation to these contexts is just as relevant to primary and secondary schools. As you will read, the degree to which younger students can be termed as self directed learners will not be the same as the extent to which adults can be independent (e.g. Roeberts et al., 2012), due to developmental, academic and maturation considerations. This means that expectations need to be appropriate and support carefully structured to match the capacities of the students. An inclusive definition of SDL is provided by Abraham et al. (2005), who investigated the SDL capacities of undergraduate students.

SDL is a process in which students take the initiative with or without the help of others in diagnosing their learning needs, formulating learning goals, identifying human and material resources for learning, choosing and implementing appropriate learning strategies, and evaluating learning outcomes In this context, product is understood to be any creations, artwork, composition, solution, concept or presentation which is the result of the learning experience. (Abraham et al., 2005: 135)

Pilling-Cormick (1997), in discussing the relationship between SDL and transformative learning, provides the most compelling reason for you to explore and engage with the notion of SDL for the students in your classes:

In self directed learning, learners determine, investigate, and evaluate their needs. When considering needs, the learner must reflect on his or her learning processes. When this reflection process moves beyond simple questioning and becomes more critical, the potential for transformative learning exists. Indeed, in order to learn how to be self directed, students go through a process of development that often must be transformative – they change their way of thinking about learning. No longer are they recipients of a teacher-directed process: they are responsible and accountable for their own development. (Pilling-Cormick, 1997: 76–77)

Transformative learning is arguably the overarching purpose of education. It involves students learning to learn, to think, to prioritise and to regulate their affect and cognition in order to complete their tasks. Tasks are self nominated and reflect learners' current learning needs. Changing students' thinking about learning demands that certain aspects of the learning process must be altered so that students are able to develop new ways of thinking about themselves as learners and about their learning process. Pilling-Cormick (1997) suggests that there are three components to SDL that have the potential to become transformative:

The degree of control the student has over their learning, in other words how self directed they are able to be. This aspect affects the other dimensions: the interaction between the student and the facilitator. A student who is demonstrating a positive attitude and sound control influences the way in which the facilitator interacts with them. Conversely, a student who has a negative attitude or lacks the skills for self directed learning also impacts on the interaction. A facilitator who is enthusiastic about SDL can influence perceptions about learning. One particularly vital aspect of this interaction is the role of reflection. What does the student need to learn? Why is the particular task so important to the student? Reflection that questions the validity of the learning itself is particularly important. (Pilling-Cormick 1997: 66)

This importance of reflection that challenges the ways in which curriculum is designed, delivered and assessed is also to be found in the later work of Schaub-de Jong et al. (2011).

In considering the particular aspects of what may influence interaction between the students and the facilitator, the following four factors appear to be influential.

- Social constraints.
- Environmental characteristics.

  o Determining needs. How much direction the facilitator provides will depend on the individual student. Facilitation strategies to prompt critical reflection of learning needs will be determined by the individual students also.

  o Availability of resources. Students may need to have opportunities that create specific circumstances around the provision of resources.

  o Outside influences. Off-campus students, part-time students and so forth have specific needs and this impacts on how their learning is facilitated in the most effective manner.

  o Time management. This is a critical aspect of SDL and skills in this area may have to be facilitated on an individual basis depending on the student's capacity to mange time effectively.

  o Group work. Students' potential anxieties and misgivings about working in groups need to be explored in collaborative and cooperative ways that respect each others' thinking and ideas need to be encouraged.

  o Room arrangement. The degree of comfort provided by the seating arrangements, lighting, easy access to resources and the appropriateness of the venue itself is important and needs consideration.

  o Comfort. Students and facilitators must be made to feel comfortable about expressing opinions, irrespective of whether they are agreeing with others or not.

- Student characteristics.
- Facilitator characteristics.

While all are important in SDL contexts and not all SDL situations are necessarily transformative, great stress is placed on the environmental characteristics as these are easily adaptable and may be a defining factor in the success of the efforts of self directed learners. Two major perspectives in SDL, learner autonomy and self regulated learning, are discussed by Lewis and Vialleton (2011) in the specific context of second language learning and are summarised in Figure 9.1. They draw on work by both Holec and Little (in Lewis and Vialleton, 2011) indicating that learner autonomy is a capacity, not just a set of behaviours. Little (in Lewis and Vialleton, 2011) goes further and indicates that although learner autonomy may be a capacity in some areas of learning, it is neither consistent in all areas of learning, nor is it a capacity that, once established, is permanent. Individuals may be able to demonstrate the capacities of learner autonomy in one instance, but it is not an unchanging, permanent characteristic.

Learner autonomy	Self regulated learning
Characteristics of learner autonomy are perceived as specific to second language learning as a capacity of interpolated behaviors (Holec and Little in Lewis and Vialleton, 2011) Learners are able to determine the following aspects of their learning:	Characteristics of self regulated learning in any discipline context are perceived as a self directed process (Zimmerman in Lewis and Vialleton, 2011) Learners are able to:
Learning management tasks Determining the objectives Defining the contents and progressions Selecting methods and techniques to be used Monitoring the procedure of acquisition properly speaking (rhythm, time, place, etc.) Evaluating what has been acquired **Issues of control** (Benson in Lewis and Vialleton, 2011) Selecting and using appropriate language learning strategies Controlling cognitive processes (e.g. attention and reflection) Marshalling meta-cognitive knowledge Determining the content of their learning	In general, students can be described as self regulated to the degree that they are metacognitively, motivationally and behaviorally active participants in their own learning process Such students personally initiate and direct their own efforts to acquire knowledge and skill rather than relying on teachers, parents, or other agents of instruction Volition, motivation or self efficacy beliefs play a role in self regulated learning Focus is on how students activate, alter and sustain specific learning practices Academic self regulation is not a mental ability, such as intelligence, or an academic skill, such as reading proficiency; rather it is the self directive process through which learners transform their mental abilities into academic skills **Three main phases** (i) Forethought, which he defines as 'influential processes and beliefs that precede efforts to learn and set the stage for such learning' (ii) Performance or volitional control, by which he means 'processes that occur during learning efforts and affect concentration and performance' (iii) Self reflection, which involves 'processes that occur after learning efforts and influence learners' reactions to that experience' **Self regulated learners attempt to control** (Pintrich, 2000 in Lewis and Vialleton, 2011) Cognition Motivation and affect Behaviour Context

Figure 9.1 Learner Autonomy and Self Regulated Learning (adapted from Lewis and Vialleton, 2011)

Elsewhere, Zimmerman (2002) discusses recently developed notions of individual learner differences and emphasises the social nature of self regulated learning. He states that the regulatory behaviours and other behaviours that comprise self regulation can be modelled by teachers, parents and peers, especially as self regulated learners often seek out the expert advice of adults and peers. The goals that students set themselves as important learning goals are socially and culturally determined, as are the strategies used to achieve them and the manner in which learning is expressed and demonstrated. However, these models are not exclusive in describing the different perspectives relating to self directed learning. Meltzer's (2007) writing on executive function has recently brought this construct out of the context of special education and clinical settings and into the mainstream inclusive classrooms.

What Does This Mean for You?

If you decide to transform the educational process from traditional teacher-led teaching and learning, then this involves conceptually moving towards student-orientated pedagogies that include self directed learning. SDL has much to recommend it. A great deal of support comes from the findings of neuroscience. Other collaborating endorsements can be found in the constructivist theories and pedagogies. Further authentication can be found in the ethical and professional standards that require you to provide an equitable education opportunity for every child. A final argument can be found in the work of theorists who are looking to the future and anticipating the skills that students will need for lifelong learning in a rapidly changing global society. Certainly, you cannot just ask students to do what they want. There need to be frameworks to guide the activity to ensure that learning occurs. However, it is a powerful strategy if you understand how to implement it successfully. There are some considerations that characterise self directed learning. These may include the following:

- The degree of control students have over the process dictates how transformative this strategy can be. They need at the very minimum to be guided towards setting appropriate, personal, academic, performance goals. Depending on their stage and competencies, they may also select their own strategies and how to demonstrate the goals they have achieved.
- Performance goals are unique to each individual and non-competitive.
- These could be planned on the SMART goal format (McGrath and Noble, 2005). Using the acronym, students need to complete the format indicating Specific, Measurable, Achievable, Realistic, Timed goals. These can be used with any age or stage of student who is literate enough to complete the format with or without assistance.

- To readily identify students' goals and successfully map students' progress, the aims, objectives, indicators or outcomes should be attached to these SMART goal records by you.
- Feedback is crucial. You need to organise your time so that you actually talk to each student individually about their work on a regular basis, not just in passing and not simply to help with difficulties or affirm the suitability of ideas or strategies. You need to build positive, professional relationships with students.
- You need to be available to anticipate the difficulties that individual students may have and mentor them in the goal setting, implementation and completion process.
- You need to set standards and high expectation for the standard of completion.
- The working environment becomes increasingly important. Resources, equipment and support materials and personnel must be easily accessed and managed.
- Students may need to be taught explicit organisational strategies. Many students, especially primary and lower secondary students, will need to have a parallel programme of skills and strategies development, and knowledge and concept exploration to support their self directed learning projects.
- Record keeping, notations, profiles and assessment records are extremely important resources for your future planning for learning. Also of importance are the feedback records and reflective journalling (even if this is only a range of drawn faces from smiley to 'oh dear') that are compiled by the students in relation to the journey they travel when working with their self directed learning goals.
- The achievement of goals, however simple or small, must be acknowledged and celebrated. Sharing with peers is an excellent means of achieving this. Records need to be kept of these and other significant learning that has been set as a goal and achieved, whether modified or not.
- Self directed learning is an important part of students developing their self knowledge, metacognitive strategies and utilising their relative strengths (if they are permitted to nominate how they might undertake the goal and the product they select as evidence of achievement) to master increased skills in areas of relative limitation.
- Self directed learning empowers students; it shifts the locus of control and redefines the roles of teacher and learner. You become a mentor and facilitator and the students take responsibility for their own learning in this specific context.

The term executive function has risen to prominence in learning contexts as a result of the increasing interest of educational practitioners in using findings from medical research into the brain to inform their teaching and learning (Denckla, 2007). However, finding a definition is not a simple task (Bernstein and Waber, 2007). Meltzer (2007: 1) comments that 'fuzzy definitions still abound' and that 'furthermore, different theories and models still compete to explain the development of executive function processes'. What can be determined, however, is that executive function is a general term that is used to identify 'the complex cognitive processes that serve ongoing, goal-directed behaviours'. It can also be determined that executive function processes are processes that are recognised as supportive of student academic learning endeavours and have been shown to improve learning outcomes. Meltzer (2007: 2–3) identifies the following traits as common elements of many of the definitions of executive function:

- Goal setting and planning.
- Organisation of behaviours over time.
- Flexibility.
- Attention and memory systems that guide these processes (e.g. working memory).
- Self regulatory processes such as self monitoring.

These fundamental skills align neatly to those described in the model offered by Dawson and Guare (2004: 2–3) and Dendy (2002). The former also offer a definition of executive skills, indicating that these cognitive processes have a major role in developing self regulatory behaviours.

Dawson and Guare (2004) believe that executive function is facilitated in two ways. Firstly, by using the specific cognitive processes and demonstrable skills acknowledged as representing executive function to determine goals and achieve them. They identify these skills as planning, organisation, time management, working memory and metacognition. The second group of executive skills, response inhibition, self regulation of emotions, task initiation, flexibility and goal directed persistence, function to modify behaviours so that goals may be successfully completed. Working together as interpolated skills, children and adolescents are able to learn more efficiently and to exhibit learning characteristics that were formerly believed to develop only in late adolescence and early adulthood. One specific perspective regarding the nature of executive function is offered by Gardner (1993b, 1997, 1999a, 1999b; Moran and Gardner, 2007), who discusses executive function in the context of one of the intelligence domains developed as his theory of multiple intelligences: intrapersonal intelligence.

Intrapersonal Intelligence: Knowledge of Self

Gardner's theory of intrapersonal intelligence (1983, 1993a, 1993b, 1997, 1999a, 1999b; Moran and Gardner, 2007) provides another, more expansive perspective on students' academic self beliefs. Intrapersonal intelligence is composed of two aspects: the sense of self that is not observable and is identified as the 'core of intrapersonal intelligence' (Moran and Gardner, 2007: 35) and the expression of self through observable skills (executive function skills). Moran and Gardner (2007: 35) define the expression of self as involving 'the second aspect of intrapersonal intelligence – the executive capacity to integrate one's goals, skills and motivation'. This executive capacity is also known as executive function (or functions) and is becoming increasingly important in educational contexts (Meltzer, 2007), especially as curriculum changes place increasing pressure on primary-aged students to become more active participants in their learning and construct their own understandings and knowledge.

While the term 'executive function' may not be used frequently in educational contexts at present, the skills that comprise the various aspects of this construct are more familiar and have attracted the attention of educational researchers for some time, as these skills are believed to be critical to the learning process. The developmental aspects of these cognitive skills, such as self regulation, task engagement and motivation, create an increasingly complex notion of the already multifaceted components of executive function.

Developmental Perspectives of Executive Function

The challenge of supporting the cognitive skills and processes that are associated with executive function is made more manageable as the result of many theorists linking the stages of development of executive function to regular cognitive developmental phases. That executive function and development are closely aligned appears to be logical. Bernstein and Waber (2007) believe that the vast majority of individual differences in executive function among children can be related to differences in maturation. They acknowledge that capacities for executive function are evident in babies and continue to develop through to adolescence. They also contend that much of children's learning in the areas of cognition, and social and emotional development, are actually evidence of the development of the skills of executive function. Additionally, they use the same type of evidence as Moran and Gardner (2007) to support the developmental nature of this construct. Both Bernstein and Waber (2007) and Moran and Gardner (2007) present evidence from neuro-imaging literature that established the fact that adults utilise different parts of the brain from children for problem solving. From the multiple intelligences perspective (Gardner, 1983, 1993a, 1999a, 1999b; Moran and Gardner, 2007), executive function grows out of sound, accurate intrapersonal intelligence that takes time and experience to develop alongside the capacity to self regulate behaviours in order to achieve a purpose. As a result, Moran and Gardner (2007) also espouse a developmental overview of executive function that would apply to most babies, children and adolescents.

Moran and Gardner (2007) recognise that the actions of babies are predominantly governed by their biological and emotional systems. As they grow, they begin to develop some sense of self, usually in the second year of life, and by the time they are ready for school, most young children have developed the ability to regulate their behaviours in response to the expectations of others, recognise and utilise a basic sense of self and remember information over a period of time (Isquith, et al., 2005). This stage is acknowledged by Moran and Gardner (2007) as the beginning of the development of executive function. From this beginning they distinguish two further phases of development: the,'master stage' and the 'apprentice stage'. The 'apprentice stage' is dominated by skill development, and a sense of self as distinct from others. Frequently this concept of 'self' may be unrealistic and idealised. They acquire the knowledge and skills that allow them to participate in society. Goals are usually set by significant adults; teachers and families, especially their parents. Children in this stage have realised that they can use their energies to achieve increasingly longer term projects as they mature. They begin to learn and understand cultural conventions and societal norms and begin to compare themselves to others in various contexts. Moran and Gardner (2007) perceive the 'apprentice stage' as being almost exclusively about meeting expectations and children being 'fundamentally conscious' (2007: 25) of the effect they have on others and vice versa. They become increasingly aware of the behaviours that promote their goals and those that are detrimental to them. Intrapersonal intelligence is developed mainly from the feedback that comes from interaction with others. However, their notion of this developmental stage may have some shortcomings as Moran and Gardner's (2007) description of the 'apprentice stage' of executive function does not appear to explicitly accommodate students' knowledge of self as learner as a major factor at this point in their development. This is particularly apparent in the following statement: 'apprentice executive function involves keeping oneself in line with expectations' (Moran and Gardner, 2007: 25).

Despite this, the notion of an 'apprentice stage' of executive function is a particularly useful framework within which to explore new ways in which students can interact effectively in school settings and develop the knowledge, skills and understandings related to the components of executive function.

Firstly, as the goals that students pursue in school settings are ultimately determined by the curriculum, school management and organisation, the learning context limits the students' capacities to exclusively select goals to pursue. As Moran and Gardner (2007) noted, the goals that students at this developmental stage are able to set are, to a large degree, culturally determined. However, a degree of student autonomy is possible within this culturally determined framework which may provide students with the opportunities they need to become more active and independent learners. As students engage with specific educational experiences in school, they are more likely to have some skills that may facilitate goal completion. The view that students can have some degree of competency in a variety of knowledge, understandings and skills without necessarily maintaining parallel competence in each at any specific age or stage of schooling is reflected in the overall constructivist notions of pedagogy and developmental considerations. It is also to be found in the practical means by which teachers assess student competencies, for example, by using the incremental terms 'not evident', 'working towards', 'working at' and 'working beyond', they provide the benchmarks for the specific educational knowledge, understandings and skills their students require to be successful in the learning process.

Towards the end of this 'apprentice stage' the role of executive function skills is to support engagement in various roles within the students' communities and to facilitate their acquisition of the skills and attitudes that will enable them to play a productive role in adult society. By the end of the apprentice stage, individuals should be able to meet the expectations of others with little conscious thought. The importance of formal goals rises to prominence at this time as behaviours and skills become automatically in line with societal expectations. While personal choices of goals are available and possible to pursue, many goals are defined by cultural expectations and authorities. Csikszentmihalyi et al. (in Moran and Gardner, 2007: 29) suggest that tensions caused by the determination of some individuals at the 'apprentice stage' to pursue personal, 'inner' goals that are outside those considered culturally appropriate may partly account for the considerable differences in young people's attitudes to motivation and planning for the future. However, some of the tensions may have physiological grounds that are important to consider as part of the developmental perspective as they are directly related to the process of maturation. A more recent study (Blakemore and Choudhury, 2006) has supported Peterson's (1988) earlier work in the area of the specific learning characteristics of adolescent development. Both studies have found that, in addition to the hormonal and physical changes that characterise puberty there are significant changes in self identity, self consciousness and, importantly, cognitive flexibility. Although empirical research into cognitive and neural changes in puberty and adolescence is in its early stages it has established that adolescents are more self aware and more reflective than prepubescent children; they also develop the capacity to think in a more strategic manner and can manage more multidimensional concepts.

There is evidence to support the hypothesis that, as changes occur in areas of the brain in adolescence, there are also changes to students' capacities to develop and improve the cognitive skills associated with executive function during this time. These skills may include selective attention, decision making, response inhibition and the capacity to multi-task. Although it is considered that different aspects of executive control may develop at different times, Anderson et al. (2001, in Blakemore and Choudhury, 2006), found that students between the ages of 11 and 17 demonstrated increased competence in tasks involving selective attention, working memory and problem solving. Other cognitive factors dependent on these parts of the brain, such as recognition of emotions, improve with pubertal development. These findings challenge the more established view that executive function develops towards the end of formal schooling (Ylvisaker and Debonis, 2000). During adolescence, a time of major change, students may temporarily experience difficulties demonstrating the behaviours associated with specific aspects of executive functioning. The most significant impact may be on the individual's capacity to cognitively process self relevant information, principally in the areas of emotion and bodily sensations and this, in turn may impair their ability to further develop the cognitive processes related to executive function, especially those that relate to the degree of attention and concentration that are embedded in the notion of optimal experience (Csikszentmihalyi, 1988, 1991).

What Does This Mean for You?

As you have read, self directed learning is a valuable teaching strategy and it is in the development of executive function skills that you are able to use it to authentically transform the nature of teaching and learning in your classroom. There have been some traditionally held notions that many of the cognitive skills that comprise executive function are not developed before late adolescence. You have just read about the theorists who dispute this and plot the development of some of the cognitive skills to very young children. The importance of Moran and Gardner's work in this instance is to highlight for you the major difference between the defining characteristics of the 'master stage' of executive function and what they have termed the 'apprentice stage'. These are significant for these reasons:

- Students are frequently given a wide variety of tasks to choose from, a set topic, limited to the strategies they can utilise or an incentive to complete the self directed learning.

- Because of the mandatory status of any school curriculum, irrespective of how loosely defined it may be, students are restricted to some degree or other regarding what they can undertake in the way of the nature of their goals that are the focus of their self directed learning. It is simply not possible to accommodate some goals in a classroom or wider school context.
- A similar situation applies to strategies. Some strategies are not able to be used in the limited time in the formal learning environment.
- As students are sensitive to the expectations of their parents, teachers and peers, they are not yet totally intrinsically or internally motivated. There is at the very least the motivation that comes from knowing that something has to be done in class and this is a preferred way of doing it.
- This does not suggest, however, that the cognitive capacities of executive function cannot be strengthened in school context. Quite the contrary. It is the perfect situation in which students can develop these skills within a framework that supports their efforts and allows them to be mentored in a meaningful, supportive manner. While they are still developing their knowledge of self, they have probably had enough experience inside and outside of the formal learning context to articulate what they like and what they don't. They gradually gain experience of learning in school contexts and begin to develop an understanding of what they are good at, how they like to learn best and which contexts and circumstances make learning easier for each of them.
- School is an ideal opportunity for transformative learning to occur as students have considerable personal control over what is to be achieved, how it might be achieved, and their degree of motivation to complete the goal tasks successfully.
- In the 'apprentice stage' of Moran and Gardner's work there is one consideration that does not apply to learning in school after a certain age. That is the developmental consideration that is allocated to prepubescent and pubescent learners. The changes they experience emotionally, physically and cognitively are not applicable to the 'master stage' but are pertinent to teachers who work with these student groups daily in teaching and learning contexts.

Goal Setting

Educational goals are generally considered to be of two major types: mastery goals and performance goals (Pintrich and Schunk, 1996; Woolfolk, 2004). Both of these goal types have a positive and negative orientation. Mastery goals focusing on achievement are planned to develop skills, improve performance and, frequently, to engage in challenges. They are designed to deepen an individual's understanding. Mastery goals with an avoidance focus stress the importance of not being wrong and avoiding misunderstanding. Mastery goals are also sometimes referred to as task goals or learning goals (Woolfolk, 2004). Performance goals are more competitively orientated. Individuals who set performance goals aim to win, demonstrate their competence, avoid failing, or gain better grades than others engaged in the same or similar tasks (Pintrich, 2000; Pintrich and Schunk, 1996). Performance goals with an avoidance focus place great stress on not losing, being last or being the slowest, depending on the specific nature of the goal that is set. These goals, like intrinsic and extrinsic motivation, are not mutually exclusive. Students may engage in mastery and performance goals simultaneously or develop goals that encompass elements of both. Woolfolk and Margetts (2007) argue that mastery goals are more likely to be intrinsically motivated, whereas performance goals are more often motivated by extrinsic motivation. They also posit that individuals who pursue mastery goals are more likely to seek and accept constructive criticism, attempt more difficult tasks, which further supports the development of their skills and academic progress. Students who plan and engage in performance goals have a tendency to set simpler goals in order to demonstrate how easily they can be accomplished or demonstrate their superiority by completing the greatest number of goals (Pintrich and Schunk in Woolfolk and Margetts, 2007). Two additional types of goals are identified. One is associated with individuals who evaluate the degree of success they have attained by the ease and speed with which they complete tasks. They have no real interest in learning or appearing to be clever. They are labelled as 'work avoidant learners' (Nicholls in Woolfolk and Margetts, 2007: 385). The final category is social goals, which can compete with learning goals for the students' time and attention. It appears, however, that the most valuable educational goals for the development of executive function skills are mastery goals.

Moran and Gardner (2007) suggest that students mature and increase the cognitive skills demonstrated as executive function by not being allowed to become too comfortable and complacent. They recommend that educators in regular classroom settings facilitate learning rather than teach. They argue that teachers should provide only the necessary support for individuals with low executive function skills and gradually withdraw this aid as students progress. They contend that students at the 'apprentice stage' should increasingly take responsibility for their own goal setting, expended energy and skill development. With support, students should begin to take responsibility for their learning. They should do this by developing increased sensitivity to 'nuances within themselves and their environment' (Moran and Gardner, 2007: 32–3), by evaluating their relative strengths and limitations of their current self regulatory behaviours and by taking opportunities to develop mental flexibility. In other words, Moran and Gardner are advocating that students use their knowledge in the intrapersonal intelligence domain to direct their efforts into discerning and utilising self relevant information in educational contexts. They posit that an individual's degree of competency in executing these processes will be expressed as the individual's capacity to demonstrate the cognitive skills of executive function.

Questions for Reflection

- Q1. Have you been involved in any self directed learning? Explain if so.
- Q2. Does your personal understanding of the role of the teacher include developing students' skills in the cognitive capacities identified as executive function? Validate your answer.
- Q3. Do you think that adolescence has an impact on how students learn? Why or why not?
- Q4. What do you think of the master stage of executive function? Do you know anyone who operates at this stage of self directed learning?
- Q5. Do you think teachers as professional practitioners need to develop and sustain the cognitive capacities associated with executive function? Validate your answer.
- Q6. Do you think you are able to support students' development of executive function skills in your preferred pedagogical practices?

Implications for Teaching

The varying perspectives on self directed learning discussed in this chapter have each got something to offer teachers in any learning context. The key to success in each of these perspectives is sound, accurate self knowledge. Anderson and Lux (2005) indicate the essential nature of self knowledge in autonomous learning, Dermitzaki and Leondari (2004) related self concept to young students' self regulatory skills in relation to their learning, Bandura (1986) and his associates have investigated self efficacy beliefs and student success but limited their efforts to the students' perceived, not demonstrated, self efficacy levels. There are numerous studies that indicate an understanding of self is important in motivation (Dweck, 2000; Eccles and Wigfield, 2002; Elliott and Dweck, 2005; Gilman and Anderman, 2006; Golan et al., 2003; Miller and Brickman, 2004), in self regulation (Boekaerts and Corno, 2005; Boekaerts and Niemivirta, 2000; Zimmerman, et al., 1996; Zimmerman and Schunk, 2001) and in other areas related to academic success in classrooms (Maitland, 2000; Murray, 2000; Ng, 1998, 2000; Sellars, 2006; Teo et al., 2001) including developing reflective processes. Few studies focus on the impact of programmes that are designed to support the development of the cognitive capacities of executive function from any of the various models. However, one study (Sellars, 2009) that focused on developing these executive function capacities, from a multiple intelligences perspective, for ten 12-year-old students provides evidence that students were not only increasingly self regulated, motivated and successful, but their learning was transformative. The students learned not only to regulate their behaviours and emotions in order to persevere and complete their self selected tasks, but became better organised, sought advice and assistance when it was needed and demonstrated improved skills in using their working memory and in their flexible thinking skills.

What Does This Mean for You?

The study that is described above requires you to adopt a teacher role that is not traditional. You must become both mentor and facilitator to your students. You have to mentor your students by:

- Discussing with them how they might plan their leaning effectively.
- Encouraging them to use their knowledge of their own relative strengths and limitations to guide their implementation of their self selected tasks that comprise their goals. You have to be able to accurately access not only their academic competencies, but also their work habits, attitudes and motivational tendencies.
- Responding to their perceived learning needs. Mentoring students involves a lot of talking about the work strategies, planning and organisation. You may easily have to support many students in their choices in addition to these other skills.
- Avoiding telling the students what to do. Discussions with your students on an individual basis should be guided by what they know and what they may explore further. Suggestions should be offered by both of you and a choice made by the students.
- Providing practical support by ensuring students have suitable materials and other resources with which to complete their tasks.
- Providing opportunities for students to present their work and explain their choices and the reasoning behind them. Allowing opportunities for students to discuss their choices with their audiences.

You need to be able to facilitate their learning by:

- Introducing the students to the basic skills, knowledge and concepts needed to explore, understand and complete their selected tasks competently. This can be done in small groups, individually or as a class so that the discussion involves peers sharing their knowledge and understandings.

- Being exceptionally well organised. This may be anticipating what your students need as resources and providing these in advance, keeping records of discussions and work sample annotations or simply modelling your own capacity to be organised, to plan and to carry through despite difficulties arising.
- Being flexible and supporting divergent and creative thinking. This requires you to be sensitive to the learning that results from errors and mistakes, to demonstrate many ways of completing a task or developing a product for presentation and to accept solutions to problems or tasks that are unconventional or unusual.
- Helping with the practicalities of a task. Developing checklists, recording and reflection sheets, providing storage space for products under completion and generally keeping track of who is doing what, when, where and how.
- Accepting a different role in situations such as this study and allowing the locus of control to be shared and different voices to be heard in relation to what individual are to be learning. The student voices are always moderated by the mandatory documents and curricula, but genuine choice has the capacity to generate transformative learning and revive students' interest and motivation in the classroom.

Questions for Reflection

- Q1. Would you consider working with your students in the way the executive function project from the multiple intelligence perspective was implemented? Validate your answer
- Q2. How well do you think the students would know themselves as learners at the conclusion of the study?
- Q3. Do you think this sort of teaching and learning has the potential to develop into transformative learning? Explain your response.
- Q4. What aspects of self directed learning such as this would be the most challenging? Can you think of ways to manage these aspects in your response?
- Q5. Can you include any of the content in this chapter in your visual organiser, i.e. mind map, concept map or other type of organiser which allows you to see at a glance how interrelated the issues for professional reflection actually are in practice? Validate your answer.

Scenario Nine

As part of an action research project, Amy and her classmates were supported in developing their own learning goals in English, selecting their own tasks and strategies, deciding on their product and presenting their work to the class. The class of 11- and 12-year-olds selected from a range of tasks developed from curriculum documents. These tasks were differentiated in content and cognitive process and students developed their goals by selecting some tasks that were easy, some tasks that would use their skills, strategies and knowledge in ways they had not used them before and some tasks that were challenging. Each student could determine what they chose in each category based on their own self knowledge of their interests, skills and relative strengths and limitations as learners.

During the time that English was timetabled in the class, Amy and two of her classmates were withdrawn from the class by the special needs teacher for additional literacy support because their reading ages were relatively low. During this time they concentrated on the foundational literacy skills and followed a commercially developed programme designed for this purpose. After several weeks the special needs teacher came to the class teacher and explained she had a problem with Amy and her classmates. Amy, who was normally very quiet and reserved, had announced that she didn't want to do the reading programme any more; it was boring and she wanted help with her self selected goal instead. The other two students readily agreed with her and began to explain about the tasks they had chosen and what they needed help with. As the special needs teacher thought the novelty of the research project and the excitement of the choices the students were being given would not last long, she had agreed to abandon the deficit programme and work on the students' requests. However, two months later, the students were still refusing to go back to the programme and remained enthusiastic as ever about their self selected English goals. Having decided to discuss the situation again with Amy's class teacher, the special needs teacher dropped into the classroom on her way past to check when they could meet. She entered the room just as Amy was about to present her work. Amy saw her, and invited her to stay for her presentation. As she sat waiting for Amy to start, she noticed that all of other students had stopped their work and were writing their names on pieces of paper. As the presentation progressed, Amy's classmates paid remarkably close attention to her PowerPoint presentation and the model she was describing. They also wrote on their pieces of paper. Amy did a fine, confident presentation and the special needs teacher was impressed. She left the classroom having arranged to meet with the class teacher after school in the classroom.

When she arrived in the classroom, she saw that Amy's class teacher was reading through the comments on Amy's presentation that had been prepared by her classmates. He offered them to her to look through as well. He explained that he had been concerned that some of the students were continuing to work on their own gaols while others were presenting. Believing that an audience was crucial to the students' focus and purpose for developing goals, he had to be creative and think of a way to entice them to be involved and to support one another. He had decided that each of the students in the audience would make comment on the presenter's work. After discussing this with them, he had designed a simple reflection sheet for peer feedback. They were organised as shown in the example below. As the special needs teacher read over the comments she thought what a productive experience this was for Amy. No wonder she was keen to get her goal organised well. Concerned that some students might write discouraging or inappropriately negative comments, she asked the class teacher what would happen in a case like that. He explained that for the first time for everyone, he was monitoring the comments before handing them to the presenter. So far there had been nothing that needed to be censored or withheld from the presenter. He believed that because all the students had to present their work and get peer feedback, it made them think about what was useful and appropriate and what may not be. It was not a competition either. Everyone's goal could be presented in any format or product so there were no onerous comparisons to be made. He added that the self directed learning had made the students develop very different relationships with him and with each other, and that these were really positive and supportive as the students all had to work hard to achieve their goals. In fact, to his surprise, during the entire six months, no one had selected a goal he had thought was too easy for them. In fact, they had made the work challenging for themselves!

Name	Presenter's Name	Date
Content (interestingly presented, clear and well structured)	Conventions (Spelling, grammar, punctuation)	Comment (What was done well and an idea for improvement)
Nice work Amy. I really am not interested in dancing but you made it okay and i can see you love it	Some full stops were missing but the power point background was good for the dancing	Next time I think you could make a bigger model and get Anna to help you with the full stops and say what the dancing words mean

Figure 9.2

Questions for reflection

- Q1. What do you think was happening here?
- Q2. What would you advise the Special Needs teacher to do next?
- Q3. What else could the class teacher do to support his students' improved learning outcomes?
- Q4. Are there any ethical or professional issues here?
- Q5. What else could you do in this situation to support your students in their self directed learning? Validate your answer.

Conclusion

This chapter discussed the various understandings of self directed learning. It introduced you to a term that may be new to you: – that of the cognitive capacities of executive function. This is really a collective term for all the attitudes and behaviours that cannot easily be separated or individually identified one from another; but are recognised as attitudes and behaviours that support successful learning on an individual basis. These also have the potential to transform learning for those students who have opportunities to work in this manner. As you can understand, there are a number of links between the ideas of self directed learning and:

- student self knowledge
- those ideas presented in previous chapters that discussed learning in the twenty-first century
- the impact of the findings of neuroscientists for education
- importance of considering the relationship of emotion and cognition in the learning process.

However, if the goals, strategies and products of self directed learning are individually selected and are socially and culturally mediated, you may wonder how self directed learning can be facilitated in diverse classroom groups. This is challenging even if you have with an understanding of the developmental considerations that will impact on your capacity to meet your students' learning needs. In the next chapter you will find a discussion of some differences that impact on students' worldviews, their every-day understandings of events in your classroom and even on their thinking as a whole.

References

Abraham, R., Upadhya, S. and Ramnaryam, K. (2005) Self directed learning. *Advances in Physiology Education*, 29 (2): 135–6.

Anderson, J. and Lux, W. (2005) Knowing your own strength: accurate self assessment as a requirement for personal autonomy. *Philosophy, Psychiatry, & Psychology*, 11 (4): 279–94.

Bandura, A. (1986) Self efficacy beliefs in human functioning Retrieved from www.emory.edu/EDUCATION/mfp/effpassages.html (accessed June 2002).

Bernstein, J. and Waber, D. (2007) 'Executive capacities from a developmental perspective.' In L. Meltzer (ed.), *Executive Function in Education: From Theory to Practice*. New York: Guilford Press. pp. 39–54.

Blakemore, S. and Choudhury, S. (2006) Development of the adolescent brain: implications for executive function and social cognition. *Journal of Child Psychology and Psychiatry*, 47 (3/4): 296–342.

Boekaerts, M. and Corno, L. (2005) Self regulation in the classroom: a perspective on assessment and intervention. *Applied Psychology: An International Review*, 54 (2): 199–231.

Boekaerts, M. and Niemivirta, M. (2000) 'Self regulated learning: finding a balance between learning goals and ego protective goals.' In M. Boekaerts (ed.), *A Handbook of Self Regulation*. London: Academic Press. pp. 589–604.

Brookfield, S. (2009) 'Self directed learning.' In R. MacLean and D. Wilson (eds), *International Handbook of Education for the Changing World of Work*. Dordrecht: Springer Netherlands. pp. 2615–2627.

Candy, P. (1991) *Self-Direction for Lifelong Learning. A Comprehensive Guide to Theory and Practice*. San Francisco, CA: Jossey Bass.

Csikszentmihalyi, M. (1988) 'The flow experience and its significance for human psychology.' In M. Csikszentmihalyi and S. Csikszentmihalyi (eds), *Optimal Experience: Psychological Studies of Flow in Consciousness*. Cambridge: Cambridge University Press.

Csikszentmihalyi, M. (1991) 'Work as flow.' In *Flow: The Psychology of Optimal Experience*. New York: Harper Perennial. pp. 143–63.

Dawson, P. and Guare, R. (2004) *Executive Skills in Children and Adolescents*. New York: Guilford Press.

Denckla, M. (2007) 'Executive function: binding together the definitions of attention-deficit/hyperactivity disorder and learning disabilities.' In L. Meltzer (ed.), *Executive Function in Education: From Theory to Practice*. New York: Guilford Press. pp. 5–18.

Dendy, C. (2002) Executive function. *Chadd's Attention Magazine* Retrieved from www.chrisdendy.com/executive.htm (accessed 12 July 2006).

Dermitzaki, T. and Leondari, A. (2004) Pre and primary students' self concept and its relationship to their self regulatory skills. Paper presented at the Third Annual International Biennial SELF Research Conference: Self Concept Motivation and Identity. Berlin, 4–7 July.

Dweck, C. (2000) *Self Theories: Their Role in Motivation, Personality and Development*. Lillington, NC: Taylor and Francis.

Eccles, J. and Wigfield, A. (2002) Motivational beliefs, values and goals. *Annual Review of Psychology*, 53 (1): 109–32.

Elliott, A. and Dweck, C. (eds) (2005) *Handbook of Competence and Motivation*. New York: Guilford Press.

Gardner, H. (1983) *Frames of Mind: The Theory of Multiple Intelligences*. New York: Basic Books.

Gardner, H. (1993a) *Frames of Mind. Tenth Anniversary Edition*. New York: Basic Books.

Gardner, H. (1993b) *Multiple Intelligences. The Theory in Practice*. New York: Basic Books.

Gardner, H. (1997) Multiple intelligences as a partner in school improvement. *Educational Leadership*, 9 (1): 20–1.

Gardner, H. (1999a) *The Disciplined Mind. What All Students Should Understand*. New York: Simon & Shuster.

Gardner, H. (1999b) *Intelligence Reframed: Multiple Intelligences for the 21st Century.* New York: Basic Books.

Gilman, R. and Anderman, E. (2006) The relationship between relative levels of motivation and intrapersonal, interpersonal and academic functioning among older adolescents. *Journal of School Psychology*, 44 (5): 375–91.

Golan, S., Henrich, C., Blatt, S., Ryan, R. and Little, T. (2003) Interpersonal relatedness, self-definition, and their motivational orientation during adolescence: a theoretical and Empirical integration. *American Psychological Association*, 39 (3): 470–83.

Heimstra, R. (1994) 'Self directed learning.' In T. Husen and T. Postlethwaite (eds), *The Encycolpedia of Education*, 2nd edn. Oxford: Pergamon Press. pp. 254–63.

Isquith, P., Crawford, J., Espy, K. and Gioia, G. (2005) Assessment of executive function in preschool-aged children. *Mental Retardation and Developmental Disabilities Research Reviews*, 11 (3): 209–15.

Lewis, T. and Vialleton, E. (2011) The notions of control and consciousness in learner autonomy and self-regulated learning: a comparison and critique. *Innovation in Language Learning and Teaching*, 5 (2): 205–19.

Maitland, L.E. (2000) Ideas in practice: self-regulation and metacognition in the reading lab. *Journal of Developmental Education*, 24 (2): 26.

McGrath, H. and Noble, T. (2005) *Eight Ways at Once: Multiple Intelligences + Revised Bloom's Taxonomy: 200 Differentiated Classroom Strategies* (Vol. 1). Frenchs Forest, NSW: Pearson Education Australia.

Meltzer, L. (2007) 'Understanding executive function.' In L. Meltzer (ed.), *Executive Function in Education: From Theory to Practice*. New York: Guilford Press.

Merriam, S. (2001) Andragogy and self-directed learning: Pillars of adult learning theory. *New Directions for Adult and Continuing Education*, 89: 3–14.

Miller, B. and Brickman, S. (2004) A model of future oriented motivation and self regulation. *Educational Phychology Review*, 16 (1): 9–33.

Moran, S. and Gardner, H. (2007) '"Hill, skill and will": executive function from a multiple-intelligences perspective.' In L. Meltzer (Ed.), *Executive Function in Education: From Theory to Practice*. New York: Guilford Press. pp. 19–38.

Murray, B. (2000) Teaching students how to learn. Retrieved from www.apa.org/monitor/jun00/howtoleran.html (accessed 19 August 2005).

Ng, C.-H. (1998) I'm motivated because of who I am: the effects of domain specific self-schemas in students' learning engagement patterns. Paper presented at the Annual Conference of Australian Association for Reearch in Education, Adelaide, Australia.

Ng, C.-H. (2000) A cross cultural comparison of the effects of self schema on learning engagement. Paper presented at the Annual Conference of Australian Association for Research in Education.

Peterson, C., Seligman, M. and Park, N. (2005) Positive psychology progress: empirical validation of interventions. *American Psychologist*, 60 (5): 410–21.

Pilling-Cormick, J. (1997) Transformative and self-directed learning in practice. *New Directions for Adult and Continuing Education* (June). 69–77.

Pintrich, P. (2000) 'The role of goal orientation in self regulated learning.' In M. Boekaerts (ed.), *Handbook of Self Regulated Learning*. London: Academic Press. pp. 452–494.

Pintrich, P. and Schunk, D. (1996) *Motivation in Education: Theory, Research and Applications*. Englewood Cliffs, NJ: Prentice–Hall.

Roeberts, C., Cimeli, P., Rothlisberger, M. and Neuenschwander, R. (2012) Executive functioning, metacognition, and self-perceived competence in elementary school children: an explorative study on their interrelations and their role for school achievement. *Metacognition and Learning*, 7 (3): 151–73.

Schaub-de Jong, M., Schonrock-Adema, J., Dekker, H., Verkerk, M. and Cohen-Schotanus, J. (2011) Development of a student rating scale to evaluate teachers' competencies for facilitating reflective learning. *Medical Education*, 45 (2): 155–65.

Sellars, M. (2006) The role of intrapersonal intelligence in self directed learning. *Issues in Educational Research*, 16 (1): 95–119.

Sellars, M. (2008) Education for the 21st century: three components of a new pedagogy. *International Journal of the Humanities*, 6 (2): 27–34.

Sellars, M. (2009) Intrapersonal intelligence, executive function and stage three students. Australian Catholic University, Sydney. Unpublished Thesis.

Teo, C., Quah, M., Rahim, R. and Rasanayagam, L. (2001) Self-knowledge education: educating gifted children in singapore on the hemispheric functioning. Paper presented at the AARE: International Research Conference: Crossing Borders: New Frontiers for Educational Research, Freemantle, 2–6 December.

Towle, A. and Cottrell, D. (1996) Self directed learning. *Archives of Diseases in Childhood*, 74: 357–9.

Woolfolk, A. (2004) *Educational Psychology*. Boston, MA: Pearson Education.

Woolfolk, A. and Margetts, K. (2007) *Educational Psychology*. Frenchs Forest, NSW: Pearson Education.

Ylvisaker, M. and Debonis, D. (2000) Executive function impairment in adolescents: TBI and ADHD. *Topics in Language Disorders*, 20 (2): 29–47.

Zimmerman, B.J. (2002) Becoming a self-regulated learner: an overview. *Theory into Practice*, 41 (2): 64–70.

Zimmerman, B. and Schunk, D. (eds) (2001) *Self Regulated Learning and Academic Achievement: Theoretical Perspectives*, 2nd edn. Mahwah, NJ: Lawrence Erlbaum Associates.

Zimmerman, B., Bonner, S. and Kovach, R. (1996) *Developing Self-Regulated Learners: Beyond Achievement to Self Efficacy*. Washington, DC: American Psychological Association.

Chapter 10: Understanding Student Diversity

- Q1. What do you understand as diversity?
- Q2. What difference do you think knowing about student diversity would make to your teaching?
- Q3. How can you accommodate diverse cultural perspectives in your classroom and in your school community?
- Q4. Do you think treating students the same is the answer to cultural, social and individual sensitivity?
- Q5. What aspects of diversity do you think impact most substantially on education and your work as a teacher?

Introduction

In the previous chapter we assumed that students would like to select their own tasks that they would enthusiastically engage with. We also assumed that education itself is valued, both as an end in itself and as a means by which to be part of the adult workforce and contribute to society. However, because social and geographical mobility have become a normal part of contemporary life, your notions regarding best pedagogy, the roles of the learner and teacher, and even the purpose of education itself may not necessarily be the same as your learners. They may also differ from their parents and caregivers, or even the local community. It is ethically imperative that, as a professional, you understand your students, parents and the wider community as well as you can so that your plans for teaching are successful and result in students learning and making academic progress. Additionally, it may well be part of your compulsory standards that you are aware of and can cater educationally for students from diverse cultural backgrounds, from different social groups and those whose physical or intellectual capacities require differentiated tasks and assessment. While it is acknowledged that each student is an individual, unique human being who constructs their own understandings and knowledge, it remains important to also recognise and accept that some students come from social and cultural backgrounds that espouse ideas about education, teaching, child rearing and a number of other matters which may be distinctly dissimilar to those held by you personally and perhaps even those held by the school and the wider community. It is, therefore, important that you are able to develop your sensitivities and be able to communicate and interact with these students and their parents in an effective, respectful manner as a professional practitioner. The difficulty that is presented when attempting to learn about other cultures, social classes and individual physical and intellectual capabilities is that the task could easily become unmanageable. This is simply because, in addition to the diverse social, cultural and individual norms that can be studied in general, your students, their families and their communities will have their own personal preferences, opinions, customs and habits. This chapter can only provide some very general information for your guidance and hopefully encourage you to explore the diversity of the students in your classrooms with this basic information to guide your efforts. As there exists such wide-ranging diversity, the information in this chapter has been organised around the ideas of cultural, social and individual differences.

What Does the Literature Say about Cultural Differences?

Cultural characteristics differ from one culture to another and influence values, beliefs and, consequently, behaviours. These cultural differences can have a significant impact on students' capacities to learn effectively in formal educational settings. Nisbett (2005) traces the historical foundations of differences to the perspectives of the Greeks, who have influenced Western thinking, and to Confucius in the East. The Greeks were the originators of the individualism that permeates Western societies, while Confucius believed there is no 'me' in isolation. This, he believed, was the result of the understanding that any one individual is the compilation of the many changing roles that they play in society; individuals are thought of as part of a very large, complex organism. In very general terms, Eastern thinking is concerned with the environment

(Chen et al., 2009; Gardner, 1991), relationships and with social harmony. There is a focus on the practical. Western thinkers have been focused on philosophical assumptions and scientific approaches, turning object attributes into abstractions. Western thinking has remained relatively static while Eastern thinking, more specifically Chinese philosophy, has been influenced through time by Confucianism, Taoism and later by Buddhism, all of which emphasise harmony and discourage abstraction. Chinese thinkers in particular hold the perspective that life and the world is constantly changing and is full of contradictions; what appears to be true now may actually be the opposite to what it appears to be. These differences in thinking affect the values and beliefs that people have about some significant issues in education and in life itself. These are manifested as behaviours, attitudes and customs. The Cultural Iceberg illustrated in Figure 10.1 indicates some of the differences that manifest themselves as three levels of cultural difference.

Culture is often likened to an iceberg in that only a small part of culture is visible. The first of these Cultural Iceberg models has been attributed to Hall (1976). and there are many interpretations and variations commonly used for different purposes in which culture has an important role to play. Figure 10.1 illustrates that the percentage of visible cultural attributes is very low in comparison to the entire complexity of cultural values and beliefs that underpin them. The emotional intensity that is attributed to the visual aspects of culture is also low in comparison to the other levels of unspoken rules, which are often highly emotional, and deep cultural beliefs and values, which are intensely emotional. At each of these cultural levels there are perspectives that impact on the routine interactions that take place in regular classrooms. The differing views and opinions that may cause the greatest dissension among peers or between teacher and students of different cultural backgrounds are, of course, those that have deep cultural rules and foundations

In order to understand the ways in which cultural differences can contrast with each other, Hofstede (1986) proposed four significant dimensions of difference. These are pertinent for teachers seeking to develop an understanding of the attitudes and behaviours that students bring to their classrooms. These are:

1. Power distance, which describes the strength of the hierarchy and the actual social distance between those who are powerful and those who are not. It also defines how societies view inequity and provide for those who are not powerful.
2. Individualism versus collectivism, which distinguishes a society that is loosely formed around nuclear families from one in which all extended family members are considered and support is expected in exchange for loyalty.

Nine-tenths of culture is not observable. The observable cultural characteristics and customs are the one-tenth that is visible. The more deeply held values and belief systems are, the more emotional intensity is attached to them.

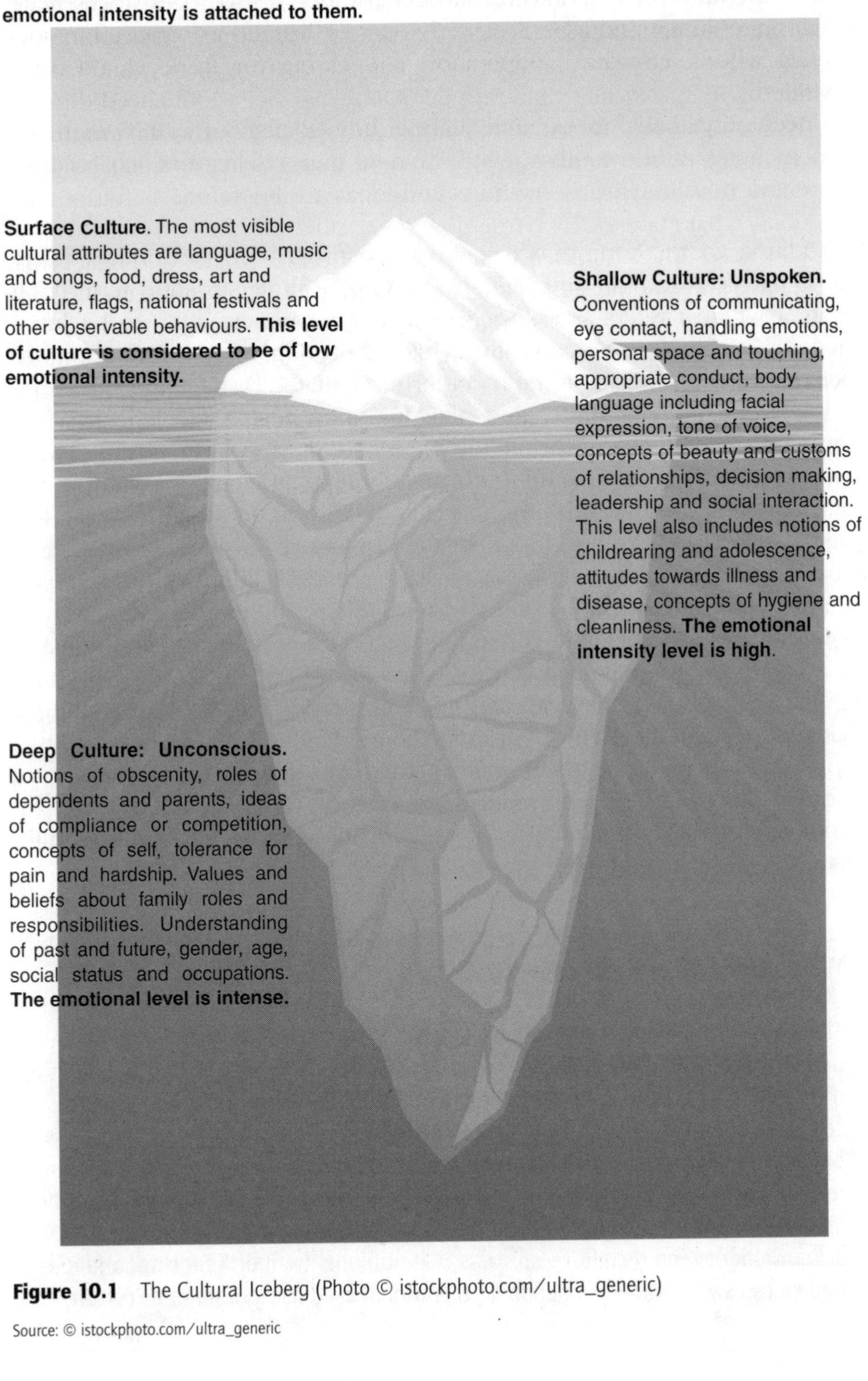
Surface Culture. The most visible cultural attributes are language, music and songs, food, dress, art and literature, flags, national festivals and other observable behaviours. **This level of culture is considered to be of low emotional intensity.**
Shallow Culture: Unspoken. Conventions of communicating, eye contact, handling emotions, personal space and touching, appropriate conduct, body language including facial expression, tone of voice, concepts of beauty and customs of relationships, decision making, leadership and social interaction. This level also includes notions of childrearing and adolescence, attitudes towards illness and disease, concepts of hygiene and cleanliness. **The emotional intensity level is high**.
Deep Culture: Unconscious. Notions of obscenity, roles of dependents and parents, ideas of compliance or competition, concepts of self, tolerance for pain and hardship. Values and beliefs about family roles and responsibilities. Understanding of past and future, gender, age, social status and occupations. **The emotional level is intense.**

Figure 10.1 The Cultural Iceberg (Photo © istockphoto.com/ultra_generic)

Source: © istockphoto.com/ultra_generic

3. Masculinity versus femininity, which is the tendency for teachers to be task orientated or person orientated. It also defines societies where materialism, courage and assertive behaviours are valued as opposed to societies where harmony, cooperation and caring for those in need are valued.

4. Uncertainty avoidance is literally about how societies and their members face change and the unknown, how rigid their behavioural expectations are and how unusual behaviours and ideas are tolerated.

In addition to the four dimensions of the original framework, Hofstede (2001) has now added a fifth dimension: long term versus short term orientation. This facet refers to a society's capacity to be 'virtuous', to be future orientated, in this case financially, while respecting or adapting traditions. Societies that are deemed to be short-term orientated respect and value their traditions but are not thrifty and plan for quick results. Societies that are long-term orientated plan for the future and adapt their well-respected traditions, believe that virtue and truth are context and time orientated, and persevere to achieve desired results. This dimension, in addition to the four original aspects, weas developed in the context of business management, not education, but it is clear to see what sort of implications this fifth dimension may have in education contexts. In a similar fashion, the sixth and most recent addition, the element of indulgence versus restraint, while orientated towards a business perspective, can help you understand the type of thinking that your students have learned in their cultural background relating to relatively free gratification of basic needs and having fun and enjoyment as opposed to very strict social norms that are diligently monitored and enforced. It is interesting to note that Hofstede (1986) maintains that the responsibility for the assimilation of students into a new culture lies with the teacher.

What Does This Mean for You?

There are considerable complexities attached to the successful integration of students of diverse cultures. One of these may be how an entire school relates to the diversity of its community by the planning of specific days to identify and to celebrate the different nationalities represented by the school population. The practice of celebrating different nationalities has been heavily criticised. One reason for this was that it was viewed as a 'token' acceptance of cultural diversity. This was based mainly on the fact that, frequently, only the surface culture was acknowledged. The second reason was that students from different nationalities and cultures were expected simply to blend in and adjust to dominant culture at all other times. This is not to say that national costumes, songs and dances were expected to replace school uniforms and curricula. Rather it was an attempt to alert educationists to the attitudes and belief systems that need to be acknowledged and accommodated on a daily basis. These might include:

1. The difficulties for students from societies and cultures with a large power difference. It may be difficult for these students to ask questions in class. They may fear implying that their teacher is incompetent and therefore offend them through lack of respect. These students would be difficult to engage in a learning dialogue as they may only answer questions initiated by the teacher. They may become distressed at the differentiation and modification strategies that are implemented in child-centred education, as may their parents. These students may not cope easily with the lack of concentration on establishing and maintaining order and may become anxious. They may also have more respect for older teachers than their peers. These attitudes may impact on the students' efforts to integrate socially with the other students.
2. Students from collectivist societies may have great difficulties when they do not request help in the classroom. They may have problems selecting their own learning tasks, engaging in critical discussion and finding their personal ways of completing tasks. They would be more comfortable being assigned tasks by the teacher, following the teacher's opinion in discussion and using strategies for task completion that have been nominated by someone in charge. They (and their parents) may expect preferential treatment because of their social connections, their wealth or their advanced competencies and skills in some areas. They (and their parents) may place a great emphasis on the winning of awards, certificates and documents that signify their achievement rather than on the potential of the achievements themselves. There are great expectations from extended families regarding loyalty and family welfare before personal interests. Contradicting or questioning the teacher's instructions, opinions or evaluations would be considered inappropriate and would possibly incur significant sanctions from parents.
3. Students (and their parents) from traditionally masculine societies may expect that corporal punishment is used judiciously, that competition is important, that praise is given openly and frequently for good results irrespective of the effort expended and that they would not be expected to join in areas of the curriculum that they view as 'female' activities. These students may resent any praise or encouragement that teachers give to students who are not so academically competent as they believe they are themselves. They may pursue subject choices that are believed to be related most closely to their choice of career. They may not select courses or subjects based on personal preferences.

(Continued)

(Continued)

4. Students that avoid uncertainty may display less enthusiasm for open-ended tasks or those with no real structures. They may not like flexibility in the time-table or curriculum planning and be unimpressed if their teacher does not have the answers for every question asked. They may not understand teacher emotion or those of their peers and have high expectations regarding the for-mality and academic correctness of their communication with their teachers. They may also demonstrate the tendency to avoid any debates, discussions or controversial issues completely or feel obliged to concur with their teacher.

As a result, students from cultural backgrounds other than your own may be more difficult to get to know as individuals. This, in turn impacts on your capacity to plan for them effectively and to develop the critical thinking skills that are required in your curriculum documents. You may not know of their learning difficulties until they produce their work and so have little opportunities to correct their misunderstandings or to plan efficiently for them. Because so many of these teacher expectations and pupil behaviours are held by the parents and extended families, you will need to develop strategies of communicating respectfully and meaningfully, despite your obvious differences. You will also have to work with these students effectively in the classroom. In the text below you will find some guidelines for developing your curriculum to incorporate strategies that will help you provide academic success for your culturally diverse groups of students.

Banks (in Howard, 2006) identifies five essential, highly related components of effective multicultural education. He lists these as:

- Content integration. This is the strategy of finding the links between other subjects, skills, strategies and knowledge that are learned in school in addition to those that are learned outside of formal learning environments.
- The knowledge construction process. This is the opportunity for students to construct knowledge and learning in their own way and for teachers to accept that there may be significant differences in the ways in which content and knowledge is assimilated and interpreted.
- Prejudice reduction. This entails not just a sensitivity to your own opin-ions and perspectives on particular issues related to cultural differences and the implications of these, but also being tolerant of students who are accustomed to doing things differently. There are obvious differ-ences in the directionality of reading and writing in other languages

which do not translate into English literacy practices at all, for example. However, other practices, such as ways of counting, directionality in measuring and other specific strategies that do not impact negatively on the outcome of the learning, need to be considered with considerable respect and understanding and perhaps allowed to continue indefinitely where practical.

- An equity pedagogy. This relates to the content and implementation of the curriculum and to the ways in which resources are selected and distributed. Narratives that depict essentially middle class white families and situations, and implicitly these standards of behaviour and beliefs, do not provide equity pedagogy, for example. Nor does the implementation of various other curricula that present only one perspective. This is a most important consideration if the single viewpoint that is discussed and accepted is that of the dominant culture.
- An empowering school culture. This component refers to a very important aspect of multicultural education. There would be a very limited impact on the students from minority cultures and also on the students from the dominant culture regarding the importance of acceptance, the undesirability of bias and prejudice if multicultural education was confined to only a few classrooms in the school. The school's policies and practices must demonstrate an authentic desire to be multicultural in all aspects of its interactions and school ethos.

Banks (in Howard, 2006) identifies the teacher characteristics that are required for providing multicultural education. These focus on the capacities of individual teachers to develop new perspectives, learn new paradigms and nurture new knowledge and skills. Richards (1981), in an explanation of some of the difficulties of teaching in multicultural educational contexts, notes that even the words that identify this context are ambiguous and the very discussion of race, culture and creed can have serious consequences depending on the political climate at the time. He identifies multicultural education as 'community education' that requires a curriculum that meets the needs and aspirations of all communities. He deplores the use of a curriculum that is predominantly developed to meet the needs of all-white, English-speaking communities. Instead, he advocates a curriculum be designed to take into account the following factors:

Ethnic diversity

The first language of the students and the fact that English is spoken as a second, perhaps even a third language

The reality of prejudice and discrimination

The expectations of the parents. (Richards, 1981: 34)

This curriculum would have three major objectives:

> To develop and improve basic skills in literacy and numeracy

> To prepare children of ethnic minority groups, who are capable of them, for external examinations in order to raise their chances of obtaining a job

> To allow each child to be proud of their ethnicity. (Richards, 1981: 34)

While aspects of Richards' model may easily appear to be outdated or naive, a degree of what he proposes remains valid for many schools that include children from diverse cultures and communities.

Questions for Reflection

- Q1. Have you experienced teaching or observing in a multicultural classroom?
- Q2. What do you think of Hofstede's dimensions of cultural difference? Discuss critically.
- Q3. Can you list what may be the implications for education when considering the fifth and sixth dimension that Hofstede added to his model at a later stage?
- Q4. Hofstede lays the responsibility for assimilation firmly with teachers. What do you think?
- Q5. What would you add, take away or change in the models of multicultural education that are presented here?
- Q6. Do you think that considerations of ethnicity and cultural differences are ethical issues for teachers?
- Q7. The models of multicultural education contain aspects of a particular pedagogical perspective. Can you identify what this is?
- Q8. What ideas do you have regarding the development or adaptation of the mandatory curricula to meet the learning needs of all students in a multicultural group?
- Q9. In which teaching and learning contexts may you have difficulties with the past actions and policies of predominantly white culture?
- Q10. Can you identify countries that may be culturally aligned to Hofstede's four dimensional model, or have you had interactions with students who have demonstrated the characteristics that Hofstede described in his 1986 model?
- Q11. Do you think that some difficulties may arise for some students and parents if you have a predominantly child-centred classroom? What strategies do you have to overcome these potential problems?

Social Diversity

A wide variety of factors has been investigated in relation to the impact of low socioeconomic status on student learning, some of it contradictory at first glance. It is important to remember that not all students from low socioeconomic backgrounds exhibit all or even any of the characteristics that are described here. As you need to know your students extremely well to meet their learning needs effectively, it is useful to know and reflect on factors that could negatively impact upon your efforts to support their learning. In fact, your views may differ greatly from these on the purpose and usefulness of schooling itself. This may not impact on their actual capacity to learn but it certainly would have some impact on their motivation. This would be especially so if they felt that the education provided by schools had little or nothing to offer them. The keys to engagement, as you have read in previous chapters, are interest and relevance. As always with matters of diversity and difference, nothing is simple. However, it is essential for you to understand how best to accommodate your differences in formal educational contexts. Without strategies to achieve this, you cannot support greater academic success for students from socioeconomic backgrounds that are considered to be low status. This aspect of reflection takes you back to the opening chapter where you were challenged to undertake critical reflection and to consider whether you believed that education was a suitable vehicle from which to promote student equity and justice (Gore, 1987; Gore and Zeichner, 1991). If you do perceive education to be an opportunity to promote student equity and justice and you understand the political and social nature of schooling, then the responsibility that you undertake is to provide suitable classroom interactions that will support a social reconstructionist perspective. In order to do that effectively, you need to know which issues may impact negatively on these students' academic progress. There are several studies that can help inform you regarding these factors, which when investigated can be grouped in terms of health, parental interaction, opportunity and expectations, and educational provision and contexts.

A summary of the research into student obesity (Sobal and Stunkard, 1989) concluded that there were strong links between student obesity and low socioeconomic status of students. There could be many reasons for this correlation. It may be that notions of appropriate diet, self image, reward and parental expectations were different from one social group to another. A review of the research into nutrition found that low iron levels affected cognitive functioning and this was found to be a common deficiency in students from low socioeconomic backgrounds. The most significant findings of the literature review were that food insufficiency was frequently a major problem among this group. They also found that students in schools who took advantage of available breakfast programmes demonstrated improved academic performance and cognitive functioning (Taras, 2005). As a result, nutrition, and educating students and families about nutrition, may be considered a factor in any plan to improve the academic success of students from this socioeconomic group. Yancey and Saporito (in Tileston, 2004) found that children from poor inner city neighbourhoods were more likely to suffer from disease and other health problems.

A study into the impact of low socioeconomic status on learning (Walker et al., 1994) point to differences in early childrearing practices and that children from low socioeconomic backgrounds had restricted language production that impacted negatively on learning outcomes in early schooling. Kolulak (in Tileston, 2004) found that when caregivers talked to children in the first three years of their life it improved their IQ. However, he also found that children in white collar families heard 2,100 words a day compared with 1,200 words heard by those belonging to working class families. Walker et al. (1994) determined that differences in time spent talking to children, the degree of attention paid to the children and the amount time spent with the children resulted in these children developing a less diverse vocabulary. They also noted that children in these groups were more frequently prohibited from talking more often than the children in other groups. Additionally, they noted that the psychological and financial stress of being a single parent impacted on the quality of interactions these parents had with their preschoolers. Other studies (Entwisle and Alexander, 1992) indicate that over the summer holidays students from disadvantaged backgrounds have less opportunities to use their mathematical knowledge and that as a result, they gradually fell behind the other students in mathematical performance. This applied equally to those who had been able to perform as well as other students during the term times. However, other reasons were also cited for lower performance during school breaks. These included lower expectations of teachers, peers and the students themselves.

Important notions regarding appropriate education for students from low socioeconomic backgrounds are contained in a report by Cotton (1996). She argued for students from low socioeconomic groups to be placed in small school settings citing the following reasons:

- In small schools, students from low socioeconomic backgrounds have:
  o More equitable access to resources and extra-curricular activities because in large schools the school community is polarised into those students who are talented, have high levels of ability and can afford

to participate and those who are not in these categories. There are no opportunities for those who would just like to participate.

o   A heightened sense of belonging because the context facilitates the development of interpersonal relationships with peers and with teachers. In large schools these students can feel alienated from the dominant culture and the organisational demands that dominate the school agenda. Alienation was found to affect self esteem and the capacity for students to develop responsibility for self direction.

o   Better attendance, improved personal and academic self concept and they experience a greater degree of care in their interpersonal relationships with teachers because of the interpersonal relationships these student are able to develop in smaller schools.

o   Teachers who are more likely to be involved in the wider community; this allows students to identify more readily with them.

o   Also, small schools are more focused on learners' needs and equity of resources than larger schools are able to be.

These reasons serve to highlight major issues that are faced by students from disadvantaged backgrounds, including being increasingly disempowered, disenfranchised and disillusioned with formal educational contexts. Gonzalez and Padilla (1997) found that the greatest predictor of academic success among resilient Hispanic students was their subjective sense of belonging in the school. Goodenow and Brady (1993) also found that peer group influence and the values of friends were not as influential in school success as their perceived sense of belonging. Hardre and Reeve (2003) investigated the presumption that lack of motivation underlies students who are predisposed to drop out of school. Their study indicated that teachers who are controlling and authoritarian act as deterrents to these students staying in school but teachers who allowed a high degree of learner autonomy and provided suitable classroom support motivated students to persevere and to stay at school. The provision of learner autonomy was also identified in another study (Skinner and Belmont, 1993), which indicated that younger students from low socioeconomic backgrounds were also motivated by autonomy support, optimal structural scaffolding and interpersonal relationships with the teachers. Additionally, this study revealed that the attention given to students who were behaviourally disengaged from their learning actually contributed negatively to the motivation to learn. The question of school 'warmth', the degree of friendliness, welcome and acceptance that students perceived to be evident in the school was also found to be associated with academic success. It was the students' participation in class that was critically important to the students' in the development their perceptions of school warmth.

What Does This Mean for You?

As an aspiring teacher, you are already making a powerful statement about your perspectives on education. It may be difficult for you to understand the attitudes and actions of parents from low socioeconomic circumstances, simply because of your own commitment to teaching. Bridging the difference is complex. Condescension, passing judgement or disdain for individuals as parents or caregivers, or for students themselves, is not only unethical and unprofessional, it is disrespectful and offensive. There may be many challenges to the standards that you espouse in relation to child rearing and education. You will have your own strategies based on your disposition and personal belief systems, but some general ideas may include the following:

1. **Don't lose sight of the bigger picture.** Does it really matter if the school socks are never white or the uniform has no colour left because it has been handed down so many times? Is the student really talking back over a disciplinary matter to disrespect you or is he just retreating to the position he needs to take at home or in his community where any show of weakness or compliance makes him a future target for bullies and other community members? Is the child's inability to wait, take turns or be patient a reflection of her home circumstances where she cannot rely on getting a share of parents' time or a turn at something special? These situations can result from a lack of routine, resources or time in her home environment. Is the student speaking to you in a casual manner because he cannot be bothered to address you appropriately or because he does not have well-developed communication skills and is not aware of the more formal tone and vocabulary that you would normally expect and receive?

2. **Take the initiative.** Develop positive attitudes towards these students yourself. This is really essential to the students feeling accepted and their sense of belonging to the school community. Take the time to get to know these students as well as the students whose backgrounds are more similar to your own and who have corresponding values regarding education. Be inclusive in your pedagogies. Do not automatically select the well dressed, the tidy, the most articulate or the most academically successful student to chat to. Building relationships that are positive, friendly and authentic is a professional tool that costs nothing, is easily transported, can be appropriate in all circumstances and which makes the most impact on these students' chances of integrating into school communities effectively. Develop a professional understanding of the impact of poor nutrition, insufficient sleep and the possible nature of the home environment and use this information daily to inform your expectations and professional demands.

3. **Implement the curriculum appropriately.** Consider what is relevant and interesting for these students. It is an ideal opportunity to develop a relationship

if you need to ask them. Do not allow the school system to take priority over your students' learning needs. Have high expectations of these students and ensure that the nature of your relationships provides a model of acceptance and inclusion for the wider class and school community. In this way you can provide the strong social support that is needed to achieve your high expectations.

4. **Facilitate optimal functioning.** Encourage these students to develop habits, behaviours and skills that support successful learning in your classroom even though this may not reflect their home situations. It may be because of this that it is important you teach students to be organised, plan ahead, to recognise and inhibit attitudes and behaviours for them that impact negatively on their potential to learn successfully. Develop tasks that facilitate 'flow' for them in order to provide an opportunity for them to enjoy a challenge. Many other challenges they face may be too difficult and not enjoyable. These students may do anything for you because they feel accepted and included. One of the most important things you can do for them is facilitate the development of a sense of 'self' which reflects their capacities, competencies and potential and which acknowledges each as an individual.

5. **Be professionally and personally aware.** Students may read facial clues and body language as a way of surviving unpleasant situations. Your expression, actions and attitudes need to reflect your capacity to develop authentic, non-judgemental relationships that facilitate students' sense of belonging to the class and school communities.

Howard et al. (2009: 31) summarise the problems that impact on children from low socioeconomic homes and compare them to what many teachers expect a normal home life would be like from their perspectives. They go further and indicate the types of behaviours these students frequently exhibit in classrooms as a result of their home experiences. They indicate the home lives of low socioeconomic families are characterised by these factors:

- Employment may be less stable, parents may work multiple jobs and shift work making scheduling and routines very difficult to establish.
- As a result of less stable circumstances children cannot rely on getting their turn to do anything or have parental attention within a reliable timeframe.
- Learning resources are very limited, parents may not have the competencies or time to support or encourage their children's learning.
- Regular meals may not be possible, nor the time and space to get enough restful sleep.

- Family time is very limited or fragmented, verbal communication skills may not be well developed or the parents' first language may not be English.
- Children may need to act on non-verbal clues and cues to know what to do.
- Children may learn that you do 'just do enough to get by'.
- Because of the demands on their time, parents may not give children instructions or be at home to supervise if they are able to follow instructions.
- Feedback from parents may be infrequent or more negative than positive.
- Asking parents questions may be discouraged for a number of reasons.

In addition to these characteristics, Payne (in Tileston, 2004: 28) identified that frequently the language of students from backgrounds of poverty or low socioeconomic status is often what she termed 'casual register'. Tileston (2004) explains that, for these students, language is about survival, unlike the 'formal register' that is characteristic of both the middle classes and the wealthy as these groups use language for negotiation and for networking respectively. She indicated that teachers may have to allow students to express themselves in their 'casual' register initially and then support the rewriting into more 'formal' register. In their study of teachers who made a real difference to their students from low socioeconomic backgrounds, Howard et al. (2009: 32) found teachers used strategies in four major areas:

Maintaining positive interpersonal relationships with students and their families

Conducting formative and summative assessments of students' skills

Integrating learning experiences (as in Marzano, 2001, learning takes many forms)

Developing a positive, democratic, learning environment which included giving students verbal and non-verbal cues, allowing real choices where possible and providing effective feedback on their work and academic progress.

The researchers found that the teachers who were more successful with these students were flexible in terms of content, process, product and learning environment, had a sense of humour, celebrated the successes of their students, and felt empowered to do small extra things that were very significant for these students.

Questions for Reflection

- Q1. Have you experienced students from low socioeconomic backgrounds in classrooms you have visited?
- Q2. Did you observe or experience any behaviour that you feel may be associated with or be the result of any of the characteristics that are described by Howard, Dresser and Dunkley?

- Q3. Why would the expectations of many teachers differ from the reality of these children's out of school lives?
- Q4. Can you add to your visual organiser (mind map or conceptual map showing the connections between one topic and others you have learned about) and weave in the information in this chapter so far?
- Q5. A great deal of responsibility for the success of students from low socioeconomic backgrounds appears to rest on the teachers and the schools. Can you list any reasons why this may be the case?
- Q6. Do you think that the responsibility for ensuring the academic success of these students is an ethical responsibility?
- Q7. Can you make explicit links with the ideas in other chapters of this text that explore the notion of social reconstructionism and the skills, knowledge and attitudes that you would need to teach students from low socioeconomic backgrounds effectively?
- Q8. Which aspects of the Holy Trinity for Teachers would you need to be accomplished in to teach these students and be successful?
- Q9. Do you think different ethics and professional skills are important in the teaching of this group of students? Validate your answer.

Individual Diversity

The notion of individual diversity is wide reaching. It would be impossible to explore all the ways in which teachers and their students are different. However, without intending to neglect the needs of your students who are gifted and who will be discussed in the following chapter, we will now focus on students who are classed as having special educational needs because of a physical or intellectual disadvantage. The ways in which students are affected by various syndromes, disadvantages and diseases are in themselves individual and diverse. It is only ever possible to gain some insight into the general manifestations of any disadvantage so that appropriate steps can be taken to ensure that classrooms and school communities are well informed and thus able to include students in a democratic and systematic manner. Including these students in a regular classroom is a matter of social justice and human rights. The process of 'normalisation' (Foreman, 2005) demands that students with a disability are treated firstly as people. In a school context this means that students who have a disability that is not a significant emotional or behavioural disorder could expect that they:

Should be allowed enrolment in regular local schools

Should be given roles that are valued by the school community

Should be provided with age appropriate activities to complete

Are educated in the least restrictive environments where they have genuine choices as provided for their peers

Are expected to learn at an appropriate rate and level. (Foreman, 2005: 8-9)

Foreman (2005) also provides definitions for terms commonly used in relation to students with a disability: 'integration' is used as a broad term to indicate that students are attending a regular school even if they are in a special class, 'mainstreaming' indicates that students are integrated while they are enrolled in a regular classroom in a school, 'inclusion' indicates that while students are already mainstreamed and integrated, the school community also focuses on how these students will be accommodated and provided for in a similar manner to the rest of the students, irrespective of their religion, race, colour, social background or gender. In an attempt to provide inclusive environments for all students, teachers at inclusive schools are encouraged to understand that disabilities are on a continuum and the range of capacities that students bring to the classroom is just the same as the other students. Students may have physical or sensory disabilities; they may have behaviour problems or learning difficulties. Each of these can vary in severity and the degree of impact on the individual student's academic progress. It is important for you to explore and understand the policies that are developed in your area regarding the education of these students, the principles and the practice. Different countries have their own understanding of these. The United States has been involved in an inclusive approach to students with disabilities and requires that each child classified as having a disability or learning difficulties has an individualised education programme developed for them. This is a very detailed document, which will be discussed in Chapter 11, which indicates how the professional healthcare services are supported by the school and how the student's achievements and goals are to be evaluated. Additionally, parents have the right to be consulted and to be involved in the educational process and there is an attempt to oversee the quality of the educational programmes provided for these students. The United Kingdom has had a slightly different approach: since the landmark Warnock Report (1978) there has been a significant move to include all children with special educational needs in mainstream schools, but the outcomes of her report's recommendations in practice have been criticised by Mary Warnock herself in 2005 (Warnock, 1978) and the UK government is mooting a move away from these statements towards a new Birth-to-25 Education, Health and Care Plan. In Australia and New Zealand legislation is not as rigorous in its nature as that in the United States. This is because it is predominantly based on the Disability Discrimination Act (1992) and not explicitly on an education act (Dempsey, 2005). There are requirements that students with disabilities are provided

Linguistic bias	Teachers need to be sensitive to the implications of what is taught in terms of content and how it is taught. Students and teachers need to be aware that: Historical and social issues need to be presented from various perspectives and with appropriate backgrounds and pedagogical strategies so that all groups involved are comfortable with the outcomes Appropriate steps need to be taken to eliminate the incorrect pronunciation of names Cultural differences in intonation, articulation and inflection may be examined and differences accepted	This may present as any language that denies or dehumanises a group or individual • Teaching history without acknowledging the minorities or other perspectives • Mispronouncing another's name to create amusement or laughter • Sniggering or giggling at an non-English speaker's attempts to speak English
Stereotyping	Students and teachers need to examine stereotyping and take steps to be aware of situation in which this type of bias may occur, most especially in teaching and learning contexts that have traditionally associated with specific groups in particular cultures or social contexts Encouraging both genders to display a variety of emotions Acknowledging that students from backgrounds of poverty often feel a sense of hopelessness over their situations. They need to be empowered by providing genuine choices where possible and facilitate an atmosphere of positive emotions in the learning environment (Payne, 2001)	Often used in relation to gender and in association with ethnic minorities • disparaging/ridiculing opposite gender students engaging in activities which may have been associated with a stereotypical notion of a particular gender, social class or culture • ridiculing students who show emotion, especially males who display a variety of emotions • dismissing students who are negative or who do not have similar views or expectations relating to education due to impoverished backgrounds or a sense of disempowerment with the school culture
Exclusion	Teachers need to acknowledge and act upon the awareness that a sense of belonging is a basic human need and, that while diversity is apparent, it should not exclude individuals or groups from mainstream teaching and learning activities	To exclude students from any group or by lack of representation in a group • Removing students to complete a special programme, often in literacy or numeracy (not counting those with special needs or disabilities who may need to access their specialist helpers)

(Continued)

(Continued)

Unreality	Teachers are required to act ethically in respect of confidentiality, respect and professional behaviours and be aware of their personal predilections in regard to unprofessional conduct	**Misinformation about a group, individual, event or contribution** • Not having high expectations for some students or groups of students • Sharing information about students with other teachers that reflects a personal opinion or bias
Selectivity	Teachers need to develop considerable skills in attribution: the capacity to understand and consider multiple viewpoints and contexts which they may not have experienced personally. This may be particularly pertinent in contexts that are countercultural to teachers' expectations of respectful behaviours, tone and register of communication	**Offering or presenting a single perspective or interpretation of an event, issue or situation** • Payne suggests that students from poor socioeconomic backgrounds cannot show fear as they feel that it is survival of the strongest. These students may laugh when disciplined and may need teachers to point out the inappropriateness of this in a school context • Students must be supported in viewing issues and situations from differing perspectives
Isolation	Supporting elitist groups or failing to systemically include students who do not have the social skills or other personal characteristics that allow them to become part of the larger group without support. Teachers need to demonstrate the 'acceptibilty' and acceptance of every student by modelling positive interactions and developing a positive relationship with each student Develop classroom culture which reflects a community of acceptance of each other as learners.	**The separation of individual or groups** • Organise groups, teams and paired activities with different students so they really get to know each other • Systematically build rapport with every student so that camaraderie and acceptance is fostered in the classroom

Figure 10.2 Detecting and Avoiding Bias (adapted from Gibbs, in Tileston, 2004: 27–33)

with an education but these are not explicit about the ways in which this may be provided.

Once a student is enrolled in your classroom, it is imperative that opportunities for participation are maximised as appropriate for the student and that the curriculum meets their learning needs as it does for other students. Differentiated activities should be developed in collaboration with the appropriate student support services and any incidents of bullying or discriminatory behaviours noted, dealt with according to school policies and the perpetrators subsequently monitored. Bullying or harassment, though unacceptable, may be more easily dealt with when it is reported as involving other students or peers. It is even more problematic when it is detected as the actions or behaviours, conscious or unintentional from adults, especially from teachers.

Tileston (2004) provides a useful framework for detecting bias or prejudice in classrooms. Using Gibbs' model, which was specifically designed to alert teachers to any type of racial, social or individual bias in the classroom, she has detailed the six types of bias that may be problematic in classrooms. There are summarised in Figure 10.2.

Many schools still exclude students into special programmes, determining that a different context allows students to concentrate better and to gain more benefit from what is offered as a special programme. This may be a valid decision for the school to make depending on the nature of the programme and the learning needs of the students who are withdrawn from class. Unfortunately, many programmes that are implemented in this manner are deficit or 'remedial' programme for students who have not reached the competencies or benchmarks that have been achieved by their peers at any stage. The issue then may become one of stereotyping, as the students themselves, the teachers and general communities regard these students as academically inept due to their obvious withdrawal from the regular activities in their usual classroom. However, there are a number of other programmes that are not so easily evaluated in terms of Gibbs' model of bias. One of these is the notion of the 'Nurture Centre' developed by Boxall (2002).

The aim of the nurture groups in schools was to provide early nurturing for students who had come to school with a number of difficulties that were significant enough to lead to their exclusion from school at a very early stage, sometimes within weeks of their commencement. Based on the students' perceived lack of readiness for learning and in response to the needs of these students, Boxall (2002) developed what was termed as 'restorative experience of early nurture' (p. viii) in an attempt to prevent a disastrous future in educational terms. In the nurture centres teachers and their assistants provide selected learning experiences in a context that is more domestic than scholastic. The rhythm of the day is not the same as the regular school day. Everything is introduced gradually and toys and other resources utilised are developmentally appropriate, focused on explicitly making the students comfortable with their learning contexts and rules, routines and timetables are established. Originally developed for the very young students from exceedingly poor areas of London, the idea of nurture groups in schools, which are staffed by their own teacher and a trained learning support aid, can now be found extensively in local neighbourhood schools throughout England and Northern Ireland, as well as other parts of the United Kingdom. Students with a range of learning difficulties are customarily included, with early intervention being the major focus of the centres. The learning environment is generally developed to resemble a living room; many also have gardens in which the students can work. Inclusion in these centres is generally on a part-time basis, when the students leave their regular classrooms and participate in activities. There appears to be an appreciation of and acceptance of these the nurture centres by parents, who give their permission for their children to participate (Sellars, 2012). Students' progress is mapped in a specially designed format known as the Boxall Profile (Bennathan and Boxall, 1998).

Another project that is being developed to support specific groups of students who are not able to adapt easily and learn effectively in regular school classrooms involves not just a centre in the school but an entire school itself. It has some parallels with Boxall's initial work, however, in that the development was initiated in response to the needs of some of the poorest children in the Sydney suburb of Redfern. The school, Redfern Jarjum College, is a primary school for Aboriginal and Torres Strait Islander students. With enrolment capped at 20 students, the aim of the school is to provide individual support and education for those students whose numeracy and literacy standards would otherwise have doomed them to be among the most uneducated Australian students (Ganter, 2012). This school will involve the community, be culturally sensitive in the implementation of their holistic curricula and require the students to attend from 8 am until 6 pm on weekdays. Both this and the nurture centre projects aim to be inclusive by removing students from regular classrooms in order to provide them with opportunities for increased academic and social progress and development.

Questions for Reflection

- Q1. Have you seen any strategies in place for students with learning difficulties or disabilities? What were the aims of these?
- Q2. Do you know the laws, policies and principles that govern the provision of educational opportunities in your area?
- Q3. What do you think are the major problems teachers face with inclusive practices? Discuss.
- Q4. What do you think of Gibb's framework for identifying bias and promoting inclusivity? Validate your answer.
- Q5. What do you think of the idea of nurture centres in schools? Indicate if you have visited one or worked in this context. Validate your opinion.

- Q6. Do you think both the projects described are being inclusive by exclusion from regular classrooms? Validate your answer and indicate the limitations, problems or advantages you would associate with these approaches.
- Q7. Can you find or name any special programmes in your area that cater for students with special learning needs? Are any of these programmes where students are withdrawn from the regular school environment for lengths of time? What do you think of these programmes? Validate your answer.

Scenario Ten

Ms Black was concerned. She had been reading a story to her class of 6-year-olds at the request of one of the girls, Lisa, whose family dog had died and been buried in the garden a few weeks previously. Lisa had seen the book often in the reading corner and now wanted everyone to hear it. There was no problem doing this. Ms Black often allowed the children to request a book and made sure she always had an ample supply of picture books of all types as a class loan from the library. She was very particular about the materials she had in the classroom as she had learners from a range of different cultural backgrounds and wanted to ensure there was something for everyone to engage with during free reading times. She had just come to part of the story where the old family dog was very ill and the vet had been called. The picture showed the family hugging the dog as the vet gave him an injection and put him to sleep. The text actually read 'put him to sleep'. All the time she was particularly keeping an eye on Lisa, who had requested the story. On the next page the picture showed the family putting their pet into a grave under his favourite tree in the garden. As she was watching the group of girls and Lisa, just in case it was upsetting, she was surprised when Janek jumped up and yelled 'No! No!'. He was very upset. Ms Black put the book down and asked what the matter was. Janek replied, 'The vet put him to sleep, you cannot bury him, he is asleep.' Ms Black and the other children quickly told John what that really meant and Lisa very calmly explained the same thing had happened to their dog and it was alright. Ms Black quickly finished the story and everyone settled to their tasks. She could not forget, however, that she had not even considered making sure all the learners in the class knew what the vet had done. She knew the story well so it was not a problem. Janek was a good example of students who spoke English as an additional language. He was fluent; he could follow instructions really well, was coping with being taught in English and was a successful learner. All this had combined to make Ms Black overlook

(Continued)

(Continued)

something she knew was basic to multicultural education: shared common meanings. Janek had comprehended what was read quite literally and the nuances of
the language and the intended meaning behind the expression. As she wrote in
her reflective journal she realised that she was preoccupied with Lisa's reaction
and forgot about this basic strategy for the others. She thought, 'I can learn from
today. I need to think things through and juggle all the students' needs in my
head at once, even though one student may have particular needs at the time.'

Questions for Reflection

- Q1. What could have been done to avoid the situation that arose?
- Q2. What would be your solution, bearing in mind that there a lot of diverse
  students in the class?
- Q3. Are there links in the content of this chapter to any information in other
  chapters? Identify these.
- Q4. Are there any professional or ethical considerations underlying the issues
  discussed in this chapter? Identify them.
- Q5. Can you add to your visual or other framework using the information you
  feel was most relevant to you from this chapter?
- Q6. What is the most personally challenging notion you have read about in
  this chapter? Why would you find this particular issue such a challenge?

Conclusion

In this chapter the notion of student diversity has been discussed as three
rather separate ideas. However, this is not often the case in reality. The issues
of diversity that were discussed in terms of cultural difference may frequently
be complicated by those that were discussed in relation to students from low
socioeconomic backgrounds. There are also cases where your students may
include a child from a different cultural background who has impairment and
is living in circumstances of poverty. In addition to the issues discussed in
this chapter, you will need to have the skills and strategies to develop programmes of work to meet the developmental and emotional needs of each
of your students while recognising their personal learning references, interests and academic capabilities. The following chapter will focus on skills and
strategies for differentiating the content, pedagogical approaches, products of

student learning and even the learning environment itself. It is these skills and strategies that will form a foundation from which you can develop your own strategies for differentiation and become confident as a professional educator in classrooms with diverse students.

References

Bennathan, M. and Boxall, M. (1998) *The Boxall Profile: Handbook for Teachers*. London: The Association of Workers for Childen with Emotional and Behavioural Difficulties.

Boxall, M. (2002) *Nurture Groups in School: Principles and Practice*. London: Paul Chapman Publishing.

Chen, J.-Q., Moran, S. and Gardner, H. (eds) (2009) *Multiple Intelligences Around the World*. San Francisco, CA: Jossey Bass.

Cotton, K. (1996) School size, school climate and student performance. Retrieved from http://upstate.colgate.edu/pdf/Abt_merger/Cotton_1996_Size_Climate_Performance.pdf (accessed 30 November 2012).

Dempsey, I. (2005) 'Legislation, policies and inclusive practices.' In P. Foreman (ed.), *Inclusion in Action*. Southbank VIC: Thomson. pp. 35–65.

Entwisle, D. and Alexander, H. (1992) Summer setback: race, poverty, school composition and mathematics achievement in the first two years of school. *American Sociological Review*, 57 (1): 72–84.

Foreman, P. (2005) 'Disability and inclusion: concepts and principles.' In P. Foreman (ed.), *Inclusion in Action*. Southbank, VIC: Thomson. pp. 3–34.

Ganter, C. (2012) 'A school with a difference.' In Alum (ed.), Vol. 3. Sydney: Australian Catholic University.

Gardner, H. (1991) *To Open Minds*. New York: Basic Books.

Gibbs, J. (1994) *Tribes*. Santa Rosa,CA: Center Source.

Gonzalez, R. and Padilla, A. (1997) The academic resilience of Mexican American high school students. *Hispanic Journal of Behavioral Sciences*, 19 (3): 301–17.

Goodenow, K. and Brady, C. (1993) The relationship of school belonging and friends' values to academic motivation among urban adolescent students. *Journal of Experimental Education*, 62 (1): 60–71.

Gore, J. (1987) Reflecting on reflective teaching. *Journal of Teacher Education*, 38 (2): 33–9.

Gore, J. and Zeichner, K. (1991) Action research and reflective teaching in preservice teacher education – a case study from the United States. *Teaching and Teacher Education*, 7 (2): 119–36.

Hall, E. (1976) *Beyond Culture*. New York: Knopf Doubleday Publishing Group.

Hardre, P. and Reeve, J. (2003) A motivational model of rural students' intentions to persist in, versus drop out of, high school. *Journal of Educational Psychology*, 95 (2): 374–56.

Hofstede, G. (1986) Cultural differences in teaching and learning. *International Journal of Intercultural Relations*, 10 (3): 301–20.

Hofstede, G. (2001) *Culture's Consequences: Comparing Values, Behaviors, Institutions and Organizations Across Nations*, 2nd edn. Thousand Oaks, CA: Sage.

Howard, G. (2006) *We Can't Teach What We Don't Know*, 2nd edn. New York: Teachers College Press.

Howard, L., Dresser, S. and Dunkley, S. (2009) *Poverty Is NOT a Learning Disability*. Thousand Oaks, CA: Corwin Press.

Marzano, R. (2001) *Developing a New Taxonomy of Educational Objectives*. Thousand Oaks: Corwin Press.

Nisbett, R. (2005) *The Geography of Thought*. London: Nicholas Brearley.

Payne, R. (2001) *A Framework for Understanding Poverty*. Highlands, TX: Aha! Process.

Richards, J. (1981) 'Multi-ethnicity and the school curriculum.' In J. Lynch (ed.), *Teaching in a Multicultural School*. Guilford: Ward Lock Educational.

Sellars, M. (2012) Interview with nurture centre teacher, Northern Ireland [unpublished].

Skinner, E. and Belmont, M. (1993) Motivation in the classroom: reciprocal effects of teacher behavior and student engagement across the school year. *Journal of Educational Psychology*, 85 (4): 571–581.

Sobal, J. and Stunkard, A. (1989) Socioeconomic status and obesity: a review of the literature. *Psychological Bulletin*, 105 (2): 260–75.

Taras, H. (2005) Nutrition and student performance at school. *American School Health Association*, 75 (6): 199–213.

Tileston, D. (2004) *What Every Teacher Should Know about Diverse Learners*. Thousand Oaks, CA: Corwin Press.

Walker, D., Greenwood, C., Hart, B. and Carta, J. (1994) Prediction of school outcomes based on early language production and socioeconomic factors. *Child Development*, 62 (2): 606–21.

Warnock, M. (1978) *Report of the Committee of Enquiry into the Education of Handicapped Children and Young People*. London: Her Majesty's Stationery Office

Chapter 11: Skills and Strategies for Differentiation

- Q1. What do you know about differentiation?
- Q2. What types of differentiation have you seen during your professional experiences? Was it aimed at a particular group or individual? Describe it.
- Q3. When and for whom would you differentiate in your classroom?
- Q4. What do you think you would differentiate?
- Q5. Have you any differentiation strategies that you have tried for yourself?

Introduction

Classrooms in which appropriately differentiated environments, curricula and pedagogies are evident are instantly identifiable as being student-centred. You have been reading about how students learn using evidence from a variety of disciplines and sources. A strong theme throughout is that students are different from each other and have different learning needs. Planning for effective student learning necessitates a reflective approach to:

- teaching and preparation of learning tasks
- efficient and stimulating environments
- the pedagogies implemented.

This may appear challenging for a class of thirty or more students, never-theless it is manageable, desirable and professionally and ethically important for you to develop skills and strategies that allow you to plan, manage, implement and assess the learning of your diverse cohort of students. This chapter presents and discusses a number of strategies that are commonly implemented by teachers in classrooms in order to meet the learning needs of their students in age appropriate, developmentally sound and academi-cally rigorous ways. The skills and strategies that comprise this chapter are not exhaustive. They are a foundation upon which you can build your own ways of accommodating your students' learning needs in the context of for-mal classrooms. Throughout the text you have been challenged to reflect and discuss a number of issues and ideas that may have been previously unknown to you or even challenging. The notion of differentiating the three major aspects of teaching (content, process and environment) could be a considerable challenge for some of you as you may be required to confront your previously held notions of what it is to be a teacher. This understand-ing challenges the traditional roles of teachers and students, and disputes the efficacy of some of the pedagogical strategies that you may have expe-rienced during your own school days.

What Does the Literature Say about Differentiation?

Tomlinson (2000a: 2) gives some wonderfully realistic, practical advice on how you might get started in your efforts to differentiate in your classrooms:

- Frequently reflect on the match between your classroom and the phi-losophy of teaching and learning you want to practise. Look for matches and mismatches and use both to guide you.
- Create a mental image of what you want your classroom to look like and use it to help plan and assess changes.
- Prepare students and parents for a differentiated classroom so that they are your partners in making it a good fit for everyone. Be sure to talk often with students about the classroom – why it is the way it is, how it is working and what everyone can do to help.
- Begin to change at a pace that pushes you a little bit beyond your com-fort zone – neither totally duplicating past practice nor trying to change everything overnight.
- You might begin with just one subject, just one time of the day, or just one curricular element (content, process, product, or learning environment).
- Think carefully about management routines for example, giving direc-tions, making sure students know how to move about the room and making sure students know where to put work when they finish it.

- Teach the routines to students carefully, monitor the effectiveness of the routines, discuss results with students and fine tune together.
- Take time off from change to regain your energy and to assess how things are going.
- Build a support system of other educators. Let administrators know how they can support you. Ask specialists (e.g., in gifted education, special education, second language instruction) to co-teach with you from time to time so you have a second pair of hands and eyes.
- Form study groups on differentiation with like-minded peers. Plan and share differentiated materials with colleagues.
- Enjoy your own growth. One of the great joys of teaching is recognising that the teacher always has more to learn than the students and that learning is no less empowering for adults than for students.

Differentiation is the act of changing or of making content, pedagogy or learning environments more personalised in order to maximise the learning of your students (Tomlinson, 1999; 2000a, 2000b). It takes into account the interests, skills and academic capacities of the learners and provides them with engaging activities within their reach as learners. Differentiating means that students are engaging with learning tasks that have an element of challenge (Dixon-Krauss, 1996; Vygotsky, 1968) and are not just based on ideas that they know already. It means:

1. that their interests may have been identified and used to provide a context within which to develop the constructs or ideas to be learned
2. that new materials are presented using pedagogical strategies that acknowledge the students' preferred ways of learning
3. that the learning environments may also be altered, changed or exchanged for a more appropriate environment in which to study, discuss or explore and complete the learning tasks.

Differentiation of Content

Content, or the basis of the syllabus documents and curriculum, is usually determined by state, regional or national authorities. However, how the knowledge, skills and concepts that these comprise are presented to students as learning tasks depends to a great deal on individual teachers. There are three main ways to differentiate content to suit different learners:

(i) The Individual Education Plan (IEP). This plan is frequently developed for learners who need some specialised or specific support, as discussed in the previous chapter. However, an IEP can be developed for any student at any stage of their education. Some teachers work effectively by developing IEPs for each of their students in the areas of literacy and numeracy, which are considered foundational understandings for other discipline areas. Specific IEPs are routinely developed for students with special needs, students who are gifted and for students who need support to become culturally assimilated. They are commonly developed collaboratively with a number of support agencies and advisors. They include details of what is to be undertaken, when and by whom, and how the effectiveness of the planned interventions is to be assessed and by whom.

(ii)   Modifying tasks. Learning tasks can be modified in many ways in order to make them more accessible or to provide appropriate challenge. Scaffolding tasks is one strategy (Dixon-Krauss, 1996; Duncan, 1995; Speaker, 1999; van der Heijden, n.d.; Vygotsky, 1968) commonly used when modifying tasks and originates from Vygotskyian theory. Scaffolds are, as their name suggests, any support that teachers give their students so that they reach the next level of their learning. These scaffolds may take many forms. They can be informal, such as prompt, cue or questioning in order to elicit responses that will help the students with their thinking. They may be interactive materials such as skip counters, fraction wheels or other equipment. They also may be specifically prepared materials. For example, in teaching a procedure such as a writing genre, some students may be able to construct their procedure with no support at all, others may need a brief outline with one word in each section to guide their writing, other student groups may need the outline with the section headers and a brief description of what might be written in each section. Other ways of modifying tasks are to:

- Alter the requirements that demonstrate the competencies and understandings of student learning. Some students may wish to present learning as a PowerPoint presentation and explanatory dialogue. Others may present as a visual format. Yet other groups may present as raps, rhymes, or songs. If an essay or written work is not acceptable, there are any number of alternatives that can be photographed, videoed or otherwise recorded for assessment purposes (McGrath and Noble, 2005).
- Alter the amount of time that is to be spent on a task to make it either more manageable for the students or to allow it to be completed to a high standard that would not be possible in limited time.
- Break the task into manageable components and only require students to complete as many as they are able at one time. They may be able to complete other parts at a later stage.

- Alter the task requirements. Some students may be able to write a narrative draft, edit it and rewrite the final product. Other students may be able to complete one or two parts of these three steps but their final product may have to be the draft or the edited draft, depending on their capacities to complete the task.
- Limit the tasks. Select carefully considered tasks that give the maximum information about the students' capacities in the areas being assessed. For some students avoid the completion of multiple tasks that illustrate the same competencies in the area of learning undertaken (Dempsey, 2005; Foreman, 2005; Hyde et al., 2011).

(iii) Different pathways. Providing different ways for students to explore and investigate new ideas and concepts has traditionally been limited to illustrating, demonstrating, writing or a combination of these. Currently, however, Gardner's multiple intelligence domains (1993) are commonly used as a means by which different pathways can be provided for diverse students. Working from student strengths allows students to work in ways that they know best and in which they find it easiest to learn. Students' learning preferences most commonly reflect the areas in which they are most proficient and allows them to confidently approach new knowledge and concepts (Anderson & Lux, 2005; Sellars, 2008b). Much of the published material on differentiation focuses on using multiple intelligence domains to support student learning (Berman, 1995; Bourke, 2001; Diaz-Lefebre, 2004; Ellison, 1992; Gabrovec, 2001; Hine, 2002; Lazear, 1999a; Lazear, 1999b; Vialle and Perry, 1995). Some of these focus on developing differentiated learning tasks by combing the two typologies of Gardner's multiple intelligences domains (1993) and the Revised Bloom's Taxonomy of cognitive processes (Anderson and Krathwohl, 2000).

What Does This Mean for You?

Much foundational learning is undertaken in the context of primary and early secondary schooling. In these years, students develop the understanding knowledge and skills that form the basis of their more specialised elective choices in their later secondary school years. As a result, considerable responsibilities are placed on the teachers of students during these years to ensure that they have utilised a wide range of strategies to support student learning. Differentiation is not just a choice, it is an ethical undertaking. One of the means of differentiating different pathways involves students being able to articulate how they learn most

(Continued)

(Continued)

effectively. As a result, this type of differentiating can offer students real choices and promote successful learning in academic and self knowledge development. Tomlinson's practical advice provides a framework from which you can start to plan how you might differentiate in one, or in each of the three ways that are discussed. Additionally, you may wish to consider other strategies that suit your particular contexts. These may include:

(i). **Resources.** What you are able to implement realistically in your teaching may not always be ideal. This is because resources, including physical space, are invariably limited to one degree or another. You may need to consider some practical questions. For example: What do you need to have readily available and in what sort of quantities? Where will they be stored? How will they be accounted for? How will you organise the differentiated activities so that you do not have music being composed while other students are trying to work in a quiet environment? What are the implications of having art supplies stored in the same area of the classroom as the electronic resources? How will you provide equitable access to students needing cameras, computers and other technological support? It is a good idea to check that you have not planned all the activities around a narrative when several students may need to access a single copy for their selected tasks, for example.

(ii). **The students.** As Tomlinson has indicated, students and their parents need to be partners in your attempts to further support academic success for your class cohort. You may have to plan to explicitly teach the skills of organisation, keeping independent records and assist students to know when they need help or confirmation of their planned strategies. Plan also so that all students do not need your support for their different tasks at the same time, but can at least get started independently. The easiest way to do this may be to develop task cards for each activity. Give examples, diagrams, tips for thinking through tricky aspects of the task and perhaps a rubric so they can see explicitly what constitutes work of a good standard for these tasks.

(iii). **Feedback** can work both ways. Plan an easy, yet informative way to allow students to communicate to you how they felt about the tasks they had self selected or you had planned for them. This can easily be facilitated by providing a strip of smiley to gloomy faces or a small proforma for other students where they can tick a box and indicate quickly how they feel, how easy or difficult the task was for them and how they are progressing. In that way you have a complete profile of what and how students are doing even if there was no time that day to conference with them. These are also useful for formative and summative assessment purposes. When you give feedback, try and ensure that you have acknowledged the best or correct aspects of the work before indicating where things may be incorrectly or poorly completed. The final aspect of the effective feedback model is to give students an idea of what you will do together to gain a greater understanding of the poor or incorrect aspects of the work and the timeframe involved. The guidance that you give is an important aspect of the feedback.

Questions for Reflection

- Q1. Have you experienced or observed any other strategies for differentiation in a classroom?
- Q2. Do you think that this type of planning can be useful or beneficial to students and to you as a teacher?
- Q3. Can you pinpoint where you might be able to start to implement a programme of differentiated content?
- Q4. What appealed to you in the reading of this section? Validate your answer.

Differentiation of Pedagogy

Pedagogy is generally understood to be the science of teaching; however, it may be more appropriate to adapt Gore's (1993: 11) understanding of pedagogy. She states 'pedagogy as the process of knowledge production also begins to draw attention to a power–knowledge connection'. How you choose to teach is important because, as the teacher, you have considerable power and this impacts on your students' capacities to learn effectively in your classroom. While you may have your own preferred pedagogies, your students may all have their preferences for how you present materials, strategies, knowledge and concepts and generally go about your teaching. If you are engaging with differentiated pedagogy, what you prefer to do will depend on your students, your context and the type of information, concepts and strategies you wish your students to think about and learn. Teaching with differentiated pedagogies involves organising your teaching strategies to implement your differentiated content in various ways. Wormeli (2011: 6) regards differentiated pedagogy as a 'mindset' not as a set of recipes. He suggests the following ideas for classroom practice:

- Tiering for readiness.
- Flexible grouping.
- Scaffolding.
- Adjusting the pacing of delivery or support so content is more meaningful and easily retained in long-term memory.
- Using respectful tasks.
- Adjusting the amount of practice for different students according to what is needed.
- Rephrasing an example so it makes better sense to a student.
- Using descriptive feedback to revise students' skills and knowledge.
- Compacting the curriculum so advanced students don't stagnate.
- Providing nutritious breakfasts to those who do not have them.
- Building prior knowledge where this is none so information 'sticks' in the mind.
- Coming to know our students well so we know what buttons to push so they learn more effectively.
- Designing lessons to increase what students capture the first time the topic is taught rather than relying on hours of remediation to fix misconceptions and build missing foundations.

You may find that there are occasions when the most effective way to teach some student groups either as a large group or as micro teaching is by modelling and direct instruction. This may be especially so when the students are learning new knowledge. On other occasions you may rely exclusively on students' prior knowledge and scaffold their exploration and their search for links with new information, concepts and contexts. You may find that a number of students are most readily engaged and more persistent when they are participating in:

- self determined tasks
- individual or group learning contracts
- pursuing self selected goals
- working from their relative strengths.

You may have to teach the same ideas in two or three different ways in order for all your students to find meaning in what they are trying to understand. There are also some differentiated pedagogies that have specific aims and methodologies, including teaching strategies and educational philosophies associated with particular schools of educational thinking and their specific pedagogical focus, such as the Steiner/Waldorf, Froebel, Montessori and multiple intelligences schools. There are various interpretations of differentiated instruction as it may be used exclusively in the context of inclusion for special needs students, when in fact it is the basis of all good teaching and learning. In the UK, for example, differentiated pedagogies are frequently used in the context of special needs students' learning, from which highly specific models of pedagogy are developed: for example, connective pedagogy (Corbett, 2006, 2011), which is a means by which special needs students are included in ways that connect their individual needs, the institutional resources and the values of the community. This notion is distinct from connective pedagogy as described by Sullivan (2011) in which teachers deliberately and explicitly link the learning matter they are currently teaching to other learning that has taken place by eliciting the links from students or by systematically making these links obvious in their teaching.

Tomlinson (in Wormeli, 2011: 39) reiterates the four underlying principles of differentiated pedagogy:

- a learning environment that provides high challenge and support
- a quality curriculum that emphasises deep understanding of content and ensures that both teachers and students recognise what is essential for students to know, understand and do
- formative assessment that allows teachers to know where students are relative to essential outcomes
- adapting instruction, using the formative-assessment data, to ensure maximum success of each learner.

In any lesson there are a number of pedagogical strategies used and as the pedagogy changes, then so do the roles of the teacher and the learners. There are a number of ways that students can be introduced to thinking and challenged to reflect on information from different perspectives. These may be termed pedagogies, but, with the possible exception of the strategies associated with teaching for multiple intelligences, these are generally acknowledged to be teaching strategies. The exception is made in regard to teaching for the holistic development of Gardner's (1993) multiple intelligences because, unlike the other models described here, it is a theory of cognition. Other paradigms or tools that can be useful to engage students in the thinking and learning processes include the following popular tools. This is not an exhaustive list, just a sample of tools to which you may have easy access. These are detailed in order to encourage you to search out strategies that suit you and your students.

- De Bono's Thinking Hats (de Bono, 2008). Used primarily in schools to help students think more creatively and to consider and reflect on the various perspectives and components that may be required to think about a topic, question or problem. The hats are colour coded and each represents a specific aspect that may need to examined, debated, clarified or reflected upon. The hats are:

- o   White hat. This hat helps students focus on data, facts or information that is provided or that is needed.
- o   Red hat. This thinking hat focuses on exploring, feelings and instincts about the topic.
- o   Yellow hat. This hat prompts students to think about their values, how useful the project or problem in question may be and encourages them to think about any possible benefits that may result from the resolution of the problem or undertaking.
- o   Blue hat. This is the management hat. It helps students to be organised and to plan the steps or procedures that will be need to be undertaken to complete the task or solve the problem.
- o   Green hat. This hat stimulates students to be creative. It encourages students to think of new ways of doing things, new perspectives and ideas, new solutions to problems, alternatives and possibilities.
- o   Black hat. This hat demands that students consider what may go wrong with a project, how and why their planning may not be successful. This is the evaluation hat.

When students become accustomed to working with the six hats in mind, they can develop skills in evaluating, organising, planning and creating within cognitive and emotional frameworks.

- Tony Ryan's Thinkers Keys (Ryan, 1990). This set of twenty 'keys' are developed to support the explicit teaching of thinking skills. They are:

  - o   The reverse. Students are asked to use cannot or never in relation to an idea.
  - o   The what if ...?
  - o   The disadvantages.
  - o   The combination. Students are asked to combine the attributes of two dissimilar items or ideas and make a totally new creation.
  - o   The BAR. Students take an item and modify it by making it Bigger, Adding something or Removing something or Replacing something.
  - o   The picture. Students add information related to what they are studying to a graphic organiser.
  - o   Different uses (for an object related to their topic).
  - o   The variations. How many ways can you ...?
  - o   The alphabet (list topic related items starting with each letter of the alphabet).
  - o   The prediction.
  - o   The ridiculous.
  - o   The commonality. Select two objects that ostensibly have nothing in common and find some commonalities.
  - o   The question. Students are given an answer and asked to provide as many questions as possible for the answer.

o The how to ...? Brainstorm different ways that something could possibly be completed.

o The construction. Students are asked to make an unusual construction of their own design related to their topic.

o The forced relationship. Problem solving using dissimilar objects.

o The brick wall. Students are provided with a commonly accepted solution to a problem and asked to provide different solutions.

o The alternative. Students are required to complete a task without using their usual equipment.

o The interpretation. Students are provided with an unusual event or scenario and have to develop an explanation for it.

o The invention. Students are asked to design something made in an unusual way. Can possibly be made if suitable.

Not all of these are used in relation to one task or topic. Their usual implementation is as practical and appropriate questions to ask regarding the problem to be solved or topic investigated. They, like the De Bono hats, can be used regularly or intermittently as you decide they are needed to promote more lateral, holistic thinking about a topic.

- Costa and Kallick's *Habits of Mind* (2000). These are attributes or perspectives on thinking and are more complex to develop in classrooms. Generally introduced one at a time, they comprise a blend of executive function skills, social sensitivities and personal competencies. They are quite complex and require a degree of maturity and competence to develop. They are the most recent paradigm discussed and include the cognitive skills, attitudes and perspectives that students will need to become successful in the current climate of change, uncertainty and global competitiveness:

o Persisting.
o Thinking and communicating with clarity and precision.
o Managing impulsivity.
o Gathering data through all senses.
o Listening with understanding and empathy.
o Creating, imagining, innovating.
o Thinking flexibly.
o Responding with wonderment and awe.
o Thinking about thinking (metacognition).
o Taking responsible risks.
o Striving for accuracy.
o Finding humour.
o Questioning and posing problems.
o Thinking interdependently.
o Applying past knowledge to new situations.
o Remaining open to continuous learning.

Differentiating the Environment

Alongside differentiated pedagogies and content you can also do a number of things to the physical environment that will support your teaching. These may include having a quiet area for reading or for students who work better when they are quietly focused. Make class rules with the students that are congruent with your ideas of how your differentiated classroom should operate. These rules should include provision for some students to be doing different activities to others, including, for example, allowing some students to be active and using equipment while others are working at their desks. Have the room overtly organised for younger students so that areas for different activities are clear and not just labelled, make sure equipment is consistently stored in the same locations and routines are consistent while allowing some flexibility. Learning out of the classroom is important also, as older students may have lots of environmental variety in their day as they move from classrooms to computer and science laboratories, studios, gymnasiums and sports fields according to the content they are studying at that time. The advantage for primary aged students is that they (and you) can customise the furniture, the wall spaces and the special areas to suit their learning and perhaps have thematic displays that transform the physical environment on a regular basis, excite and motivate students and make everyone's contribution to the learning space valuable and respected. This may be harder to achieve in secondary school teaching and learning spaces that may be shared by large numbers of students and staff members.

Questions for Reflection

- Q1. Are there any strategies discussed here that you think would enhance your teaching and enrich the learning of your students?
- Q2. If so, would you be able to plan them and implement them in a classroom?
- Q3. What would you have to personally consider before engaging with a differentiated curriculum?
- Q4. Would you agree that the physical environment is important in differentiated learning contexts? Validate your answer.

Differentiating and Technology

There are many benefits to providing students with access to digital tools (Maddux and Johnson, 2011), and it makes good sense to incorporate aspects of technology into your classroom practices. A significant number of studies that report on the capacity of various technological tools to improve aspects of teaching and learning include those related to emotional intelligence (Furger, 2001; Goldsworthy, 2002), learning in multicultural classrooms (Lin and Ward, 2011; Maddux and Johnson, 2011), teacher reflection (Clegg et al., 2003; Gurol, 2011; Prestridge and Watson, 2004) and the development of critical thinking skills (Butchart et al., 2009). Buchanan (2011), in a critique of the Australian government's plans to incorporate technology into schools at an ever-increasing rate, summarises the push for teachers everywhere to provide a technology-dependent education for their students. This is in response to increasing globalisation and its focus on choice, competition and performance. Buchanan nominates three ways in which students today in developed countries are promoted as being different from previous generations (Buchanan, 2011: 68). She suggests that the literature presupposes:

- that students are not merely familiar with technology but are voracious consumers of it
- that the ways in which students have been exposed to digital, techno-logical tools may well have altered the physiology of their brains due to the extreme neuroplasticity of the nature of the brain
- that, as a result, these students will learn differently than those of previous generations, indicating that they need highly technologically driven instruction.

She challenges these notions, indicating that there is lack of research evidence to support these claims and that the discourse around 'digital natives' leads to the stereotyping of young people while obscuring some key differences that are pertinent to education. She writes:

> I contend that the digital native motif not only imposes a particular identity upon the current generation of learners, but that in so doing, it confounds the social justice goals of education by erasing key differences between young people – such as differences in access to technology, gender, race, ethnicity, geographic location and socio-economic status. (Buchanan and Chapman in Buchanan, 2011: 72)

However, it appears that young people are actually spending considerable time creating digital identities by engaging in the social networking aspects of technology outside of the school environment in comparison to information gathering. They do not spend nearly as much time using digital technology for academic purposes. There are still advantages in using technology in classrooms if it enhances the learning experience and informs students' thinking. It appears, however, that the reality is that computers in classrooms are put to various uses. Yelland (2001) in her report on the use of technology in relation to numeracy, noted that research evidence indicated that the 'role and style' of the teacher was the defining factor in the successful integration of technology into classrooms. These teachers integrated computer use throughout the curriculum and the computers became a tool that was part of daily classroom life. Using computers to occupy students who finished work early or as a reward for some students was seen as not only poor practice but actually harmful as students then associated the machines with circumstances other than educational knowledge gathering. Computers are seen to be a tool to enrich good pedagogy and may improve students' outcomes in that they are a ready source of data and other materials with which to engage higher-order cognitive processes such as interpreting data, investigating, reasoning, writing, solving real problems and conducting scientific enquiries (Becker in Yelland, 2001: 10).

In response to this need to integrate technology into everyday classroom interactions in teaching and learning, Mishra and Koehler (2006) developed a framework for teachers known as Technological Pedagogical Content Knowledge (TPCK). Using Shulman's (1987) model of integrating pedagogical knowledge and content knowledge (PCK), which prioritises the relationship of these two aspects of teacher knowledge and results in teachers being able to effectively teach what they know, TPCK had the addition of technology knowledge. The authors argue that currently technological knowledge is considered a separate knowledge domain in much the same way as pedagogical knowledge and content knowledge were prior to Shulman's (1987) seminal work. The new model they are suggesting integrates technological knowledge with the other two knowledge domains. They acknowledge that, in many ways, in the past content knowledge and pedagogical knowledge was more 'fixed' and less prone to the constant updates and advances that characterise technological knowledge. Despite this, however, they argue that the impact upon connections to and limitations of technology in its relationship to the other knowledge domains must be considered in order to incorporate technology meaningfully in teaching and learning contexts. Each discipline demands unique pedagogies and these are the basis of effective teaching. Pedagogical knowledge and content knowledge, in specific learning contexts, take account of students' skills, prior knowledge, difficulties and which concepts they might find difficult to learn. Content knowledge incorporates:

- an understanding of the frameworks and theories and also of the nature of content knowledge
- methods of enquiry, and
- facts.

Pedagogical knowledge includes:

- understandings of methods and processes in learning and teaching
- acknowledgement of the relationship between these, and
- management

- planning
- assessment
- evaluation.

As a result, technological knowledge is not simply the skills required to operate the technological tools. It also requires knowledge of: ·

- the computer systems
- software applications
- how to produce a variety of documents
- how to archive a variety of documents.

Mishra and Koehler (2006) indicate that technological content knowledge is knowing:

- what the technology available can do to change how the content matter is presented
- how it is represented to allow students other perspectives and greater understanding.

Pedagogical technical knowledge is described as being able to assess the 'goodness of fit' of software for specific purposes in addition to knowing how the technology operates. Describing TPCK as a completely new class of knowledge, they write:

> TPCK represents a class of knowledge that is central to teachers' work with technology. This knowledge would not typically be held by technologically proficient subject matter experts, or by technologists who know nothing of the subject or of the pedagogy, or by teachers who know little of that subject or of technology. (Mishra and Koehler, 2006: 1029)

TPCK can be described as a subtle interweaving of all three knowledge domains; there is no one combination for any subject matter or context that can be successful for all contexts. The knowledge that is the result of the interweaving of all three knowledge domains is, in the authors' opinions, the core of quality teaching with technological tools.

Questions for Reflection

- Q1. What do you think about the TPCK model?
- Q2. Does it help you understand the ways in which technological tools need to integrated into your classroom practice?

(Continued)

(Continued)

- Q3. Are you equally as knowledgeable about your technological tools as you are about the other two other dimensions of your teaching?
- Q4. Do you agree with Buchanan's argument that a government initiative to place technology in schools is actually masking issues of inequity? Give your reasons.
- Q5. Does this section change your perception regarding technological tools in school? Validate your answer.

Differentiation for Gifted Students

The provision for gifted students in schools has had rather a chequered past. It was thought by some educationalists that:

- gifted students were able to learn sufficiently well on their own
- planning for giftedness was succumbing to overly ambitious parents
- it was breeding some sort of elitism in what was perceived to be an otherwise democratic process. (Brody and Stanfield, 2005)

You may also think that in a successfully differentiated classroom or school that specialises in the promotion of inclusive practices or the development of the holistic learner that gifted learners would be adequately catered for but Brody and Stanfield (2005) disagree. What is clear is that gifted students do not necessarily demonstrate genius, nor do they have to possess outstanding potential in every area of learning. The behaviours and attributes of gifted students need to be acknowledged and identified so that they are provided with opportunities to engage with challenging tasks (Callaghan and Miller, 2005), irrespective of their specific learning context. There have been a number of models developed to guide educators in the identification of support of gifted students (Greenberg and Coleman, 1993; Kornhaber, 1999; Teo, et al., 2001), with some of these being reviewed very positively by research evaluators (Henderson, 2005; Iii and Ford, 1991; Moss, 1990), but the most widely accepted and implemented model at this time is Gagne's (2004) Differentiated Model of Giftedness and Talent. Developed from Gagne's earlier work (1985, 1995) and critiquing Renzulli's model in addition to Cohen's model of giftedness, Gagne clearly distinguished between and defines the constructs of giftedness and talent. He defines giftedness as the possession and use of untrained superior talents in at least one domain that results in the individual being ranked in the top 10% of their peers. Talent is defined as the mastery of trained skills in one domain that places the individual in the top 10% of peers with similar training (Gagne, 2004). This model of giftedness is inclusive of areas that are not academic. Gagne (2004) lists four areas of giftedness:

- intellectual
- creative
- socioaffective
- sensorimotor

He indicates that students can be determined as gifted if they show a high degree of natural competence in any of these four areas. Noting that this is most strikingly observed in the very young, he attributes this to the limited impact of environment factors and systemised instruction. Talents are understood by Gagne (2004) as developing from the high aptitudes that students have as the result of their education or training and observes that this is easily observed in school-aged youth. As this is a developmental model, Gagne (2004) proposes that talents develop from these naturally high attributes or gifts. He asserts, however that the rate of underachievement in students is evidence that gifts cannot be developed from talents. It is the systematic learning and repeated rehearsal of gifts that transforms them into talents. This however, does not happen by osmosis.

Gagne (2004) indicates there are two types of triggers in this process:

- Intrapersonal catalysts, which are the physical and psychological factors including heredity, executive function skills and temperament and environment. This includes the entire context in which the student lives: social, geographic, demographic and family personality and parenting style. Every factor in the student's environment is considered under the category of milieu.
- Added to this are other persons, provisions and events. In other words, environmental factors include all the circumstances in a student's life, including the element of chance, which could be incorporated into any of the four other environmental categories.

Although there is not any explicit responsibility placed on educators to ensure that the gifts of students are not disregarded or wasted and are indeed developed appropriately as talents, there are expectations. As schooling is the major pathway for most children and young people, the responsibility of all teachers, from those engaged in the earliest forms of childhood education to those working with the most senior students, is clear. Gifts need to be nurtured, challenged and celebrated into lifelong talents using the differentiation strategies that you have reflected upon, tried and testing and that are comfortable for you.

Questions for Reflection

- Q1. Do you think that gifted students could be adequately catered for in all schools without a specific programme to support them? Validate your answer.
- Q2. Do you find Gagne's model of giftedness a reasonable way to understand these students and to support their development? Validate your answer.
- Q3. Were you, or do you know any students who were or are, classed as gifted? If so, what do you think they would want in the way of school support?
- Q4. Do you think there are any ethical issues in the ways in which you teach in relation to the provision of specific learning tasks for gifted students?
- Q5. Do you think the entire issue of differentiation demands you to be competent in all three areas of the Holy Trinity for Teachers? Why or why not?
- Q6. Can you incorporate the new information discussed in this chapter into your visual organiser?
- Q7. What strategies might you have for identifying gifted students in each of the four categories identified by Gagne?
- Q8. What would your priorities be in the situation where you need to include gifted students in your classroom practices and community?

Scenario Eleven

Miss Grey surveyed the room from where she had placed herself strategically to work with a small group of her 11- and 12-year-old students. They were working on fractions but some of her students really did not have the concept at all. Others had really robust knowledge. She was working with a group who had some ideas, but needed monitoring as they also had a great deal of misinformation between them. As she checked over the classroom quickly, she noticed the Orange group were settled into their tasks that were designed at a lower level than that of the rest of the class. The Blue group was managing their task of developing or discovering the rule that they could apply to these particular fractions and making a poster explaining this for the other students and illustrating how it might work. The Red group were working beyond the stage of the syllabus that the rest of the class were working at and they were discussing their problems and planning strategies. The Green group that she was working with needed to clarify their ideas and develop a strategy that worked for them. The problem that they began with was:

There are 35 small chocolate bars left over at the party and Mrs Smith decided to share them among the children who had younger siblings at home. There were seven younger siblings at home. How many would Alex get if he had three siblings at home?

The students in Green group could all agree that the siblings at home should get equal shares. They could articulate that the 35 chocolates should be divided by 7 and then Alex got 3 shares. One for each of his siblings at home. They could independently compute that the correct answer was 15. What they could not do was represent this notion symbolically. They looked totally horrified when Miss Grey wrote the following for them and asked if they could offer any ideas on how they might find the answer. She wrote $\frac{3}{7} \times 35 = 15$.

Deciding at that point that the Green group were not taking that leap of understanding alone, Miss Grey decided to talk them through the symbolic representation. They knew that $\frac{3}{7}$ was three-sevenths. They also knew that they needed to work out the answer to $\frac{3}{7}$ of 35. The next step was for Miss Grey to get out the counters. These came in two colours. On long strips of paper the students began to lay out the 35 counters they had counted out in groups of seven. When they had finished, Miss Grey established, by asking some specific questions, that they wanted to know how many three out of every seven would be. One student pulled three counters out of every seven to one side and drew a ring around them. Another took three out of every seven and placed them into a margarine container. Another exchanged three counters in every group for counters of the other colour. They could all see that the answer was 15 and were really surprised! Miss Grey then introduced a planner page for recording their work. Divided into four diagonally, in one section they wrote the number story they had started with, in another section they drew or photographed what they did and in a third section they wrote the symbolic representation. The final quarter was reserved for a statement about what they learned. They could start anywhere on the page. As she watched the students each start where they wanted to, she thought about the individuals in the group. There was no reason why these students should not have developed these understandings previously. Unlike the Orange group who had some specific learning difficulties and were genuinely not ready for this work, this Green group had been able, with a few minutes' guidance, to make sense of the ideas straight way. Her thoughts were interrupted as one of the students asked, does this work all the time? Well done, she smiled to herself, let's see. She gave the student another similar algorithm. The others said they would have another also, so she gave different algorithms of the same type to each of them. In a few minutes, they brought back their answers. They were all correct. The next step was to complete a planner for the second algorithm. As she left the group to complete the task independently, she thought what a useful learning experience this had been for the students and for her. As she checked

(Continued)

(Continued)

and read the planners later, she would be able to see if the really understood what they were doing by reading the story they had developed to accompany the symbolic representations she had deliberately given without any context. In less than twenty minutes, these students had changed from fearful, reluctant participants in the mathematics lesson into engaged, motivated young people who were actually discussing their working with peers and using language to make sense of their learning experience and new understandings.

While some days were certainly better than others, Miss Grey was satisfied that all the work, the effort and the determination she had expended into developing her differentiated classroom had been worth it. Now to check that Red group; they would have a go at anything. They were very confident in maths so they had to be really challenged, but it was always wise to make sure they were on the right track with their thinking as they charged ahead ...

Questions for Reflection

- Q1. What considerations regarding student learning are embedded in this scenario? List them.
- Q2. What other strategies can you devise to support student learning in situations similar to these? Identify their potential to support student learning.
- Q3. How could Miss Grey identify that the students showed a degree of readiness?
- Q4. Why might she ask the Green group to use the planner that she gave them?

Conclusion

The notions presented in this chapter are just the beginning of the multiple ways in which you can support student learning in your classroom. Ideas for altering tasks, amending pedagogies and transforming your classroom are not prescriptive, although the frameworks discussed here can easily be used as a starting point. The opportunity to differentiate all three aspects of practice (content, process and environment):

- presents itself in all classrooms
- can work effectively within the inflexible structure of mandatory curriculum
- can empower students to become increasingly successful, self directed and motivated learners.

Although there is a general view that newly graduated teachers at the beginning of their careers can be extensively focused on the more technical aspects of teaching, meeting mandatory standards, gathering evidence of curriculum implementation, attending to student misbehaviours and generally settling into the profession, the notion of differentiating aspects of classroom interaction, getting to know students' learning needs well and establishing a successful learning environment must also become the predominant mindset if you wish to be assessed as ethical members of the profession.

References

Anderson, L. and Krathwohl, D. (2000) *Taxonomy of Teaching and Learning: A Revision of Bloom's Taxonomy of Educational Objectives*. New York: Longman.

Anderson, J. and Lux, W. (2005) Knowing your own strength: accurate self assessment as a requirement for personal autonomy. *Philosophy, Psychiatry, & Psychology*, 11 (4): 279–94.

Berman, S. (1995) *A Multiple Intelligences Road to a Quality Classroom*. Melbourne: Hawker Brownlow Education.

Bourke, J. (2001) *The M.I. Series: Using Multiple Intelligences in the Classroom: Countries of the World*. Greenwood: Ready-Ed Publications.

Brody, L. and Stanfield, J. (2005) 'Youths who reason exceptionally well in mathematics and/ or verbally.' In R. Sternberg and J. Davidson.(eds), *Conceptions of Giftedness*. New York: Cambridge University Press. pp. 20–36.

Buchanan, R. (2011) Paradox, promise and public pedagogy: implications of the federal government's digital education revolution. *Australian Journal of Teacher Education*, 36 (2): Article 6.

Butchart, S., Forster, D., Gold, I., Bigelow, J., Korb, K., Oppy, G. and Serrenti, A. (2009) Improving critical thinking using web based argument mapping exercises with automated feedback. *Australasian Journal of Educational Technology*, 25 (2): 268–91.

Callahan, C. and Miller, E. (2005) 'A child responsive model of giftedness.' In R. Sternberg and J. Davidson (eds), *Conceptions of Giftedness*. New York: Cambridge University Press. pp. 38–51.

Clegg, S., Hudson, A. and Steel, J. (2003) The emperor's new clothes: globalisation and e-Learning in higher education. *British Journal of Sociology of Education*, 24 (1): 39–53.

Corbett, J. (2006) Connective pedagogy. *British Journal of Special Education*, 28 (2): 55–9.

Corbett, J. (2011) *Supporting Inclusive Education: A Connective Pedagogy*. London: Routledge Falmer.

Costa, A. and Kallick, B. (2000) *Habits of Mind*. Retrieved from www.artcostacentre.com/html/habits.htm (accessed 12 December 2012).

de Bono, E. (2008) *Six Thinking Hats*. London: Popular Penguin.

Dempsey, I. (2005) 'Legislation, policies and inclusive practices.' In P. Foreman (ed.), *Inclusion in Action*. Southbank, VIC: Thomson.

Diaz-Lefebre, R. (2004) Multiple intelligences, learning for understanding and creative assessment: some pieces to the puzzle of learning. *Teachers College Record*, 106 (1): 49–57.

Dixon-Krauss, L. (1996) *Vygotsky in the Classroom: Mediated Literacy Instruction and Assessment*. White Plains, NY: Longman Publishers.

Duncan, M. (1995) Piaget and Vygotsky revisited: dialogue or assimilitation? *Developmental Review*, 15 (4): 458–72.

Ellison, L. (1992) Using multiple intelligences to set goals. *Educational Leadership*, 50 (2): 69–72.

Foreman, P. (2005) 'Disability and inclusion: concepts and principles.' In P. Foreman (ed.), *Inclusion in Action*. Southbank, VIC: Thomson. pp. 3–34.

Furger, R. (2001) *Digital Technology: Tools to Enhance Emotional Intelligence*. Retrieved www. edutopia.org/digital-technology-tools-help-enhance-emotional-intelligence (accessed 19 October 2012).

Gabrovec, J. (2001) *The M.I. Series – Using Multiple Intelligences in the Classroom: Farm Fun*. Greenwood, W.A.: Ready-Ed Publications.

Gagne, F. (1985) Giftedness and talent: reexamining a reexamination of the definitions. *Gifted Child Quarterly*, 29 (3): 103–12.

Gagne, F. (1995) From giftedness to talent: a developmental model and its impact on the language of the field. *Roeper Review*, 18 (2): 103–111.

Gagne, F. (2004) Transforming gifts into talents: the DMGT as a developmental theory. *High Ability Studies*, 15 (2): 119–47.

Gardner, H. (1993) *Multiple Intelligences: The Theory in Practice*. New York: Basic Books.

Goldsworthy, R. (2002) Supporting the development of emotional intelligence through technology. *Computers in the Schools*, 19 (1/2): 119–48.

Gore, J. (1993) *The Search for Pedagogies*. New York: Routledge.

Greenberg, K.H. and Coleman, L. (1993) The cognitive enrichment network program: goodness of fit with at-risk gifted students. *Roeper Review*, 16 (2): 91–95.

Gurol, A. (2011) Determining the reflective thinking skills of pre-service teachers in learning and teaching process. *Energy Education Science and Technology Part B-Social and Educational Studies*, 3 (3): 387–402.

Henderson, L. (2005). Unleashing talent : an examination of VanTassel-Baska's (1995) integrated curriculum model in an inclusive classroom. Unpublished Thesis. Parkville Vic: University of Melbourne.

Hine, C. (2002) *Developing Multiple Intelligences in Young Learners*. Retrieved www.early-childhood.com/articles (accessed 10th November, 2002).

Hyde, M., Carpenter, L. and Conway, R. (eds) (2011) *Diversity and Inclusion in Australian Schools*. Melbourne: Oxford University Press.

Iii, J. and Ford, D. (1991) Identifying and nurturing the promise of gifted Black American children. *Journal of Negro Education*, 60 (1): 3–18.

Kornhaber, M. (1999) Enhancing equality in gifted education: a framework for examining assessments drawing on the theory of multiple intelligences. *High Ability Studies*, 10 (2): 143–63.

Lazear, D. (1999a) *Eight Ways of Teaching: The Artistry of Teaching with Multiple Intelligences*, 3rd edn. Melbourne: Hawker Brownlow Education.

Lazear, D. (1999b) *Eight Ways of Knowing: Teaching for Multiple Intelligences*, 3rd edn. Arlington Heights: Skylight Professional Development.

Lin, L.-M.G. and Ward, C.L. (2011) The integration of Web2Quest technology into multicultural curriculum in teacher education: a potential for globalization. *International Journal of Online Pedagogy and Course Design*, 1 (2): 12–28.

Maddux, C. and Johnson, D. (2011) Future trends in information technology in education. *Computers in the Schools*, 28 (2): 87–91.

McGrath, H. and Noble, T. (2005) *Eight Ways at Once: Multiple Intelligences + Revised Bloom's Taxonomy: 200 Differentiated Classroom Strategies* (Vol. 1) Frenchs Forest, NSW: Pearson Education Australia.

Mishra, P. and Koehler, M. (2006) Technological pedagogical content knowledge: a framework for teacher knowledge. *Teachers College Record*, 108 (6): 1017–54.

Moss, E. (1990) Social interaction and metacognitive development in gifted preschoolers. *Gifted Child Quarterly*, 34 (1): 16–20.

Prestridge, S., & Watson, G. (2004). Developing classroom teachers' understanding of multi-literacies : the role of reflection. *Australian Journal of Educational Technology*, 19 (2): 227–40.

Ryan, T. (1990) *Tony Ryan's Thinkers Keys*. Retrieved from http://learningplace.com.au/uploads/documents/store/resources/res_40022_Thinkerskeys.pdf (accessed 12 December 2012).

Sellars, M. (2008) *Using Students' Strengths to Support Learning Outcomes: A Study of the Development of Gardner's Intrapersonal Intelligence to Support Increased Academic Achievement for Primary School Students*. Saarbrucken: VDM Verlag 97.

Shulman, L. (1987) Knowledge and teaching: foundations of the new reform. *Harvard Educational Review*, 57 (1): 1–22.

Speaker, R. (1999) *Reflections on Vygotsky*. Retrieved from http://ed.uno.edu/Faculty/RSpeaker/Epistemologies/vygotsky.html (accessed 24 August 2005).

Sullivan, P. (2011) *Teaching Mathematics: Using Research-Informed Strategies*. Camberwell: ACER Press.

Teo, C., Quah, M., Rahim, R. and Rasanayagam, L. (2001) Self-knowledge education: educating gifted children in Singapore on the hemispheric functioning. Paper presented at the AARE: International Research Conference: Crossing Borders: New Frontiers for Educational Research, Freemantle, 2–6 December.

Tomlinson, C.A. (1999) Mapping a route towards differentiated instruction. *Educational Leadership*, 57 (1): 77–114.

Tomlinson, C.A. (2000a) Differentiation of instruction in the Elementary grades. *ERIC Digest* ED443572. Retrieved from www.eric.ed.gov (accessed 29 April 2005).

Tomlinson, C.A. (2000b) Reconcilable differences? *Educational Leadership*, 58 (1): 6–11.

van der Heijden, M.K. (n.d.) *A Holistic Vygotskian Operational Definition of Approach Behaviour for the Study of Personality and Learning*. Retrieved from http://psych.hanover.edu/vygotsky/heijden.html (accessed 23 August 2005).

Vialle, W. and Perry, J. (1995) *Nurturing Multiple Intelligences in the Australian Classroom*. Melbourne: Hawker Brownlow Education.

Vygotsky, L.S. (1968) The problem of consciousness. *Collected Works of L.S. Vygotsky*. Retrieved from www.markists.org/archive/vygotsky/works/1934/problem-consciousness.htm (accessed 23 August 2005).

Wormeli, R. (2011) Differentiated instruction: setting the pedagogy straight. *Middle Ground* (October). Retrieved from www.amle.org/portals/0/pdf/publications/Middle_Ground/oct2011/article10.pdf (accessed December 2012).

Yelland, N. (2001) *Teaching and Learning with Information and Communication Technologies (ICT) for Numeracy in the Early Childhood and Primary Years of Schooling*. Australia: Research and Evaluation Branch, International Analysis Division, Department of Education Training and Youth Affairs (accessed 20 May 2012).

Chapter 12: Beginning Your Teaching Career

- Q1. What do you think are the major challenges faced by beginning teachers?
- Q2. Do you feel adequately prepared to cope with these challenges?
- Q3. In your opinion, what are the major differences between beginning teachers and experienced teachers?
- Q4. Do you think any one aspect of the Holy Trinity for Teachers is more important for beginning teachers than others? Justify your response.
- Q5. What do you think you will be reading about in this chapter?

Introduction

Teaching is demanding in terms of ethical decision making, pedagogical choices, engaging with the planning cycle, organising your classroom and all the other roles and responsibilities that are teachers' work. What you take away from your preparatory courses is frequently challenged as you attempt to adapt what you have learned to suit specific cohorts of students. Staton and Hunt (1992) argue that this is the process of learning to teach: the process of change and adaptation that you have to experience to bring your theoretical learning and understandings to the reality of your current position in the school. This process includes learning to manage your classroom, bringing together your pedagogical, technological and content knowledge at the same time as meeting the expectations of colleagues, communities and systems. Part of meeting these expectations is your response to the process of socialisation. This process occurs when a newcomer to a setting adopts the beliefs, values and attitudes of those who are already members of the group to which the newcomer would like belong (Staton and Hunt, 1992). In order to become an effective member of the staff of any school, you need to acknowledge and understand the current belief systems and values that underpin the school and its staff. The means of adaptation that you may undergo is a process of enculturalisation. The degree to which you adopt the current belief systems and attitudes of the teachers and principal with whom you begin your career may depend on your own personal history and social background, especially when it concerns matters of student control (Zeichner and Grant, 1981).

Zeichner and Grant (1981) challenge a prevalent notion that beginning teachers, such as you, are rather vulnerable, are easily socialised into the status quo and consider themselves relatively uninformed. They argue that this is not always the case. Staton and Hunt (1992) agree. They suggest that the development of beginning teachers is not linear and is an ongoing 'multi-dimensional' progression and that newcomers and existing staff mutually influence each other throughout this relationship. The degree of enculturalisation and the impact of the existing school culture on you personally, appear to depend on the 'closeness of fit' between your belief systems and attitudes and those that are demonstrated in the school's policies, practices and ethos. In many ways, the beginning of your practice as a teacher and the degree of personal satisfaction you experience depend on your capacity to understand the hidden and overt curricula that dominate the culture of your school and to recognise how this supports or differs from your own value systems and beliefs.

What Does the Literature Say about Beginning Teachers?

There are several areas of research and commentary that relate to beginning teachers. One of these focuses on how new teachers can best be orientated into the profession. In most other professions, newcomers are assigned to more experienced employees as assistants. From this junior level they have opportunities to work closely with another professional as they are orientated into the profession. They have someone with whom to consult about difficult matters and for advice when problems arise. Although there are many mentoring and induction programmes for new teachers, unlike other professionals, you are essentially alone in your classroom from your first day's teaching. You have to make relatively instant decisions about matters that require your attention without necessarily having the time to consult with someone more senior or more experienced. Additionally, you have an almost unique responsibility among professionals in that there is an unequal balance of power in the context in which you spend the majority of your working day and you may be allocated the most difficult assignments or students (Carter and Francis, 2001). These circumstances require you to have a heightened sensitivity in regards to your personal ethics, belief systems and values. As a newcomer to the profession, you need to be able to reflect accurately on your practice, thoroughly and constantly using your knowledge of self, of content and of your students. Simmons and her colleagues (Simmons et al., 1999) found, in the context of teachers in primary schools teaching the science curriculum, that this degree of reflection was not always apparent. Their findings showed that beginning teachers have a range of ideas and opinions about how teachers should develop relationships with their students. They had views on what teachers should be doing in classrooms and could articulate their beliefs and philosophies about teaching. When asked about their own classroom practice, they could discuss how they perceived themselves as teachers. They invariably described themselves as student-orientated teachers. However, when their classroom practices were analysed, the observation notes provided evidence that their actual work was teacher-centred. The reflection process in which these beginning teachers had engaged was not significantly critical to allow them to appreciate that their ideological thinking and understanding was not actually reflected in their decisions about how to teach. They did not perceive the discrepancy that existed in reality; that their intended purpose was not, in fact, being supported by their actions.

What Does This Mean for You?

In the teaching profession, the aspects of your work that are most frequently assessed may be your planning and assessment records. Much of what may concern you most is planning and assessing to match the curriculum demands and other mandatory documentation. Novice teachers often prepare a 'special' or exciting lesson when expecting a mentor, principal or colleague to observe their lesson. While that almost certainly creates a positive learning experience for the students and a good impression for the evaluator, it is important that you strive to offer what you personally believe to be best practice for your students consistently. This means engaging in reflective practice that asks pertinent, challenging questions. If you believe that the purpose of education is to help each student reach their unique potential, these questions may include:

How are the learning needs of each of my students reflected in my planning?

What strategies have I used to allow students to grow in knowledge, skills and concepts and that provide each student with an equitable degree of challenge?

Which teacher role am I undertaking, especially in class discussion and the development of the students' thinking skills (Cam, 1995; Langrehr, 1999; Pohl, 1997)?

What consideration have I given to the specific cultural and social contexts of my students given that these will determine both what I can do with the content and subject matter and what students will do with the content and subject matter (Posner, 2005)?

If I have photographs of my class members in front of me as I plan, what considerations would I ethically be bound to make in this planning to accommodate the diversity and differences among my class(es) of students?

Have I planned for student reflection or feedback to become a pivotal part of pedagogical strategies?

Have I panned assessment tasks and strategies that are varied and that allow students to communicate what they know, not what I think, or the curriculum dictates is important about the topic or understanding being taught?

What do I know about my own capacities to implement this planning successfully, be sensitive to student diversity and differences and manage the classroom environment effectively in order that the learning that takes places has meaning for the students?

Irrespective of how you understand the role of the teacher, there are reflective questions that can be asked more generally to focus your thinking about aspects of your professional work and a greater degree of congruence between your understanding of teachers' work, the mandatory restrictions and restraints and your personal values and belief systems. You are in a uniquely privileged situation in a classroom, and among the questions you might ask as reflection are:

Is my planning for learning truly reflecting what I believe to be good practice?

Have I individualised the learning goals so that all students are truly included (Janney and Snell, 2004)?

(Continued)

(Continued)

Are my selected resources and other results of my professional decisions a clear indication of how I see my role as a teacher?

Am I able to implement what I have planned and stay true to my professional ethics, values and belief systems?

Where do I have to compromise, change or develop a deeper understanding of myself and my contribution to maintaining best practice in my specific context?

How can I proceed ethically if and when my teaching context is not a good 'fit' with my personal values and beliefs relating to the teaching profession?

As a professional, am I open to new ideas, practices and suggestions that will cause me to develop my understanding of the nature of teachers' work?

While your professional reflection is intrinsically personal, you are not entirely alone in determining what to do and how you might proceed as a beginner in the profession. Many strategies have been developed by educational authorities to support you. Gordon (1991), in commenting that many of the significant difficulties that beginning teachers experience are environmentally orientated, indicated the strategies described in a successful induction programme. These included:

- Beginning teachers being provided with explicit details of the roles and responsibilities that they would be expected to undertake. As teachers' responsibilities are not confined to classroom interactions, details of playground duty, responsibilities at the beginning and the end of a school day, such as breakfast duty, after-hours sports and other training or instruction, are important for newcomers to the school to know.
- Newcomers being made aware of the details of key policies in addition to mandatory curriculum documents and systemic and school requirements in a variety of areas. These may include personal expectations such as dress codes, arrival and departure times, and communication with parents and the school community. They may include procedures to be followed in case of teacher or student illness, accident or misconduct
- Other suggestions focus on the need for new staff members to be welcomed appropriately. Gordon (1991) suggests celebrating the newcomer's arrival, planning opportunities for staff to get to know each other socially as well as professionally and build rapport. He suggests that

orientation days, nominated mentors and guidance from the principal are all important ways to support beginning teachers in the profession.

There is some debate around the question of induction into teaching for newcomers. Wang and her colleagues (2008) suggested that there was little evidence to show that induction influenced teacher practice or student achievement, although it did impact on beginning teachers' perceptions and ideas about teaching. Luft and her colleagues (2003) suggested that the benefits of teacher induction programmes could be maximised by the development and provision of programmes that had a specialised focus. The debate relating to mentors and mentoring programmes is somewhat similar. Hobson and her colleagues indicated that the usefulness of mentoring programmes for beginning teachers relied heavily on the selections and training of the mentors. Carter and Francis (2001), in a study of mentoring programmes, concluded that formal mentoring in particular contributed significantly to the wellbeing and success of beginning teachers, providing them with much needed support and guidance. Inman and Marlow (2004), reporting on a study designed to explore the reasons teachers stayed in the profession, concluded there were four areas of positive support that benefited beginning teachers and increased retention rates. These were opportunities to interact and work with:

teacher education mentors

colleagues with similar ideas about teaching and working cooperatively

administrators who encourage and promote teachers' ideas

a community which feels positive about the educational system and those involved.
(Inman and Marlow, 2004: 610)

DeWert and her colleagues (DeWert et al., 2003) came to similar conclusion regarding the potential of online mentoring to improve workplace performance and satisfaction for beginning teachers. Although there are numerous issues that could provide material for discussion with mentors, it appears that beginning teachers have common areas of concern. Veenman (1984) indicated eight areas of difficulty that reflect various aspects of what is known as the 'reality shock', a collective term for areas that appeared to be highly problematic for beginning teachers. They are:

Classroom discipline

Motivating students

Dealing with individual differences

Assessing students' work

Relationships with parents

Organisation of class work

Insufficient/inadequate teaching materials and supplies

Dealing with the problems presented by individual students (Veenman, 1984: 144)

He considered teachers as beginning teachers for their first three years of full-time teaching. In his discussion of the notion of 'reality shock', Veenman uses Müller-Fohrbrodt et al.'s (1978) understanding of the term, which is detailed in Figure 12.1.

Aspect	Description
Perceptions of problems	This includes all the subjectively experienced stress and anxieties, including workload, stress and psychological and physical complaints.
Changes of behaviour	This refers to changes of beginning teachers' behaviour due to external pressure. These changes are contrary to the behaviours that would reflect these teachers' own beliefs. Various studies discussed indicated that beginning teachers had changes from their more liberal, student-centred strategies for teaching to more authoritarian, teacher directed procedures as a result of experiencing difficulties in this area. Effective classroom management strategies were a difficulty and as a result more authoritarian measures were put in place.
Changes of attitude	These attitudinal changes are changes in the beginning teachers' belief systems about teachers' work, interactions with students and pedagogies. Findings showed that many teachers who held idealistic, progressive notions of teaching tended to swing most markedly to the conservative, custodial teacher role most readily if they were disillusioned. However, the individual variables of personality impact on these outcomes with young teachers who are uncommunicative or withdrawn being those who exhibit the most attitudinal changes. It is also noted that revision of attitude is not solely the province of teachers beginning a career; others entering professions from a liberal university background had undergone similar experiences. Innovative, progressive young teachers had the most difficult working relationships with their colleagues and supervisors but maintain their original attitudes and capacity to be innovative in contrast to their more traditional peers.
Change of personality	This refers to changes in beginning teachers' emotional states and self concepts.(It is useful to note here the work completed by Day et al., (2006), indicates that teacher personality, emotional states and efficacy changes throughout their careers in response to other factors in their life, career and personal circumstances. They suggest teacher personalities are neither intrinsically stable nor fragmented.)
Leaving the profession early	The disappointment and disillusionment may be so great that teachers leave the profession before having a teaching career.

Figure 12.1   Model of Reality Shock for Beginning Teachers (after Müller-Fohrbrodt et al., 1978, adapted from Veenman, 1984: 144–7)

While this information may paint a rather gloomy picture of life for beginning teachers, it must be remembered that teaching is a very demanding profession and that these research projects are more than a generation old. This model is included for reflection for several reasons:

- It reinforces the necessity for you to be aware of the 'goodness of fit' between your philosophies of teaching and the context in which they are working.
- Although dated, it does reflect some ongoing difficulties that you may experience depending on the circumstances in which you start your career.
- It explicitly links classroom management and the development of less student-orientated pedagogies that result in more teacher directed and authoritarian classrooms.
- It emphasises the struggle that beginning teachers have experienced when their working contexts cause them to be disillusioned. Many of these factors are not necessarily school or classroom based but are due to demands of systems and policies that mandate specific activities, for example national, compulsory, standardised testing of even young students and then advertising the outcomes and results (Darling-Hammond and Wise, 1985).
- It reassures you that although progressive, unconventional pedagogies, attitudes and belief may attract some derision among your colleagues and create difficulties with parents, the wider school community and even your students, planning, perseverance and management can prevent disillusionment.

What Does This Mean for You?

Throughout this book, you have been challenged to reflect on your personal beliefs about issues and concepts that are foundational precepts for your work. You have had the opportunity to analyse and discuss different perspectives and approaches to your chosen profession. In an ideal world, all theory would easily translate into effective practice. However, there is no recipe or formula for teaching effectively in all situations, with all students and in all communities. You need to be realistic about your own expectations. You will need to examine your own ethics, beliefs and value systems systematically and identify areas of relative strength and those of relative limitation and realistically assess the impact that both of these have on your professional work. Key points worth remembering as a beginning teacher may include the following:

(Continued)

(Continued)

- Teaching, while being satisfying, is emotionally and physically demanding. Teachers have not been awarded substantially more paid annual leave by accident. There are good reasons for this.
- If you fail to plan, you plan to fail. Not all your plans will be as successful as you might wish, but many of the areas of difficulty listed by Veenman (1984) can be mediated by thorough planning.
- Value your teacher education programme and your professional experience opportunities (Baird, 2008; Cleak and Wilson, 2004; Darling-Hammond, 2006). Learn how to join the dots and connect your learning in disparate courses in order to develop a deep understanding of your work as a teacher. Celebrate your qualification and accreditation status. Teachers who have accreditation qualifications actually facilitate increased student success (Darling-Hammond et al. 2001). Be responsible and make a commitment. Research shows that teachers who view teaching as a long term commitment feel responsible for student learning and have confidence that they have strategies to facilitate this; they are more successful and so are their students (Darling-Hammond et al. 2002).
- Use what you have learned and valued about how the brain is wired, how learning takes place and the circumstances, values and attitudes that facilitate student development and learning most successfully. It is unlikely that you will have an opportunity to work with 'pure' pedagogical models or theory unless your first position is in a Steiner, Montessori, Waldorf, Froebel or MI (Multiple Intelligences) school. That does not mean you cannot use what you learn and value as a blended or eclectic model to suit your circumstances, your students and your professional philosophy, even if it does require some compromises.
- Remember that educationalists have a right and a responsibility to change and grow, even as beginning teachers (Darling-Hammond, 1996, 1998) and it is important to bring something new or progressive to your context and expect it to earn a degree of success if you introduce it and plan it effectively. In your career you will experience different policies and contexts and these may be a catalyst for educational change and reform (Darling-Hammond, 2009).
- Think about the Holy Trinity for Teachers and ensure that you know your content and how to teach it. Ensure that you know your students as well as you are able, have reflected on their diverse perspectives (Darling-Hammond, 2000) and you are actually facilitating learning for each of them and know yourself. Acknowledge the sources and influences of your beliefs, opinions and perspectives as they change and you grow personally and professionally in response to the rewards and celebrations, frustrations and challenges that invariably accompany the initiations and rites of passage that redefine

you from a student teacher to a novice teacher and then to an accomplished teacher and beyond.

- Try to reflect on and in practice critically using the Personal Reflection Model. There are many means by which these reflections can be recorded and referred to later. Be aware of the steps that Newman and Pollnitz (2002) and others have provided as frameworks for thinking purposefully about ethical dilemmas, especially in regard to your personal, professional and legal responsibilities.
- Be determined to be positive in your thinking about your challenges and problem solving. The power of positive thinking can provide you with intuitive and creative ways in which to approach your dilemmas (Fredrickson, 2000, 2001).
- Be organised. Be aware of the factors that may negatively impact on the potential success of your planning and how you might minimise the opportunities for this to occur.
- Develop your model of classroom discipline within the boundaries of your ethical perspectives, the school and system policies and the law. Be aware of the cultural diversity, student subcultures and their attitudes to school and education in general, the issues of fairness and any beliefs you hold regarding the organisation of education for either (i) social reproduction (maintaining the status quo) or for (ii) social justice (overcoming social inequities (Wadham et al., 2007).

Classroom Discipline

The top of the list that Veenman (1984) compiled as the most frequently reported area of difficulty for beginning teachers is classroom discipline. Difficulties with motivating students to learn can result in boredom, disenchantment and disillusionment. These in turn can easily lead to students demonstrating inappropriate classroom behaviours that detract from the potential of others in the class to learn optimally or even effectively and prevent the perpetrators themselves from engaging with teaching and learning. Learning to motivate students can therefore be understood as a classroom management and student discipline strategy. As you have read in previous chapters, knowing your students is critical to understanding what and how to plan and implement tasks and strategies to support their learning. This also includes catering for diversity and individual difference. It would appear that the top three challenges indicated by Veenman are all focused around understanding your students as individual learners and respecting their differences in your planning for learning. This is not to suggest that planning suitable learning tasks that capture students' interests, are personally meaningful and sensitively scaffolded will automatically dissolve student resistance and motivate the most recalcitrant learners. Sometimes students have to be encouraged, coaxed or reminded of the possible consequences of non-cooperation in order for them to initially engage with the learning tasks, but that does not necessarily detract from their learning or their opportunity to undergo an optimal learning experience (Csikszentmihalyi, 2000). The decision to encourage, coax or remind of consequences for non-compliance in class depends heavily on your personal beliefs and value systems, your professional ethics and the frameworks dictated by schools and systems (Edwards and Watts, 2010). The following models allow you to critically reflect on these aspects of your professional work in an intensely personal manner and consider the possible impact of each of these on the students in your classrooms.

Models of Behaviour Management

There are a number of theories that address this topic. Some models commonly found in classrooms are detailed in Figure 12.2. Each has its particular background in specific educational and psychological theory (with the exception of Decisive Discipline) and its own relative shortcomings. The

Theorist	Theory	Criticisms
The Kounin (1970) Model of Withitness and Organisation	Kounin's model is entirely focused on the competencies of the teacher to manage the learning environment and the students. The major ideas in this model are: (i) the teachers' response to the inappropriate behaviour of one student influences the subsequent behaviours of the others (Ripple effect), including (ii) the teachers' capacities to be aware of what is going on in all parts of the room irrespective of where they are or what they are doing – he indicates that teacher behaviour is more powerful than what is said (Withitness); (iii) effective management of transitions from one lesson to another or one section of the lesson to another (Movement management); (iv) the teachers' abilities to monitor groups and attend to two issues at once (Overlapping); (v) teachers' ability to ensure that each individual has contributed to the work (encouraging accountability); (vi) planning activities that require a high level of student participation (High participation format lessons); (vii) pacing the learning activities appropriately teachers planning for flowing lessons (Momentum smoothness); (viii) dialoguing with individuals while retaining the attention of the rest of the class (Group alerting).	Criticism of this model focuses on the lack of direct instruction it gives for teachers to deal with students who are misbehaving. While it certainly has the components of a positive learning environment, there is no strategy or guideline for redirecting misbehaviour.

ABA (Applied Behaviour Analysis) developed from the work of Skinner (1977)	This theory is based in behaviourist strategies. Positive, productive behaviours are reinforced by praise or other pleasant consequences. Negative or non-productive behaviours result in unpleasant consequences such a punishment. Four main strategies are commonly used in classrooms: (i) Positive reinforcement – the behaviour is rewarded with something the students desires or values. (ii) Negative reinforcement – something that the student dislikes is removed or modified as a reward. (iii) Presentation punishment – an added condition or component that the student dislikes is included as a punishment. (iv) Removal punishment – something the student likes is withdrawn from the situation as a punishment. Details of developing a structured ABA programme can be found in Arthur et al. (2003)	Deals only with overt, observable behaviours and the immediate causes. It does not consider the thinking and feelings that underpin the behaviour.
Assertive Discipline Model of Canter (1988)	Teachers have to control students as they are not capable of controlling themselves. Teachers should insist on decent, respectful behaviours. Those who fail to maintain discipline are failing as teachers. Firm, strict boundaries are important for students and it is an error to think otherwise. Parents and school executives need to support the teacher. Students have the right to learn in optimal learning environments without inappropriate behaviours from others and to have teachers who ensure this is the case. In order to implement this model successfully teachers need to develop a range of assertive behaviours.	Based on the teacher as an authoritarian. Only considers the rights and needs of the teacher, not the students (Render et al., 1989).
Teacher Effectiveness Training Gordon (1989)	Teachers are trained to understand that students are capable of self control and that self discipline can be taught and supported in line with student ethics and beliefs. It actively seeks to provide non-aggressive strategies for conflict resolution. The development of self discipline is supported by maintaining positive teacher student relationships and establishing good communication techniques. Gordon suggests that there are several techniques that are foundational to these aims. He suggests: (i) Removing roadblocks – the behaviours and attitudes that impede the development of good communication and positive relationships. (ii) Engaging in active listening – this is a problem solving technique that allows the students to solve problems for themselves but not by themselves. Teachers listen emphatically, respond with short affirmative comments, frequently paraphrase the student's words to confirm common understanding and respond to the issue emphatically. (iii) I-messages – these have three components: they describe the behaviour, indicate its effects or consequences and express how the behaviour makes the teacher feel.	The major critique of this theory is that its focus is exclusively on solving conflict after it arises. There are no suggestions for planning in advance or preventative strategies. Additionally, the use of I-messages could be interpreted in such a way that it implies blame or actually blames the other person. This has a negative impact on the development of positive relationships which is a central tenet of the theory.

(Continued)

Figure 12.2 (Continued)

| Choice Theory Glasser (1998) | Behaviour is part of human life and is comprised of four parts: thinking, acting, feeling and physiology. Glasser suggests that students have some control over their thinking and feeling and all the choices they make are aimed at satisfying needs. He developed a basic human needs model (not dissimilar to Maslow's) and suggest that apart from basic needs, humans need:

(i) to belong – to be connected to others and be loved;
(ii) to have power – to be significant and be competent;
(iii) to have freedom – some degree of autonomy;
(iv) to learn to have fun.

Students choose their behaviours to meet these needs. Communication, dialogue, negotiation, mutual respect and collaboration are key notions. Teachers are to be 'lead' teachers or teacher facilitators and develop caring relationships with students and discuss inappropriate behaviours with them. Schools and systems need to change to meet the needs of their students. It calls for quality schools and quality curriculum negotiated and based on students' needs. It recognises the importance of student empowerment. | This theory raises questions of how teachers can develop optimal environments for all the diverse students in any class. The environment may be ideal from the teachers' perspective but the student may still choose to misbehave. The restraints of systems and mandatory curriculum on schools and teachers make this model difficult. |
| Goal-centred Theory Dreikurs (1998) | Built on the initial work of a colleague (Adler), who understood all behaviour as 'goal directed', with the goal of 'belonging' being the overreaching objective. Adler believed that individuals naturally prefer to behave in socially acceptable ways and that it is only when they feel discouraged and unable to belong, or to be important to someone that they begin to behave in anti-social ways. Dreikurs proposed that students misbehaved when discouraged and that the resultant consequences only serve to reinforce their belief that they are not important or accepted. He lists four goals of misbehaviour:

(i) to be noticed by attention seeking;
(ii) to be influential by winning or controlling;
(iii) to get fairness by taking revenge;
(iv) to be nurtured by becoming dependent or escape from mortification by withdrawing.

In order to promote positive behaviours, Dreikurs proposed four major strategies:

(i) develop class rules in negotiation with the students;
(ii) problem solve by engaging in group discussion;
(iii) encourage (not praise) each student regularly;
(iv) explicitly plan to meet the needs of the most vulnerable students.

A clear distinction is made between logical consequences for misbehaviour and punishment. Punishment is considered an arbitrary response whereas logical consequences link the behaviour and consequences in a cause and effect manner so the outcomes of misbehaviour are clearly indicated in the resultant penalty. | The major criticism is that this approach takes time to become effective and is not practical to manage a situation that requires an instant response. Some students may actually want to be in control and actively seek to be powerful and the goal of their misbehaviour is not easily discouraged. |

| Decisive Discipline Rogers (2003, 2007, 2011) | This is a very practical model that draws on a number of theorists and is based on the interrelationship of rules, rights and responsibilities. Rogers' practical approach includes:

(i) expect disruption and respond according to the level of disruption – (a) low level or (b) high level;
(ii) try to decipher the reason for the individual student's behaviour and
(iii) how they are different from those who do not exhibit those behaviours;
(iv) acknowledge which type of teacher you are, this determines what action you will take to discipline the student;
(v) understand that teachers are part of the classroom ecology and can be predominantly proactive or reactive;
(vi) decisive teachers plan and respond in specific ways. They determine how intrusive to be according to the degree of disruption caused, have a step-by-step plan in place for dealing with disruption that is skilfully graduated from least intrusive (ignoring the behaviour) to most intrusive (invoking a severe penalty). They understand that implementing their plan requires specific communication skills such as appropriate language use, close proximity to the misbehaving student, use of hand gestures and body language and eye contact. The intervention plan is to be implemented consistently, with fair warning, calmly and without malice or prejudice. | The lack of an underlying, uniting principle or theory is considered problematic, as is the use of humour. Whilst humour is generally agreed to be positive, it is a very personal trait and does not lend itself easily to transfer. What is funny to one person or in one situation is not to others. What one teacher can do humorously may not work for another. |

Figure 12.2 Theories of Behaviour Management in Schools

models described also reflect the values and belief systems of those who developed them. The means by which you manage the behaviours of your students reflects your own personal values and belief systems, including what you believe to be the purpose of education and what you understand to be the role of the teacher in this process. Theorists are listed in chronological order and the range of perspectives may reflect a shift in how teachers have been encouraged to view their students' behaviours as perceptions of the role of education and the work of teachers change over time.

What Does This Mean for You?

This review of models of classroom management has several implications for teachers in general and for beginning teachers in particular. It challenges you

(Continued)

(Continued)

to reflect on (i) the type of teacher you want to become, your values and belief systems and your own personality; (ii) what you believe about students' capacities to become self disciplined given appropriate support; (iii) how skilled you are personally in the development of positive relationships with students; (iv) the quality and consistency of your communication skills; (v) your capabilities in planning, implementing and assessing strategies to help students modify their misbehaviours, develop authentic feelings of belonging to your class and remain positive about their learning environment and experiences. It also introduces the notion that classroom management is not all about student behaviours. Teachers contribute to the classroom interactions, develop desired cultures or allow them to be dictated by others and are generally expected to be in charge of maintaining a classroom environment that is physically and emotionally safe for all the participants. Steps you can take to fulfil this responsibility include:

- Know your students. Ensure that you are aware of any circumstances that may trigger off-task behaviours, confrontations, displays of aggression or non-compliance.
- Plan. As discussed in previous chapters, plan lessons that excite, engage and are differentiated to provide a reasonable challenge for each student and implement them creatively. Plan to manage also. Cope (2005) suggests that both proactive and reactive strategies need to be considered in a management plan. As it is neither practical nor realistic to expect any one model to suit diverse contexts, teachers and students, he presents four aspects of planning for management: proactive, supportive, maintenance and reactive. The proactive measures are organisational and depend heavily on practical arrangements, developing students' interpretation of the rules as common understandings and maintaining a positive, professional demeanour. The supportive aspect focuses on developing students' sense of belonging and empowerment, modelling desirable behaviours and positive relationships, and assessing student responses to the selected strategies. The maintenance strategies are designed to encourage students, to remind them of rules, to remain visible and supportive and to gain the attention of students at key times. The reactive strategies require you to know the school rules and policies, to establish logical consequences and to determine how intrusive your intervention may have to become in response to high level misbehaviours.
- Know yourself. Be aware of how you are presenting yourself to students. Determine the degree of personal information you need to disclose in order to establish positive respectful relationships. You may have students who are highly academic and all they may wish to know about you is how well you

know and teach the subject matter you are responsible for. Other students may have to see a more personal side of you in order to become sufficiently motivated to engage positively and attempt a challenge in your classes.

- Be practical. Be organised with resources, sensitive with your lesson timing and use of physical space in order to maximise the potential of the learning environment. Plan for areas of heavy traffic, wet areas, specific resource accessibility and physical space when considering the layout of the classroom. Try to anticipate difficulties such as limited views of shared teaching resources such as electronic whiteboards and areas that you use for demonstration and modelling. Consider the size and developmental stage of your students and allow for sufficient personal and physical space.

- Be flexible. The body language of students is as powerful as that which you use to convey messages. Students often show signs of boredom, tiredness, frustration before they actually misbehave. Sometimes it can be more beneficial to take notice of these warning signals even if you have to cut an activity short or return to it at another time. Use all your knowledge about the brain and learning in addition to your curriculum knowledge and pedagogical strategies to support students' success.

There is no formula that suits everyone, all contexts and all teaching situations. There are, however. some constants, such as the need for you to consistently act fairly, be sensitive to the causes of problems that are presented as classroom misbehaviours, consider the triarchic taxonomy of ethics (Haynes, 1998) and reflect on the decisions you make and the alternative options that may have been present. This may appear cumbersome. However, if you understand that every decision you make reflects your professional and personal ethics, beliefs and values, has implications for your classroom discipline and influences your classroom culture, then you are beginning to realise the complexities of teaching. Some of these decisions can be made before you set foot in your classroom. These relate to your planning for teaching and learning – a substantial part of the overall concept of classroom management. The Handy Management Plan (Figure 12.3) may help you think clearly about your planning and organisation for a successful classroom.

Assessment, Feedback and Communicating with Parents

There a number of ways that authentic assessment can be organised. Marzano and his colleagues (Marzano et al., 1993) provide a comprehensive model that evaluates five aspects of students' progress and development in

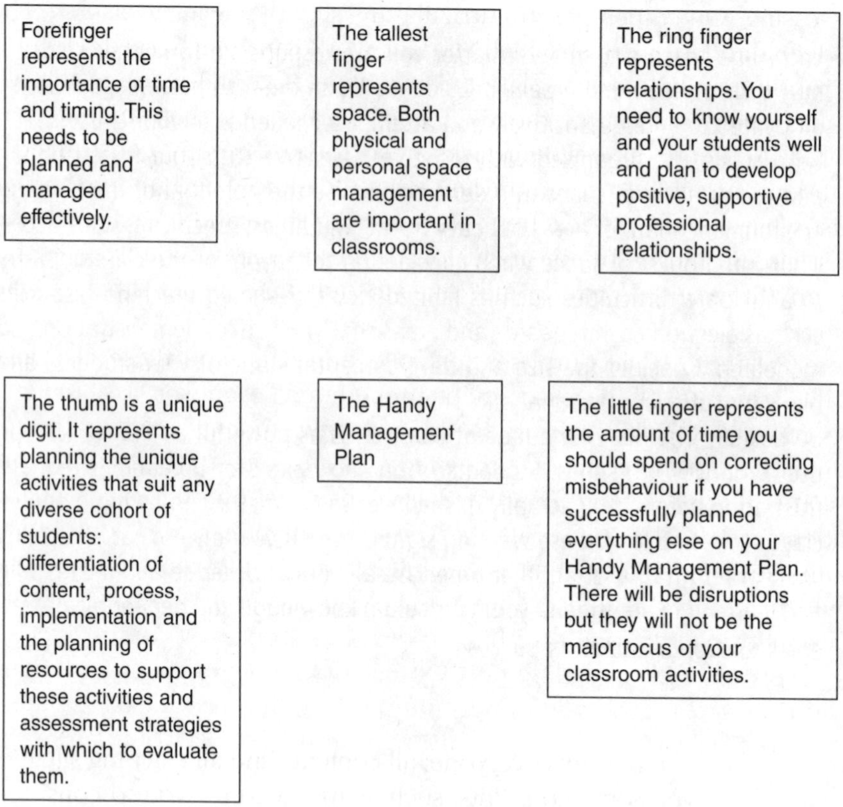

Forefinger represents the importance of time and timing. This needs to be planned and managed effectively.

The tallest finger represents space. Both physical and personal space management are important in classrooms.

The ring finger represents relationships. You need to know yourself and your students well and plan to develop positive, supportive professional relationships.

The thumb is a unique digit. It represents planning the unique activities that suit any diverse cohort of students: differentiation of content, process, implementation and the planning of resources to support these activities and assessment strategies with which to evaluate them.

The Handy Management Plan

The little finger represents the amount of time you should spend on correcting misbehaviour if you have successfully planned everything else on your Handy Management Plan. There will be disruptions but they will not be the major focus of your classroom activities.

Figure 12.3   The Handy Management Plan

schools. These are: (i) how positive they are about learning in general and being in school; (ii) how they have progressed in the development of their thinking skills and problem solving strategies when learning and integrating new material; (iii) to what degree they have developed complex thinking skills identified as higher-order thinking; (iv) how skilled they have become in using newly acquired knowledge productively; and (v) the degree to which they have progressed in the development of their cognitive skills of executive function. To assess these, students must have participated in teaching and learning activities that supported these skills. The critical factor in assessment is that what is taught matches the intended lesson aims or outcomes and what is assessed matches what is taught.

Records of students' learning that are created from your observation notes, conferring with students about their thinking and learning, and carefully analysing a variety of work products may produce a mass of information. The key to sorting through this is to have a clear focus on what exactly you are assessing. Outcomes-based curricula are slightly easier to assess. They set a clear standard against which student work can be assessed. Developing a rubric may help you isolate the key aspects of the learning that you hope has taken place and the degree of proficiency that students have exhibited. Authentic assessment tasks need to be carefully constructed so that students are able to communicate what they know and understand and not just what you, as the teacher, select to ask. This can be easily achieved in most circumstances by the inclusion of the question, written or oral, 'Is there anything else you would like to tell me about [the selected learning]?'

There are three basic purposes for collecting data, and these also influence the structure of the assessment procedure. Diagnostic assessment is always constructed with the purpose of indicating students' relative strengths and limitations in the concepts, knowledge, skills and strategies of the area in which you are teaching. Formative assessment is the ongoing evaluation of students' work as it is in progress. This assessment can also contribute to the summative assessment that is designed at the end of any unit or topic and which requires a final evaluation of students' progress. Assessment is not designed to be a 'one size fits all' test. It is important to consider students' levels of work in a differentiated classroom. Assessment is designed to indicate progress and to inform future planning for individuals, groups or entire cohorts of students. Any product can be the subject of analysis, any demonstrated behaviour can be purposefully observed and any conversation between you and your students can be indicative of students' thinking and executive function capacities that cannot be observed. Each of these strategies contributes to the students' learning profiles and is collated with the others to give an accurate account of progress.

One significant aspect of assessment already discussed is the use of the information to inform you about students' learning needs. Another is to allow you to give accurate feedback to the students and the parents and caregivers. Feedback to students should be couched in appropriate terms, include comment on which aspects were completed well and which needed some further attention. The final component of effective feedback is future planning. The strategies planned to support students' learning should be clearly communicated to them with the details of type of intervention planned, the time and place, so that they are aware that you are treating each of them as individuals, have a professional interest in their progress and are prepared to spend time supporting their efforts to improve the outcomes they are working on. As Veenman (1984) found that communication with parents was perceived to be a problematic area for newcomers to the profession, it may be useful to outline some guidelines for respectful communication. These may include:

- Being sensitive to the different attitudes and understandings that you and others may have regarding (a) the purpose and value of education, (b) notions of childrearing and parenting, (c) the role and responsibilities that you, as a teacher, undertake, (d) the context and conditions in which you work and (e) that expected standards of behaviour can vary between home and school.
- Acknowledging the diversity of opinion that is the result of socioeconomic, individual and cultural differences and remaining unbiased, non-judgemental and positive in your communication with parents.
- Recognising that there are various means of communicating and that body language, tone of voice, facial expressions and gestures are all powerful indicators of how you feel about the interaction.
- Understanding that, in general, much of what teachers do goes unnoticed by all but the trained observer and many parents do not know a great deal about teachers' work.
- Accepting that parents focus on their own child's wellbeing and progress and do not have to consider issues of equity, fairness or professional ethics in the same way that you do.

It is always easier if you ask to see a parent, as you can prepare for the communication session beforehand. If a parent requests the communication, it is useful to establish the focus of the discussion in advance as it gives you time to reflect and prepare. In either case, many beginning teachers feel more comfortable to have an experienced member of staff or mentor sit in on the interview or phone conversation or to read through email or written correspondence before it is sent to parents. You will feel more at ease with collegial support.

Resources

The issue of school resources and their impact on student performance has been widely investigated (Hanushek, 1997), particularly in relation to technological and digital resourcing (Condie and Miunro, 2007). However, an international study (Hanushek and Luque, 2003) conducted with data from countries with diverse incomes has indicated that only one particular resource impacts significantly on students' achievement: the quality of the human resources, that is – the teachers. While these findings may challenge those of other studies, they are not totally unreasonable. In other chapters you read about the importance of teacher quality and the characteristics that define them. Quality teachers work conscientiously and creatively with the resources that are available to create meaningful teaching and learning environments for their pupils because they care about them in a professional manner. Similarly, another study found that students' academic performances were positively impacted by employment of quality librarians as additional staff in school libraries (Lance et al., 2000). Quality teachers would be expected to understand that technological resources require a different pedagogical approach, as discussed in an earlier chapter, in order to seamlessly integrate it into their teaching and learning. They would engage with professional learning to become increasingly confident with its use and appreciate that technological support is one of the prerequisites for its effective and efficient use (Yelland, 2001). Even everyday resources such as textbooks, reading materials and photocopiers can be misused or implemented to support teaching and learning effectively. The ways in which photocopiers are used reflects your understanding of your role as a teacher. Quality teachers do not let worksheets do the teaching. They use the photocopier to support teaching, as detailed in Figure 12.4.

Resources	Sheets that support student thinking, e.g. graphic organisers, nets for 3D solids, formats for writing different genre
Reference	Sheets that contain information from which to work, e.g. facts about marine life, chemical symbols, or sheets of directions, e.g. how to save work to a disc or thumb drive, how to work the digital camera
Recording	Sheets for organising results, e.g. tally sheets, games scores, results of science experiments and chance and data investigations
Response	Sheets for gathering opinions, answers to questionnaires and variations to questions asked, e.g. How would you define a trapezium?
Reflection	Sheets on which students can indicate their feelings and thoughts about their work, e.g. faces with expressions, Likert scales from Great! to Oh Dear, open-ended responses to questions designed to support student reflection

Figure 12.4 Materials for Photocopying

Conclusion

Although this chapter presented the many difficulties that face beginning teachers, its purpose was not to discourage you. It was concerned with challenging you to reflect on what you have read, discussed and reflected upon in the course of your preparation to teach. It also served to prepare you as you change from student teacher to beginning teacher by detailing strategies that may be useful to you at the start of your teaching career. The discussions of models of discipline, organising programmes, managing classrooms and working with the parent community are provided for your reflection. As you can see, a key characteristic of successful teachers is their capacity to be prepared, whether they are planning for teaching, meeting with parents and caregivers or dealing with the inevitable disruptions to their teaching or their routines. You can also understand from this chapter and from the discussions throughout the book that much of what really effective teachers do actually happens outside of the classroom itself. It is this professional reflection, planning and commitment that allows you to support students' learning outcomes productively in your classroom and to promote the positive professional relationships that have the potential to engage and motivate even the most reluctant learners and begin your professional career as a teacher of quality.

References

Arthur, M., Gordon, C. and Butterfield, N. (2003) *Classroom Management: Creating Positive Learning Environments*. Southbank, VIC: Thomson.

Baird, B. (2008) *The Internship, Practicum and Field Placement Handbook*, 5th edn. Upper Saddle River, NJ: Pearson Education.

Cam, P. (1995) *Thinking Together: Philosophiacl Discussion for the Classroom*. Sydney: Hale and Iremonger.

Canter, L. (1988) Let the educator beware: a response to Curnin and Mendler. *Educational Leadership*, 46 (2): 71–73.

Carter, M. and Francis, R. (2001) Mentoring and beginning teachers' workplace learning. *Asia-Pacific Journal of Teacher Education*, 29 (3): 249–262.

Cleak, H. and Wilson, J. (2004) *Making The Most of your Field Placement*. Melbourne: Nelson Australia.

Condie, R. and Munro, B. (2007) *The Impact of ICT in Schools – A Landscape Review*. Strathclyde: Becta Research.

Cope, B. (2005) *How to Make a Classroom Management Plan*. Frenchs Forest, NSW: Pearson Springprint.

Csikszentmihalyi, M. (2000) Happiness, flow and economic equality. *American Psychological Association*, 55 (10): 1163–4.

Darling-Hammond, L. (1996) The right to learn and the advancement of teaching: research, policy and practice for democratic education. *Educational Researcher*, 25 (6): 5–17.

Darling-Hammond, L. (1998) Teachers and teaching: testing policy hypotheses from a National Commission Report. *Educational Researcher*, 27 (1): 5–15.

Darling-Hammond, L. (2000) How teacher education matters. *Journal of Teacher Education*, 51 (3): 166–73.

Darling-Hammond, L. (2006) Constructing 21st-century teacher education. *Journal of Teacher Education*, 57 (3): 300–14.

Darling-Hammond, L. (2009) 'Teaching and educational transformation: Second International Handbook of Educational Change.' In A. Hargreaves, A. Lieberman, M. Fullan and D. Hopkins (eds), *Teaching and Educational Transformation*, Vol. 23. Dordrecht: Springer Netherlands. pp. 505–20.

Darling-Hammond, L. and Wise, A. (1985) Beyond standardization: state standards and school improvement. *The Elementary School Journal*, 85 (3): 315–36.

Darling-Hammond, L., Berry, B. and Thoreson, A. (2001) Does teacher certification matter? Evaluating the evidence. *Educational Evaluation and Policy Analysis*, 23 (1): 57–77.

Darling-Hammond, L., Chung, R. and Frelow, F. (2002) Variation in teacher preparation. *Journal of Teacher Education*, 53 (4): 286–302.

Day, C., Alison, K., Gordon, S. and Sammons, P. (2006) The personal and professional selves of teachers: stable and unstable identities. *British Educational Research Journal*, 32 (4): 601–16.

DeWert, M., Babinski, L. and Jones, B. (2003) Safe passages: providing online support to beginning teachers. *Journal of Teacher Education*, 54 (4): 311–20.

Dreikurs, R. (1998) *Maintaining Sanity in the Classroom: Classroom Management Techniques*, 2nd edn. Levittown, PA: Taylor and Francis.

Edwards, C. and Watts, E. (2010) *Classroom Discipline and Management*. Milton, QLD: John Wiley and Sons .

Fredrickson, B. (2000) Cultivating positive emotions to optimize health and well-being. *Prevention and Treatment*, 3: article 0001a. Retrieved from www.rickhanson.net/wp-content/files/papers/Cult Po.Emot.pdf (accessed 24 July 2013).
www.unc.edu/peplab/publications/Fredrickson_2000_Prev&Trmt.pdf

Fredrickson, B. (2001) The role of positive emotions in positive psychology. *American Psychologist*, 56 (3): 218–26.

Glasser, W. (1998) *Choice Theory: A New Psychology of Personal Freedom*. New York: Harper Perennial.

Gordon, S.P. (1991) *How to Help Beginning Teachers Succeed*. Alexandria, VA: Association for Supervision and Curriculum Development.

Gordon, T. (1989) *Discipline that Works: Promoting Self-Discipline in Children*. New York. Plume.

Hanushek, E. (1997) Assessing the effects of school resources on student performance: an update. *Educational Evaluation and Policy Analysis*, 19 (2): 141–64.

Hanushek, E. and Luque, J. (2003) Efficiency and equity in schools around the world. *Economics of Education Review*, 22 (5): 485–502.

Haynes, F. (1998) *The Ethical School*. London: Routledge.

Inman, D. and Marlow, L. (2004) Teacher retention: why do beginning teachers remain in the profession? *Education*, 124 (Summer): 605–15.

Janney, R. and Snell, M. (2004) *Modifying Schoolwork*. Baltimore, MD: Paul H. Brookes.

Kounin, J. (1970). *Discipline and Group Management in classrooms*. New York: Holt Rinehart & Winston.

Lance, K., Rodney, M. and Hamilton-Pennell, C. (2000) *Measuring up to Standards: The Impact of School Library Programs and Information Literacy in Pennsylvania Schools*. Greensburg, PA: Pennsylvania State Department of Education, and Office of Commonwealth Libraries.

Langrehr, J. (1999) *Teaching Your Children to Think*. Elsternwick, VIC: Wrightbooks.

Luft, J., Roehrig, G. and Patterson, N. (2003) Contrasting landscapes: a comparison of the impact of different induction programs on beginning secondary science teachers' practices, beliefs and experiences. *Journal of Research in Science Teaching*, 40 (1): 77–97.

Marzano, R., Pickering, D. and McTighe, J. (1993) *Assessing Student Outcomes: Performance Assessment Using the Dimensions of Learning Model*. Alexandria, VA: Association for Supervision and Curriculum Development.

Müller-Fohrbrodt, F., Cloetta, G., and Dann, H. (1978) *The Transition Shock in Beginning Teachers*. Stuttgart: Klett.

Newman, L. and Pollnitz, L. (2002) *Ethics in Action: Introducing the Ethical Response Cycle*. Watson, ACT: Australian Early Childhood Association.

Pohl, M. (1997) *Teaching Thinking Skills in the Primary Years*. Cheltenham, VIC: Hawker Brownlow Education.

Posner, G. (2005) *Field Experience: A Guide to Reflective Teaching*. Boston, MA: Pearson Education.

Qualter, P., Whiteley, H., Hutchinson, J. and Pope, D. (2007) Supporting the development of emotional intelligence competencies to ease the transition from primary to high school. *Education Psychology in Practice*, 23(1): 79–95.

Render, G., Padilla, J. and Krank, M. (1989) Assertive discipline: a critical review and analysis. *Teachers College Record*, 90 (4): 607–30.

Rogers, B. (2003) *Effective Supply Teaching: Behaviour Management, Classroom Discipline and Colleague Support*. London: Sage.

Rogers, B. (2007) *Behaviour Management: A Whole-School Approach*. London: Sage.

Rogers, B. (2011) *Classroom Behaviour: A Practical Guide to Effective Teaching, Behaviour Management and Colleague Support*. London: Sage.

Simmons, P., Emory, A., Carter, T., Coker, T., Finnegan, B., Crockett, D. and Labuda, K. (1999) Beginning teachers: beliefs and classroom actions. *Journal of Research in Science Teaching*, 36 (8): 930–54.

Skinner, B. (1977) Why I am not a cognitive psychologist. *Behaviorism*, 5 (2): 1–10.

Staton, S. and Hunt, S. (1992) Teacher socialisation: review and conceptualisation. *Communication Education*, 41 (2): 109–137.

Veenman, S. (1984) Perceived problems of beginning teachers. *Review of Educational Research*, 54 (2): 143–78.

Wadham, B., Pudsey, J. and Boyd, R. (2007) *Culture and Education*. Frenchs Forest, NSW: Pearson Prentice–Hall.

Wang, J., Odell, S. and Schwille, S. (2008) Effects of teacher induction on beginning teachers' teaching: a critical review of the literature. *Journal of Teacher Education*, 59 (2): 132–52.

Yelland, N. (2001) *Teaching and Learning with Information and Communication Technologies (ICT) for Numeracy in the Early Childhood and Primary Years of Schooling*. Australia: Research and Evaluation Branch, International Analysis Division, Department of Education Training and Youth Affairs.

Zeichner, K. and Grant, C. (1981) Biography and social structure in the socialization of student teachers: a re-examination of the pupil control ideologies of student teachers. *Journal of Education for Teaching: International Research and Pedagogy*, 7 (3): 109–137.

Index